KV-030-321

CRITICAL DIALOGUES

Thinking Together in Turbulent Times

John Clarke

in conversation with

Wendy Brown, Allan Cochrane,
Davina Cooper, Larry Grossberg,
Wendy Larner, Gail Lewis, Tania Murray Li,
Jeff Maskovsky, Janet Newman,
Anu (Aradhana) Sharma, Paul Stubbs
and Fiona Williams

First published in Great Britain in 2019 by

Policy Press
University of Bristol
1-9 Old Park Hill
Bristol
BS2 8BB
UK
t: +44 (0)117 954 5940
pp-info@bristol.ac.uk
www.policypress.co.uk

North America office:
Policy Press
c/o The University of Chicago Press
1427 East 60th Street
Chicago, IL 60637, USA
t: +1 773 702 7700
f: +1 773-702-9756
sales@press.uchicago.edu
www.press.uchicago.edu

© Policy Press 2019

British Library Cataloguing in Publication Data
A catalogue record for this book is available from the British Library

Library of Congress Cataloging-in-Publication Data
A catalog record for this book has been requested

ISBN 978-1-4473-5098-9 paperback
ISBN 978-1-4473-5097-2 hardcover
ISBN 978-1-4473-5100-9 ePub
ISBN 978-1-4473-5101-6 Mobi
ISBN 978-1-4473-5099-6 ePdf

The right of John Clarke to be identified as author of this work has been asserted by him in accordance with the Copyright, Designs and Patents Act 1988.

All rights reserved: no part of this publication may be reproduced, stored in a retrieval system, or transmitted in any form or by any means, electronic, mechanical, photocopying, recording, or otherwise without the prior permission of Policy Press.

The statements and opinions contained within this publication are solely those of the author and not of the University of Bristol or Policy Press. The University of Bristol and Policy Press disclaim responsibility for any injury to persons or property resulting from any material published in this publication.

Policy Press works to counter discrimination on grounds of gender, race, disability, age and sexuality.

Cover design by Hayes Design
Front cover image: © Freepik
Printed and bound in Great Britain by CMP, Poole
Policy Press uses environmentally responsible print partners

For Stuart, whose voice lives on

Contents

Acknowledgements viii

Introduction: 'Voices in my head':
Thinking critically as dialogic practice 1
Voices in my head 2
Thinking critically, but not alone 5
Thinking critically: with and against 7
Dialogic selves: thinking subjects 10
Introducing the voices 12
The missing voices 14
Listening to voices; or, how to use this book 18

1   Tania Murray Li 21
A collaborative-working puzzle 22
Making concepts work 30
Questions of conservative rule 33
The problem of work 34

2   Larry Grossberg 37
Talking through differences 38
Taking positions provisionally 42
The pains and pleasures of collaboration 44
Looking for the popular 49

3   Wendy Brown 53
Talking theory 54
The seductions of theory 57
Between theory and politics 62
A moment of ambivalence 66

4   Anu (Aradhana) Sharma 69
Thinking with multiple resources 70
Subjects behaving badly 72
What is an NGO? 76
Having troubling thoughts 80

5   Jeff Maskovsky 87
Paradoxes of popular politics 88
On political trajectories 91
Politics, certainty and ambivalence 94

6   Paul Stubbs   103
        Being dragged out of place   104
        Who studies policy?   107
        Making up things – and places   111
        The work of agency   113
        The threat of being found out   117

7   Allan Cochrane   119
        The Open University as a space for critical thinking   120
        Opening up possibilities   125
        Disciplines and interdisciplinary thinking   126

8   Fiona Williams   135
        Coming to terms with social policy   136
        Resistances and refusals   138
        On contradictions and complexity   143
        Back to social policy   148

9   Davina Cooper   151
        In a world of disciplines?   152
        Thinking beyond boundaries   154
        The consequences of talking to people   157
        Emerging projects and emerging identities   162

10   Gail Lewis   165
        Thinking with others   166
        Between certainty and uncertainty   170
        Thinking with and through race   172
        Dimensions and dynamics of crisis   180
        Imagining other connections   183

11   Wendy Larner   185
        Conversations within and beyond disciplines   186
        Changing institutions   188
        Unorthodox formations   191
        On discourse as the practice of articulation   196

12   Janet Newman   203
        On collaboration   204
        The pessimism of critique   208
        The Marxism and feminism thing   210
        Looking for the current moment   212
        Between collaborative and dialogic processes   216

Contents

Afterword	219
Keywords	225
References	231
Index	237

Acknowledgements

First and foremost, my thanks to the 12 people who generously agreed to take part in these conversations – and then put up with my requests for checking, clarifications and the rest. They exemplify so well why thinking together matters. I am also grateful to Policy Press for taking this somewhat odd publication on. Emily Watt listened (again) to my weird ideas and pursued them. Sarah Bird took the process over while Emily was on maternity leave and has been a great support. Thanks also to Sarah Connolly and Laura Cope for their help. Thanks, too, to Ruth Wallace for her fast, constructive and helpful editorial work on the manuscript, and to Vaarunika Dharmapala who saw it through to the end. A very special thank you to Richard Freeman, who demonstrated that the reviewing process can also be conversational rather than antagonistic. His comments on the first draft were generous, thoughtful and very helpful in trying to make the book interesting and useable. Even better, they were also funny.

Thanks also to what was the Faculty of Social Sciences at the Open University (subsequently transformed into the Faculty of Arts and Social Sciences). It generously supported the early phases of this work with some travel money, while the Centre for Citizenship, Identities and Governance provided support for the transcription of the first six conversations. Page Six Services did impressive work with all the recordings despite my sometimes garbled interruptions and a bewildering array of extraneous sounds (building sites, helicopters and motor mowers).

A rather different thank you to all the many people I talked to about the project who encouraged me to see it through, especially those who expressed disappointment about not being among the dozen conversations! It has always felt like a weird and self-indulgent sort of thing to embark on – and the generously supportive reactions have helped me to make it happen. And finally, a different sort of thank you to Janet Newman in her other role – as the person who has had to live with it (and me) for the last five years, while waiting, more or less patiently, to be the final dialogist. I might easily have lost my way without her support.

INTRODUCTION

'Voices in my head': thinking critically as dialogic practice

This book is strange in many ways. It has been a different sort of book to produce and will, I am certain, be a strange book to read. However, it has also been a joy to produce: it features conversations with a dozen leading academic thinkers *talking about thinking*. The 12 voices contained here are people who have inspired many of us across a range of disciplines and fields, from political theory (Wendy Brown) to social policy (Fiona Williams), and from geography (Wendy Larner) to anthropology (Anu Sharma). More particularly, these voices belong to people who have helped me to think about the problems of doing critical intellectual work in hard times. These conversations explore the difficult relationships that are in play between politics, theorising and the practice of academic work.

As a consequence, this is necessarily a strange sort of book. Although academics talk all the time, we rarely record our conversations – as opposed to the public presentation or the structured interview. Yet conversation is intrinsic to our way of working: it involves thinking out loud, responding to questions, provocations and arguments, taking account of others and thinking 're-on your feet' (even if sitting down). Some of my most memorable academic moments have come from watching people whom I admire engaging with the question and the questioner, trying to re-articulate their arguments, trying to make connections or explore differences. Quite a lot of those who gave me such memorable moments are present in this book, precisely because they (literally) embody the qualities of thinking through talking and thinking out loud.

So, the book partly emerges out of a puzzle: given what a significant part this sort of dialogue plays in our lives and our work, why does it so rarely feature in the public forms and formats of academic work? I suspect this is partly a product of how the forms and formalities of academic work combine in creating the varieties of 'finished work' that represent our public face: the article, the book, the presentation or even the carefully crafted interview. But so much of our real work takes place in this other mode – arguing in research teams, negotiating with co-authors, discussing with audiences or even just fretting about some elusive topic over a cup of coffee or a drink. This book represents a chance to make this practice of 'thinking out loud' more visible and more audible. It is also about the way in which such thinking is not the rarefied reflections of the brilliant individual but an *intersubjective* process – a dialogue in which things develop dynamically. That too is missing from most accounts of academic work, which still celebrate the heroic individual who thinks great thoughts in splendid isolation.

Voices in my head

This project has a number of inspirations, most of them deriving from disconcerting moments of realisation. The first emerged at a workshop with a group of researchers at the Open University ('early career researchers', to give them their current organisational designation) on the topic of working collaboratively. As we explored the pleasures and problems of collaboration, I said that one of the great joys of collaborative working was that I had never had an original thought in my life. This evoked polite protests from several people and led me to clarify what I had intended by the statement. Since arriving as a postgraduate student at the Birmingham Centre for Contemporary Cultural Studies (CCCS) in 1972, I have been privileged to work in collaboration with a wide range of people in a variety of research, writing and teaching projects. These collaborations have generated lots of original ideas and innovative work, but the generative processes were collective ones. They involved discussion, argument, criticism and iterative processes of drafting and development. I will have more to say about such processes later, but the question of 'original ideas' made me think about how our views of intellectual work are overshadowed by highly individualistic conceptions of thinking and working. One of the purposes of this book is to unsettle those conceptions and open out the collective and collaborative processes by which so much critical thinking is done in practice.

The second trigger for the project took the form of another phrase that I find myself using with increasing frequency when talking about my work – a claim that it is constantly shaped by 'voices in my head'. This is, of course, a profoundly ambiguous observation: it is a way of paying tribute to those whose voices travel with me, reminding me of what we know and think, prodding me to do better and always providing a sort of location device, connecting me to a set of relationships in which thinking takes place. On the other hand, it also evokes images of hearing voices as a psychological disorder, a different and unsettling image that requires the normalising conception of the unique and coherent thinking individual (McCarthy-Jones, 2012). While I do not intend to underestimate the distress and disorientation that people suffer from the experience of 'hearing voices', I do want to borrow the phrase for my purposes. As several authors working in the field have argued, hearing voices may be a much more common phenomenon than its psychiatric pathologisation implies and may, indeed, point to much more heteroglossic (multi-voiced) senses of the self (from *very* different starting points, see Billig, 1987; Longden, 2013; and McCarthy-Jones, 2012 and 2017). In what follows, I will connect these 'voices' to my understanding of the processes of intellectual work as a dynamic and relational practice of thinking with and against others.

This brings me to my third starting point, which emerged in discussions about 'critical thinking' in a class at Central European University. This lovely group of smart and engaged students were exploring issues and approaches loosely clustered under the heading of 'Critical Policy Studies', when it became clear to me that all of us were extremely good at the critical deconstruction of positions and arguments. Each of the chosen readings could be taken apart, weighed and found wanting in important ways. In an effort to interrupt our collective power of criticism, I suggested that whoever introduced one of the readings for the class also had to include a comment about what they had gained from the reading. This proved to be a challenge: some rose to it with more grace than others but it memorably culminated in one student reminding me of the rule after I had launched into a long and hostile attack on one of the papers we were looking at: 'Didn't you say that we were supposed to also think about what we had got out of it, rather than just what's wrong?' The rest of the group smiled and looked expectantly at me … It took me back to significant moments of my own postgraduate work in cultural studies in Birmingham when I would be recurrently impressed by Stuart Hall's capacity to dig out the 'good sense' of positions and analyses that I had learned to deconstruct and dismiss. That capacity, that willingness to think *with*, as well as *against*, seems to me to be one of Stuart's gifts, and one that is central to the process of thinking critically.

I was reminded of it as I began work on this book in the shadow of Stuart's death and the problem of accounting for one of the most salient voices in my head. At that point, I read David Scott's beautiful and moving book written to, and about, Stuart: *Stuart Hall's Voice* (2017). I will say more about Stuart – and David's idea of an 'ethics of receptive generosity' – later in this Introduction, but the possibility of 'thinking with' provides one of the cornerstones of this project. The voices collected here are ones that have regularly helped me to think.

They are in my head in complex and rewarding ways, but it might be worth noting other ways in which such voices might be imagined. At an event at the University of Leeds held to celebrate the retirement of Fiona Williams (one of the voices in my head), Fiona talked about the same experience, but in terms of having her interlocutors perched on her shoulder, whispering in her ear.

The final prompt for this project was my retirement from the Open University in 2013, which gave rise to considerable thinking – and talking – about the people, processes and practices that had filled my working life and had enabled me to do the sort of work that I had enjoyed (the commodification and managerialisation of higher education notwithstanding). It made me want to settle accounts with the relationships that had supported and sustained critical thinking in a range of settings, and to draw some of the people who played important roles in those processes into thinking out loud about critical thinking and thinking together. I had the ambition to find a dozen people and spend time with them and an audio recorder to try to reflect on these experiences. Of course, I found my 12, who appear here: Tania Murray Li, Larry Grossberg, Wendy Brown, Anu Sharma, Jeff Maskovsky, Paul Stubbs, Allan Cochrane, Fiona Williams, Davina Cooper, Wendy Larner, Gail Lewis and Janet Newman.

However, the process was not straightforward. I say more about two 'missing voices' (Stuart Hall and Doreen Massey) below, but there is a wider sense of absent voices too. I have worked collaboratively with many people since my first immersion in the pleasures and problems of the process in the subcultures group at CCCS (see Hall and Jefferson, 1976). There were other collective projects at the Centre, notably the 'mugging group' that produced *Policing the Crisis* (Hall et al, 1978). I have spoken (and written) elsewhere about the collective processes that were fundamental to the Centre's work – organisational as well as intellectual (Clarke, 2016a). Subsequently, there were many course teams (later renamed module teams) at the Open University that proved to be an education in themselves as we struggled to cope with the demands of being a collective teacher and with the pedagogic puzzles of teaching at a distance. There have been research projects and writing collaborations with many wonderful people, all of whom have helped me to think – to think better, to think differently and, perhaps most importantly, to think *again*. Critical thinking, I will suggest, cannot, and should not, stand still.

Thinking critically, but not alone

In trying to work out what this book might be about, I thought it might be about the process of 'critical thinking', but then I discovered that, like most academic terms, the phrase was already owned and occupied. This, too, took me back to the practices of cultural studies: none of the topics or issues on which we worked was readily available to an emergent approach. On the contrary, everything from literature to television, from youth cultures to the state, already existed as someone else's territory, with all the established canons, hierarchies and proprietorial claims that such academic institutionalisation implies. As a result, cultural studies often felt like a practice mobilised through cross-border raids in which we (and this was certainly a way in which the collective identity really mattered) would turn up somewhere to explain how much more interesting and significant topic X would be if only it was turned around and reconfigured through a cultural studies framing. While cultural studies was certainly an emergent approach, it was also an insurgent one. So let me briefly return to this mode of reframing – what in cultural studies terms might be called re-articulation – in relation to 'critical thinking'. Critical thinking is currently organised and circulated as an approach to thinking systematically about any issue. The capacity to do critical thinking is now widely viewed as a set of skills that are indispensable for success in education, professional training or life in general, and is articulated through a wide range of books and courses, of which my current favourite is *Critical Thinking for Dummies* (Cohen, 2015). Systematic guidance about how to do critical thinking is offered in a range of books and pamphlets and through websites such as *The Critical Thinking Community*. Drawing from a statement by Michael Scriven and Richard Paul adopted by the National Council for Excellence in Critical Thinking in 1987, they note that

> Critical thinking is the intellectually disciplined process of actively and skillfully conceptualizing, applying, analyzing, synthesizing, and/or evaluating information gathered from, or generated by, observation, experience, reflection, reasoning, or communication, as a guide to belief and action. In its exemplary form, it is based on universal intellectual values that transcend subject matter divisions: clarity, accuracy, precision, consistency, relevance, sound evidence, good reasons, depth, breadth, and fairness. (Scriven and Paul, 1987)

In the current epistemological crisis there are many points to celebrate here, and challenges to ill-informed and biased intellectual short cuts do have to be maintained. Nonetheless, there are troubling assumptions here about how critical thinking is to be performed and judged. It is firmly lodged in the Enlightenment framework of rationalist and positivist reason, despite the occlusions, limitations and problems associated with that universalising view of reason. Equally, it is to be treated as a normative standard against which almost all thinking necessarily falls short:

> Everyone thinks; it is our nature to do so. But much of our thinking, left to itself, is biased, distorted, partial, uninformed or down-right prejudiced. Yet the quality of our life and that of what we produce, make, or build depends precisely on the quality of our thought. Shoddy thinking is costly, both in money and in quality of life. Excellence in thought, however, must be systematically cultivated. (Scriven and Paul, 1987)

For me, this juxtaposition of critical thinking and its opposite short-circuits important questions about framings, dispositions, political and affective investments and the limitations of both available information and dominant ways of knowing. Most noticeably for a 'cultural studies boy', the problematic relationships between knowledge and power have disappeared, which leads me to puzzle about what the word 'critical' is doing in the phrase 'critical thinking'. Presumably the critical thinkers celebrated in this model are, in fact, critical of those who think less well? But, for the purposes at hand, I am most struck by what a lonely process this version of critical thinking is: it is undertaken by a disciplined intellect, separating itself from its social contexts, rising above local biases and arriving at its conclusion (and its fulfilment) through a process of individualised ratiocination. At its very (unexamined) core, this is the critical thinking *self*: 'Critical thinking is, in short, self-directed, self-disciplined, self-monitored, and self-corrective thinking' (Scriven and Paul, 1987). I am sure there are people who think in such a way, or at least who understand themselves as thinking in such a way. But it feels a long way from my experience of what Michael Billig has described as the necessarily entwined processes of arguing *and* thinking. As he puts it, 'humans do not converse because they have inner thoughts to express, but they have thoughts to express because they converse' (Billig, 1987: 111).

I want to draw two conclusions from this process of thinking critically about critical thinking. The first is the simple proposition that thinking *critically* might be socially and politically motivated, driven by a desire to challenge formations of power and knowledge; to unlock ways of knowing that obscure, deny or legitimate inequalities and injustices. That is, I would like to redeem the word 'critical' for political purposes. The second is to insist that thinking is *necessarily* social, both in the sense of being conditioned by contexts and in the sense of being intersubjective. Even when we are thinking alone, we are engaged in forms of argument; we are in conversation with the voices in our heads. Or, to put it in more formal terms borrowed from Mikhail Bakhtin, our thinking is both dialogic and heteroglossic: each of us contains, works with and negotiates multiple voices.

Thinking critically: with and against

I suggested earlier that many versions of thinking critically or engaging in critique involve a practice of deconstruction that demonstrate the thinker's superiority over X or Y's approach. I am not about to suggest that such processes of challenge and deconstruction are unnecessary – as our post-Brexit, post-Trump, post-Modi world reminds us, there is still much that needs to be challenged, criticised and deconstructed. There are also plenty of critical approaches that leave me feeling frustrated and grumpy. Among my friends, colleagues and students, I am well known for such frustrations and my tendency to dramatise them as conflicts that are simultaneously personal and political. And yet, there is always another dimension. I remember once being introduced to someone at a conference as 'this is John: he's a contrarian. He will begin every sentence with "yes, but …".' And I think there is some truth in that: it speaks to a desire to hold more than one thought in play at once. So I can both be frustrated by Foucault's unwillingness to pay attention to how power works in practice (whether he is talking dismissively about the 'witches' brew' of what happens in the prison or the business of governing rather than the neoliberal programme, see Clarke, 2009) and still think it impossible to deal with the relations between knowledge and power, for example, without him. One doesn't have to be a Foucauldian to think with Foucault … Indeed, I am not sure how one thinks without Foucault after Foucault, any more than I can imagine how to think without Marx after Marx. Both reorganised intellectual and political horizons in decisive ways, but so too do many other individuals and movements, such that the challenge of thinking critically is to work, creatively, carefully, collaboratively, with the tensions, possibilities and gaps that surround us. Thinking critically is, then, something other than taking down a much-loved theory and saying here's another example of how right it is. Such mechanical deployments engage in the problems of the moment (whenever that moment is or was) in only the thinnest sense, even if they are deeply satisfying to the ones doing the deploying. One result is the disconcerting intellectual oscillation between the desire to claim that everything is new (we have now arrived at an era of ...) or that this is just another instance of what we already know. Instead, many of the conversations in this book engage with the problems, and pleasures, of having to think again.

These relationships between theory, thinking and the moment are a continuous theme of Stuart Hall's work, as David Scott makes clear when he calls Stuart 'a theorist of the *contingency* of the present' (Scott, 2017: 55, italics in original). But Scott also insists that what is to be gained from Stuart is a disposition to thinking as a dialogic process – of listening and answering in an open-ended practice of 'clarification':

> Clarification is a way of approaching thinking – and learning – that aims to make us more aware of what we are thinking or doing ... That is to say, clarification involves endlessly saying the *next* thing, never the last thing. Clarification therefore does not presume the possibility of resolution; on the contrary, there is no presumption of closure, only successive provisional resting points along the way where we gather our thoughts for further dialogic probing. (Scott, 2017: 16, italics in original)

Two points flow from this. First, it describes a process of thinking with as well as against – and, in some respects, the 'with' is more significant, since it implies a commitment to maintaining an engagement, a relationship with the other (whether the other is a person or a text). It implies a necessary willingness to avoid 'closure': that moment of declaring the process over with a definitive verdict (after which the issue, theory or text can be put away). I remember the sheer shock – and joy – of a collaborative project in Paris, organised by the French anthropologist Catherine Neveu, which involved Catherine, Evelina Dagnino, Kathy Coll and me working around questions of citizenship (see Clarke et al, 2014; Neveu et al, 2011). One vital dimension of our work together was to explore readings on the topic that we would discuss, and then return to the following day, or the following week, in a drawn-out process of 'clarification'. Academic work is rarely so generous with its time and temporal rhythms, but in this instance we found and made use of the time/space to work in a manner that was both intense and slow – and, I believe, productive.

Second, Scott's observation makes visible the important difference between 'closure' and 'provisional resting points': the points that are necessary in order to be able say something other than the next round of clarification. Thinking together in this sense is a process that underpins and makes possible interventions into debates, discussions and issues, but such interventions are always, and contradictorily, provisional. Interventions – be they comments in discussions, blogs or full-length books – are necessarily provisional: they are 'the best we can do for now', rather than the definitive statement. One of the features of the Birmingham Centre when I went there was its house journal, whose title, *Working Papers in Cultural Studies*, has always struck me as an indispensable reminder of this provisionality – and I do not think I have written anything since that has not been a working paper in this sense. But provisional is not the same as tentative: I write and say things that are assertive, that make claims and that argue for positions. I have no doubt that some will find them frustrating, dogmatic or wilfully wrong-headed. But they are, nevertheless, provisional, with the intention of intervening in a discussion or issue to 'clarify', to move the argument along or to open it up to new possibilities. And by the time it has been published (even in the digital age), I may well have had occasion to think again. There is, then, a paradoxical combination of assertiveness and provisionality involved in this model of clarification and conversation.

Finally, the notion of *conversation* plays a significant role in this view of thinking as a dialogic process. It has both a real and a symbolic quality. On the one hand, dialogue implies a conversational relationship – and this book is a tribute to the importance that conversations have played in my life. It is also a theme that runs through David Scott's book on/ to Stuart Hall, given the central role that both voice and listening plays in his account of Stuart's way of working and way of being. But the idea of the conversation also plays another role in academic work where we imagine ourselves as 'joining in' or even 'starting' a conversation by writing an article or book. These, it should be said, are rather strange conversations. Sometimes our arguments get noticed and commented upon; occasionally they may be reviewed or even referred to in someone else's work (and sometimes those doing the referring get the idea at stake). But writing in academic forms also resembles sending a letter in a bottle, or broadcasting messages into outer space, and wondering if there is anyone out there. At best, these are oddly disjointed and dislocated forms of conversation – although they do, as a consequence, allow plenty of room for replies that begin 'I have had more time to think about this …'. But academic writing strains to be dialogic and all too easily turns into a monologic mode of address. My friend Ann Davis once commented on the draft conclusion for a book that I was writing by saying 'Are you writing for friends? Are you hoping to persuade people? If so, why are you shouting at them?' She was, of course, right; and the conclusion was revised into a slightly more conversational style. But there are reasons why talking *with* has rewards that are different from writing *to*, or even writing *for* – and one aim of this book was to show why talking about thinking has been a significant part of my life.

Dialogic selves: thinking subjects

The book rests on an underlying theory: that we are all 'dialogic subjects', who think, reason, reflect and argue as a fundamental condition of our sociality. This view derives from the work of the Russian linguist and literary theorist Mikhail Bakhtin (Holquist, 1981), who took the view that utterances and texts emerged out of a condition of heteroglossia – the coexistence (not necessarily comfortable) of different voices and ways of thinking. My connections to Bakhtin's work have been enabled by a number of intermediaries, especially Michael Billig in his development of a linguistic or discursive approach to social psychology, and Dorothy Holland and Jean Lave, whose collection of essays *History in Person* (2001) demanded that we think about subjects who 'answer back' rather than simply being the bearers and reproducers of dominant ideologies. They found Bakhtin's view of the dialogic creation of selves – what Holquist (1981) calls 'dialogism' – a foundation for grasping how individuals both were socially produced and played active parts in their own formation.

> History in person can in no way be confined to discrete persons. Durable intimate formations result from practices of identification in historically specific times and places. Dialogism insists upon the always-engaged-in-practice, always-engaged-in-dialogue, unfinished character of history in person. The person is necessarily 'spread' over the social environment, becoming in substance a collection point of socially situated and culturally interpreted experience. And herein lie important sources of stability and thickening. Weaker parties to struggles, as well as the strong, can

durably create their own discourses, practices, and emblems of struggle.

Given the uneven playing fields of power depicted in this volume, it is important that dialogism provides a way to think about a generativity that 'fills up the space between transgression and reproduction' (to borrow Willis's borrowing of Aretxaga's phrase from the seminar). In the course of local struggles, marginalized groups create their own practices. Participants in these groups both are identified by these practices and often identify themselves as 'owners' of them. These practices thus provide the means by which subjectivities in the margins of power thicken and become more developed and so more determinant in shaping local struggles. (Holland and Lave, 2001: 18–19)

Dialogism builds on Bakhtin's view of heteroglossia as a condition of sociality – that we all inhabit a complex (and shifting) landscape of multiple languages, voices and ways of thinking about the world and our place within it. Bakhtinian subjects are active participants: reasoning, negotiating, anticipating others' arguments and arguing back. This view has been helpful and productive for me: that idea of a 'space between transgression and reproduction' invites us to think about subjects as complex, social and creative, rather than either dupes or revolutionaries. Rather, it raises the possibility of thinking about the multiple ways in which people live their subordination, sometimes consenting, sometimes refusing but more often finding accommodations and distancing devices and living with/in ambivalence. During a research project on the emergence of citizen-consumers in public services in the UK, we described our respondents as 'little Bakhtinians' as a way of describing the complex capacity to negotiate and reason about the different messages, images and interpellations in play (Clarke et al, 2007: 142). The same issues – and the value of Bakhtin's view of the dialogic subject – were also important in a subsequent research project where we asked advisers working in Citizens Advice Bureaux how they understood the 'citizen' in 'Citizens Advice' (Kirwan, McDermont and Clarke, 2016). Here, too, we found people borrowing creatively from diverse repertoires about citizenship (conditionality, systems of rights and responsibilities, its links to nationality and so on) to offer alternative accounts of who might be a citizen. Most recently, Janet Newman and I have been writing about aspects of Brexit, including an article about political subjectivity in which we have again borrowed from Bakhtin (and Holland and Lave) to resist views of people as singular and coherent political subjects (Clarke and Newman, 2019). For me, the idea also has productive echoes of Gramsci's view of 'common sense' as a plural noun – common sense contains many diverse (heteroglossic) elements on which people and political projects draw, selectively, creatively but not necessarily coherently or consistently.

All of this emerges in the context of trying to make sense of subjects 'out there', encountered in research projects or political situations. But I do not think we (academics) should be in the business of having theories about people 'out there' in which we cannot simultaneously recognise ourselves. One of the great advantages of Bakhtin's dialogism, from my point of view, is that it works equally for thinking about the 'in here' – in the world of the academy and inside my own head. We – working academics – are also social subjects, not transcendent individuals. And we proceed through thinking, negotiating, arguing, anticipating and accommodating across a heteroglossic terrain. We may do so more formally, conditioned by a set of codes about how to articulate our thoughts and reasoning (with added references and footnotes), but we are also contextually produced subjects and dialogic – intersubjective – ones. One of the aims of this book is to make this more visible and more explicit: that I (and we) think dialogically, both in conversations with others and in imagined conversations with those others in our heads. Which brings me back to the voices.

Introducing the voices

When the idea for this project (my retirement project, remember) came to me, I started to make a list of people with whom I would like to record conversations, both for the pleasure of talking with them and to mark the ways in which talking to them had shaped my thinking. After a week or so thinking about this, it became clear to me that a multi-volume series was probably not viable: the list was simply huge, and so began the harder task of limiting myself to a dozen possibilities. Several criteria shaped the final selection. They should be people with whom I was currently in some engagement, rather than past collaborators no matter how significant they had been (this ruled out a lot of friends and collaborators from my early cultural studies days). Second, they should be relatively accessible to me. This turned out to mean I could access people in the UK and in North America, thanks to a travel grant from the Open University's Social Science Faculty that extended a trip to a conference in San Francisco. That excluded friends and collaborators in continental Europe – such as Catherine Neveu, Fabian Kessl, Prem Kumar Rajaram, Mikko Lehtonen – and beyond, such as Margaret Wetherell in New Zealand. Finally, they should be willing; and I am delighted to say that all those whom I approached agreed to take part, though not without some initial puzzlement at times: 'what, just sit and talk??'. Or at least, those were the original organising criteria. I had missed out a further critical one, that they should be alive. In the time between having the idea and putting it into action Stuart had died, followed by Doreen Massey just as we were talking about when to meet. I talk about these and other 'missing voices' in the next section, but here I am just going to say something briefly about the dozen who are present here.

Most obviously, they are all Anglophone, though they work in and on very different places: from the US to India, from the UK to Indonesia. That points to something important about the skewing effected by the model of 'conversation' in play here: conversations tend to be monolingual, even if dialogic. They are also generationally skewed, missing out younger scholars encountered at conferences, workshops and through both Central European University and the Open University. The selection is slightly biased towards anthropologists (3 out of 12: Tania Murray Li, Jeff Maskovsky, Anu Sharma). This reflects my later-life seduction by anthropology, which played a role in taking me beyond the 'little Britain' tendencies of both cultural studies and social policy. I was lucky in the anthropologists that I fell among on my first visit to a mega-professional conference (Washington, DC in 2001), who have sustained me since then in a spirit of considerable generosity. But the dozen also includes cultural studies people (Larry Grossberg), social policy scholars (Fiona Williams, Janet Newman, Paul Stubbs, even if he would rather be an anthropologist), legal scholars (Davina Cooper), geographers (Allan Cochrane, Wendy Larner) and those in politics (Wendy Brown) and psycho-social studies (Gail Lewis). But, in some ways, these disciplinary categorisations are misleading: all of them are more than those designations might imply, and indeed I suspect that these conversations are possible because people both outrun these disciplinary classifications and operate on their margins, making friends across such boundaries.

My conversations with all of them start from happy encounters – from standing behind Wendy Brown in a queue for accommodation at a conference to being told by Stuart that I should try to find Larry Grossberg in deepest Illinois when I went to the US in 1986 (Urbana-Champaign is indelibly lodged in my memory). They have different temporalities: I have known Allan Cochrane the longest (since an encounter in Catherine and Stuart Hall's living room in Birmingham in 1976 to discuss whether a Birmingham branch of the Conference of Socialist Economists might be set up – no), and we subsequently shared an office and much else at the Open University for over 30 years. And they have different rhythms and intensities: I live and write with Janet Newman, which gives it a sort of daily character, where others are more interrupted and intermittent. But they are inextricably linked by the sense that, without them, I would not think as I do. Each gets a slightly fuller introduction at the beginning of their chapter.

The missing voices

As I noted earlier, there are many missing voices who have shaped my work and thinking by adding to the overlapping, intersecting and unsettling conversations through which I have discovered things. Those things include topics (from being drawn into work on youth subcultures with Tony Jefferson, Dick Hebdige and others in 1972, to research on school inspection with Jenny Ozga and others in 2010); keywords and concepts, from taking citizenship seriously with my 'three sisters' – Kathy Coll, Evelina Dagnino and Catherine Neveu – to contemplating legal consciousness with Morag McDermont and Samuel Kirwan; and different domains and practices (finding social psychology through people like Margaret Wetherell and Mick Billig); and constantly being invited to think about social movements and social relations by activist-intellectuals who helped me to de-normalise my place in the world (as a white, male, able-bodied and straight academic). From Richard Dyer to Ann Phoenix, John Cho to Linda Gordon, I have benefited from the generosity of 'clarifications' that have helped me to ensure that – in thinking, at least – biology is not destiny. I could write a long intellectual-political personal history that traced these intersections and their transformative effects, but this is not the place for it. Rather, I need to pay a little more attention to the two missing voices – those 'absent presences' who, as Althusser suggested, are visible in their effects: Stuart Hall and Doreen Massey.

The first – Stuart – is both exceedingly simple and overwhelmingly complicated. It is simple in the sense that I would not be here today, doing this, without Stuart. The Birmingham Centre rescued me after a dismal undergraduate experience. Under Stuart's leadership (he became Acting-Director as I arrived), the Centre provided me with friends, collaborators, confidence and a sense of why it was worth bothering (some of this is explored in interviews with Hudson Vincent, 2013, and Kieran Connell, 2015). Stuart was also personally central to how all this unfolded – as a supervisor, mentor, collaborator, colleague and friend from 1972 until his death in 2014. As so many others have said, he was a brilliant, passionate, inspiring and wonderful person with whom to spend time, and with whom to think. He was also a rather frustrating exemplar, at least for me. His sustained personal, intellectual and political generosity set a standard that is difficult to match. I still clearly remember those moments in Birmingham where I would have bad-temperedly wrestled with some new source, arriving at my very crabby dismissal of their failings and limitations, only for Stuart to turn things on their head and tease out what we might gain from taking them more seriously. He was, of course, usually right – both substantively and in principle. But the accumulated frustrations of a would-be radical and critical scholar are also part of this learning process. By the time I (and often we) had got to our diagnosis of the problems of Althusser, Poulantzas, Foucault – that is, the moment of 'thinking against' – Stuart was ready for thinking 'after Foucault', both with and against. He still sits in my head as both the impossible standard and the eternal support, insisting that yes, we can think better ... and that it matters to try. This, I think, is my more ambivalent take on David Scott's wonderful articulation of Stuart as a practitioner of an 'ethics of receptive generosity'. He is right when he reminds us – and Stuart – of how this ethics was

> already there in your particular practice of thinking aloud with others, your style of speaking that is simultaneously a hermeneutics of listening. To my mind, you are an exemplary receptive giver insofar as you strive to practice a mode of effecting change among others that is, at the same time, a mode of changing yourself through the influence of others ...
>
> I don't think anyone would need much persuading, Stuart, that you were a generous self in exactly this sense of a receptive giver. You were never merely a privatised intellectual self, but also a *builder* and *sustainer* of intellectual community. And as such you were never-not sharing yourself with those around you, enabling, shouldering, bolstering and supporting them in the common endeavors in which you were together engaged ... But at the same time you would have been the first to tell me that all of this giving was also, reciprocally, a paradoxical kind of receiving as well. You, Stuart, were an *insatiable* learner. You were a *congenital* borrower of the ideas of others. You were never so closed or proud as to be unable to gain something from others. You had no false conceit about originality. You had

no misplaced fear of recycling. And I think this liberated you into a kind of modesty, and courtesy, a sense of proportion really, that was your true gift. (Scott, 2017: 140–41, italics in original)

It should be clear that I share the view of thinking as a dialogic process that underpins this celebration of Stuart's capacity to do it in practice: he modelled a distinctive version of how to be a public intellectual, not just in terms of making interventions into the public realm, but as an embodied mode of conduct and a way of being with others. This is a mode of conduct that remains depressingly uncommon among intellectuals, and among male intellectuals in particular. But I am grateful for having been exposed to it for such a long time – and to the voice that carried it. There are many more substantive gains from working with Stuart: about why Gramsci matters, about how articulation works, about how it is impossible to grasp the British social formation without its racialisation, and more. I suspect I am also 'a congenital borrower', though my intellectual borrowing is probably more shameless than modest. But I certainly continue to try on, and try out, other possibilities for thinking about the present in a process that Alistair Pennycook nicely called 'borrowing, bending and blending' (Pennycook, 2007: 47). In a recent collaborative project on transnational policy flows (Clarke et al, 2015) we took Pennycook's phrase as a perfect description of the unfinished process of theorising that our book offered. Others, it should be said, took a different view, suggesting that our lack of overall coherence and rigorous theorisation fell short of proper standards and ignored the overwhelming claims of particular intellectual schools (Actor Network Theory, most notably). But I have lived long enough in Stuart's ambit not to find this the most upsetting thing to have been said about my work.

Stuart is inextricably linked to Doreen Massey in my head, partly through their joint working lives at the Open University, following Doreen's arrival as Professor of Geography in 1982, which regularly featured political-intellectual discussions in Stuart's car on the drive to and from Milton Keynes. But they were also connected in the search for a new politics – after Thatcherism and after neoliberalism, originally through *Marxism Today*, then as co-founders (with Michael Rustin) of the journal *Soundings*. They similarly took responsibility for *The Kilburn Manifesto* (Hall, Massey and Rustin, 2015). Doreen, quite simply, taught me to think about space – an experience I share with many others. For me, space was where things happened – a series of passive contexts for action, events, movements and more. Doreen was a passionate advocate for the necessity to think actively about space and, more particularly, to think about space as relational – beautifully and powerfully argued in her book *For Space* (2005). I have written a farewell to Doreen elsewhere – in *Cultural Studies*, at the prompting of its editor, Larry Grossberg, who also knew Doreen and her work well (Clarke, 2016b). I don't want to go over that ground again, except to say that I stressed the conversational qualities of her thinking, arguing and writing. She had a dialogical style well suited to the collaborative and collegial world of the Open University as well as the socialist and feminist milieux in which she was formed and to which she remained committed.

I will, though, pause over one facet of our relationship: we spent a lot of time thinking and talking about the 'conjuncture'. Stuart developed the idea from Gramsci's work and it became a focal point for one version of cultural studies (see *Policing the Crisis*, for example). It provided a way of focusing attention on the complexity and contingency of the current moment in economic, social, political and cultural terms. It underpinned much of Stuart's work and formed a key element for how the triumvirate of Stuart, Doreen and Michael Rustin approached the work of *Soundings* and *The Kilburn Manifesto*. Doreen, Michael and I were also involved in organising a couple of workshop events on the theme of the 'current conjuncture' in the vibrantly dusty setting of the Marx Memorial Library in London. They were stimulating and frustrating in equal measure but acted like refuelling stops for longer conversational journeys about what it meant to think conjuncturally, and how to do it. Doreen and I last talked about these things on a panel at a Goldsmiths College conference to celebrate Stuart's life and work (Henriques et al, 2017). Our conversation included a promise to meet again and talk more about how time and space were configured in a conjuncture – and to record the conversation as a part of this book. Doreen died before we could make it happen and my gesture towards that conversation is now published in a collection of essays for and about Doreen, appropriately titled *Critical Dialogues* (Werner et al, 2018).

There can be no doubt that this book would be different if Stuart and Doreen were two of the conversations available here. Both of them thought in wonderfully conversational ways and were committed to thinking as a dialogic practice. But they are not here and we have to continue to think without them, though they have gifted us wonderful resources with which to do our thinking. That includes giving us models for how to do thinking, critically, collaboratively, creatively and focused on the social and political challenges of the present. For those reasons, as well as the remembered pleasures of their wonderful voices, they remain active as voices in my head.

Listening to voices; or, how to use this book

And so, to the substance of the book itself. The chapters are highly edited versions of much longer conversations recorded between 2013 and 2018. Each of the conversations is exactly that – a conversation, rather than an interview with a structured format. My aim was to explore the issues that the specific person and I had in common and how we went about thinking about them. As a consequence, although there are overlaps and intersections, each dialogue develops in its own unique direction. This makes their transformation into 'chapters' a somewhat strange process. They do not look or read like the finished pieces of academic work that we normally see in print. On the contrary, they are full of overlaps, interruptions, hesitations and, especially, short cuts that emerge because the person speaking and I already share some common points of reference. The editing process has involved addressing some of the dilemmas of turning 'talk' into 'text', involving exchanges between me and the dialogists. All of them have expressed frustrations that the transcribed conversations do not catch them at their best: they are less fluent, coherent, explicit or systematic than they would wish (I should note that it's even worse for me, as I keep reappearing …). I think this is intrinsic to the format – conversations between people who know each other are less structured or systematic than a formalised interview, and certainly less so than a polished and revised written piece of work.

So, the following chapters are the edited highlights from much longer conversations that lasted between one hour and three hours. I made the original selections from the transcribed conversations, aiming at chapters of around 6,000 words, and sent them to the dialogists. Some accepted my selections, others suggested alternatives that now form part of the chapters. People have taken slightly different approaches to 'tidying up' the edited texts, ranging from the minimalist to more developed polishing aimed at overcoming some of the difference between talk and text. I have allowed them to make their own judgements, and the editing is marked in the chapters by ellipses … that mark segments taken out and the use of square brackets to identify clarifying or contextualising additions. I have also edited them for what might best be called verbal tics … those little devices such as 'yes', 'indeed', 'mmm', 'I mean', 'I think' and 'you know' that act as spacers, connectors and acknowledgements during conversations but take up a lot of space on the page. They are of interest to conversational analysts but don't help with making the chapters readable. I have also added some clarifying footnotes about people, topics or issues that pass thought the conversations. Nonetheless, despite these efforts of housekeeping, they are a strange read!

I have left some time markers in the chapters to give a rough guide to where they appear in the sound recordings. The full versions of these dialogues – only edited to tidy them up sonically and remove the occasional embarrassments that can occur in relaxed conversation – are available as audio files (at https://soundcloud.com/bristol-university-press/sets/critical-dialogues). I was meeting with a group of Larry Grossberg's graduate students in Chapel Hill when this project was just beginning and told them about my plans. One of them, Chris Dahlie, who also worked as a sound engineer, was appalled that I was planning to record these conversations in order to merely produce much briefer textual versions of them. His first suggestion was that I should video them all, but, given that I share my mother's reluctance to be either photographed or videoed (both of us on the basis of very strong evidence), I declined this suggestion – on technical as well as personal grounds. But the more I thought about the potential uses of a series of audio recordings with interesting intellectual figures, the more it became clear that we should work out a way of making them available. I am grateful both to the dialogists and to the publishers for making this possible.

The characteristic of dialogic thinking – that it is emergent and open ended – gave rise to discussions with the publishers about how best to present the conversations. I have resisted suggestions that the dialogues might be cut up and arranged thematically because I fear that would lose the point of them being conversations. My aim has been to give the reader/listener the chance to see/hear the process of thinking together. As a result, the chapters are arranged in nothing more complicated than the order in which they were recorded, beginning with Tania Murray Li and ending with Janet Newman. I cannot think of a 'principle' that would take precedence over sequence, but, of course, that does not mean that the chapters should be read in that sequence. Each reader has the possibility to bring their own interests and orientations to the selection and ordering of the material. Fascinated by feminist political theory? Then start with Wendy Brown. Excited by the prospect of cultural studies 'old lags' in conversation? Then start with Larry Grossberg. Different routes can be plotted across this landscape: ones that follow existing connections (anthropologists first?) or bring new juxtapositions into being (try Wendy Larner alongside Anu Sharma for different geopolitical displacements). If you are seeking a thematic way through the dialogues, then we have tried hard to construct an index that enables such thematic tracing.

In his comments on the first version of the book Richard Freeman rightly pointed to the way in which key ideas and concepts slip and slide through the chapters without being explicitly discussed. This too is a feature of conversation: such terms work as points of reference, connection and, occasionally, disagreement, rather than being the focus of sustained explanation or development. To redress this a little I have added a section – called 'Keywords' (after Raymond Williams, 1976) – at the end of the book. It is not a glossary, in the sense that it does not provide a singular or clear definition of any of the terms included. Rather, it offers a reflection of the significance and potential (and shifting) meanings of some of the words that make a significant appearance in the conversations.

I have gained great pleasure from this project. Talking with each of these people reminded me about why I value them and of the ways in which they help me to think. I hope they do some of those things for you.

Recording and editing: a technical note

For technically minded readers, the recordings were made using an Edirol (Roland) R-09HR recording device, in 16bit .wav format. They were professionally transcribed by Page Six Services, then edited by me and subsequently reviewed with the interlocutor. The sound recordings were edited using Audacity software and are stored in 16bit .wav format.

1

Tania Murray Li

Tania Murray Li is a Professor of Anthropology at the University of Toronto. Her work has explored changing forms of land use and governing in South East Asia. In particular she has worked on questions of culture, economy, environment and development in Indonesia's upland regions. She has written about the rise of Indonesia's indigenous peoples' movement, land reform, rural class formation, struggles over the forests and conservation, community resource management and state-organised resettlement. Among her publications are *The Will to Improve: Governmentality, Development, and the Practice of Politics* (2007) and *Land's End: Capitalist Relations on an Indigenous Frontier* (2014). With James Ferguson she has produced a remarkable, thought-provoking pamphlet about work, welfare, subsistence and the politics of distribution (themes touched on in this conversation; Ferguson and Li, 2018).

I first met Tania at an anthropology conference in 2002 and became fascinated by her ethnographically grounded deployment and development of concepts like governmentality and assemblage. This fascination triggered a series of encounters and conversations that continue.

Further details can be found at her home page: https://anthropology. utoronto.ca/people/faculty/tania-li/.

This conversation was recorded in Toronto on 25 March 2013.

Themes and topics

- A collaborative-working puzzle
- Making concepts work
- Questions of conservative rule
- The problem of work

A collaborative-working puzzle

Tania: You know, the first thing I came across of your work was in collected things coming out of cultural studies which were multi-authored, and in my discipline, anthropology, that's a very rare thing. Now recently I've started to co-author things but it's very unusual and I wonder about that, working in groups at a young age, how formative that was? How do you think about the possibility of a group of people hammering out something together? Or was that actually what was going on there? When a string of names appeared on those publications, what was the process that you were all involved in?

John: *It's a great starting point. It was absolutely formative and it still drives me to think that working and writing collaboratively is the best thing I do. I mean, time consuming, difficult in all sorts of ways, but it delivers things that I would never do by myself. That holds for me because it's a way of working which is more than just, 'Oh you write that bit, I'll write that bit and we'll put some "ands" and "buts" in'; it is about reworking things together, that changes them, that reworks the substance as well as just the words.*

Tania: So what was the labour process? You would go in a room and have a topic or … how did you actually do that?

John: *It would start with a topic. It would start with some shared readings and arguments. So the writing has a sort of hidden set of precursors in trying to think together I guess, and work our way round questions and issues and puzzles and problems. Often I think they started with dissatisfactions, with, 'But you couldn't possibly think like that.'*

Tania: With each other or with something you'd read?

John: *With something we'd read.*

Tania: So something would –

John: *Provide a sort of hinge to doing something different and then we would go away and somebody might do a draft. It would come back and somebody else would do another draft and this is in the days of typewriters so this is a slow, cumbersome process. It's easier with word processors and that makes me a little suspicious about the speed with which it's possible to redraft. But at its best I think it's generative of something that none of us could have done by ourselves. Even working with Stuart Hall, I think there are things that happened that were even beyond what Stuart would have known and been able to do and that seems to me to be a thrill, a joy, for me anyway, and a chastening reminder about the limits of the individual intellect, as the source of new thoughts and new knowledge. So why is it rare in anthropology, do you think?*

Tania: I think partly because of the nature of our field data. I was there, I have all my notes in scratchy semi-literate form. I've often worked in places without any electricity so I don't have typed notes. The archive is very personal. Also, anthropologists have what we call 'head notes' as well as 'field notes' and it's your recollection of a scene and a moment which may never have been written down but you recall it and can draw on it. So that's part of it, it's the archive. But also it's ... I would say there's no disciplinary tradition of that. And also, intellectual formation. I came through the Cambridge system, so as an undergrad, the input from my supervisors was wonderful in the sense that it was, 'Here's an essay topic, five things you should read', so I learned to be an autodidact. That's to say someone would give me suggestions, really helpful ones because I would have no way into these literatures without someone prodding me and saying, 'I think you should read this, this and this and this is the interesting question that you should think about this week and write an essay.' So it was wonderful but it was very solitary and the supervisions were never conversations, because I was an 18-year-old. We don't have grounds for such a conversation, I didn't feel I did. The PhD process was also very solitary. No course work, none of what our students go through in terms of hammering out ideas together in seminars. So that was my normal way of working until about the mid-'90s when I started publishing things and I acquired this wonderful group of interlocutors who were willing to read drafts of things and give me usually – because we were thousands of miles away – I mean you're one of them and you know most of the others – give me really tough feedback on my writing (laughs). So it was dialogic but it was over my attempts at written work which people were generous enough to take seriously, to tear to pieces and say, 'I think you're really missing this, you should read that ...,' you know, 'You've got to work some more on that.' So I learned the benefit of critical input from colleagues, but it still wasn't face to face, actually being able to hammer it out together. That's something I've started to do more recently.

[0:06:27]

John: *Tell me about that and why it feels different, if it feels different.*

Tania: I co-authored a book with two people on land issues and that's the first time I've actually tried to co-author something.[1] We started with two two-day meetings and then a ten-day meeting where we worked together. And so your experience of it's more than the sum of the parts – if I look at the book now I think, 'I couldn't have done that.' In fact, none of us could have. But it's a pretty good book and it shows our different training. One is a geographer, one is a political scientist. It shows our common interests. We were all on the same page, I would say, probably politically, but with very different skills, knowledge, expertise … so that was hard work but worth it. Now I'm starting a co-writing project with Jim Ferguson and we've decided that we have enough common interests that we're going to try. I don't know if it will work or not, but every time we meet and we talk for two or three hours we both end up thinking, 'I've moved along.' What I came out with after this intense discussion is different from the way I was thinking about this topic three hours ago.

John: *Yeah.*

Tania: So I think it's what you say; it's the sense that you're being pushed in your thinking.

John: *It's interesting because there's two different dynamics. One is, you were talking about having critical interlocutors on your work and giving you tough criticism that pushes you. And I think part of the dialogue for me is the ability to combine that with the – I don't know, the generosity of spirit that you were talking about in the possible collaboration with Jim, which is – it's also a gift that you offer people –*

Tania: Oh it's huge.

John: *That changes the possibilities. And yet actually it's probably true that you don't know if it will work.*

Tania: Well, and also not everyone's receptive to it. Victor[2] thinks I'm crazy in the extent to which I seek critical input on my

---

[1] Co-authored with Derek Hall and Philip Hirsch: *Powers of exclusion: Land dilemmas in Southeast Asia.* University of Hawaii Press/National University of Singapore Press, 2011.

[2] Tania's husband: Victor Li, Professor of Comparative Literature and English at the University of Toronto.

work, but I've become addicted to it, because I know that it'll get better if I'm prepared to hold on to it for another year (laughs) and work through all of this, these ideas. I think it's not bad, but you know, there's more. I've only once felt with one thing that I wrote that I actually went too far in the sense that the initial boldness of the argument became so modified by me trying to work through different points of critique, and kind of not exactly please people but – I got pushed and pulled to the extent where I thought, 'Ah! Actually at the end of the day this is very mealy mouthed, this isn't actually what I – it's lost something of the kind of boldness.' So there's a point where you could perhaps go too far with it, but I think it's rare to get to that point –

John: *No, I'm sure that's fair.*

Tania: First of all you have to trust your interlocutors and your interlocutors have to trust you to not take umbrage at the criticism, right? And not to be cross because someone's saying you're not there yet. So it takes a lot of personal trust. I think I'm really going to take up my red pen on John's piece because I know he's not going to hate me for it and actually he'll make good use of it; it's worth my time and it's worth his time. So that relationship of mutual trust, in that sense it's kind of personal.

John: *Well, I think it's personal but this is going to sound strange, but I also think it's political that – I mean not in a precise politics sense, but that you are likely to work with interlocutors who will in some ways speak the same language and I – and I think part of that is finding people with whom you would not be cross and –*

Tania: Ideologically, you wouldn't start out on a different page. We have the same project, it's just we're struggling to –

John: *Yeah, and the sense is then that we're struggling together to make something of it. I remember when I first went to the Open University, which doesn't write collaboratively but produces teaching materials collectively, and so there's a lot of rounds of discussion of drafts which I thought was just normal, I thought it was what you did, but for a lot of people it was a very vulnerability-inducing process and they became, I thought, bizarrely defensive about their particular words. And my view was well, the words were just stepping-stones on the way to getting somewhere and if people could tell me to do them better it was a good idea. But it reintroduced me, I guess, to the notion of how proprietorial academics are about their words, and so finding people with whom it's possible to make things move seems to me to be a critical bit of the process.*

[0:12:27]

Tania: Now I've introduced this into my teaching a lot and into my collegial work here; not in that sort of intensive one-on-one format but I run these dissertation workshops where students give input to each other on their dissertation proposals and I facilitate. You'd think there's no one more vulnerable than a grad student trying to articulate their ideas – they love it! And they're such good interlocutors for each other, even with very little experience. Every time I set this task and they do written comments on each other's work at the beginning before we meet, and I'm always so amazed and proud of their skill actually in spotting what's working and not working. They're very respectful and delicate and sometimes they are spot on. So they know how to do this. It's a question of developing formats in which we routinely pay someone the compliment of saying, 'We're going to have a go at your draft of something – you know four or five of us will read it and we'll give you what we can.' So I organise it among my colleagues as well. We have an ongoing work-in-progress workshop and when I first started it some of my senior colleagues said, 'Oh, the un-tenured people, they'd never want to share their half-baked work-in-progress because they would be afraid of being judged,' and I said, 'Well let's try.' You try stopping them! (John laughs) Everybody wants to put their work into the workshop because you get so much out of it; it's such a good exchange and even people you may think are in a vulnerable position don't seem to feel that, from what I can tell, because they keep on coming back. They don't seem to feel, 'Everybody jumped on me and –'

John: *So it does seem to me that one of the really critical things is creating the setting, the context, in which people think that receiving criticism is generous rather than an attack. ... And I think if you can create that, it is shockingly productive and engaging for people and they learn a set of skills about receiving and taking criticism in the process. And that's one of the things that cultural studies did for me, was make me think that was a process by which you worked and by which you got better.*

Tania: It wasn't part of my formation but I got there eventually, just improvising and because of the people I fell in with and some techniques I learned. The workshop I got from David Szanton at Berkeley, who devised this format and taught it to me, and I've been using it and it's really been working for lots of people. There are different ways you learn how to do these things but it's surprising that it's not actually the routine core of academic life. Because I think (John laughs) for those of us who have become addicted to it, it's so obvious. But the other part of it though is that – there's the question doing your homework. Before I wrote *The Will to Improve* I did an intensive period of reading on state and governmentality and so on and I was prodded to that by colleagues, by Donald Moore and Arun Agrawal, and we were actually reading the stuff together at one point. In fact I hadn't even met Donald at that stage but we still had this intensive discussion. They basically helped me devise a reading list. Then I spent an entire summer sitting in this chair just reading. So there's a point at which you've got to pull back from all this dialogue and actually equip yourself with the vocabulary and the sort of basic training. Maybe that's also part of a Cambridge training in the sense that we didn't do course work, I felt leaving Cambridge that my knowledge base was extremely narrow and thin. But I always felt I could teach myself when I needed to. So when I needed to read about the state and governmentality I realised that I really didn't know this literature at all, but it had become important for something I was trying to get at in my work and I had kind of a glimpse of the corner of it but I'm really thin there. If I'm going to do this, I need to really read this literature and not just be on thin ice or dropping terms left and right, which I haven't really worked through. So that's kind of solo work, that's just doing your homework, it's just doing the reading and …

[0:17:25]

John: *I like the 'doing your homework' idea – and it is about re-equipping, expanding possibilities. But I'm interested by your description of it as a set of capacities generated by Cambridge and I think – not my first degree, but cultural studies did some of that for me. We were always, as it were, having to go into somebody else's repertoire to find stuff, to work our way through things. And it did, I think, leave me with – I don't know, somewhere between a confidence and an arrogance that if I needed to I could turn up somewhere and … engage with the literature of the field and make some sort of cultural studies-ish sense of it, which might not be becoming part of the field, but turning it into something slightly different for my purposes. So there is, I think, something about … the capacity to spread widely rather than, by doing homework, having to stay at home. And so I want to push you about thinking about disciplines and boundary-crossing moments because you said you were working collaboratively with a political scientist and a geographer, so how was that?*

Tania: This was a book we wrote about land issues in South East Asia and it started with a conversation I had with a political scientist, Derek Hall, when he came to my office one day and we had a two-hour conversation in which it turned out we'd read all the same stuff. I had just spent a whole summer – one of my re-equipping summers – reading the agrarian studies literature, thinking, 'You know I dance around this topic but it's a while since I've done this, I did some of this as an undergrad,' so I had just read a slew of stuff and I read some very formative things. Like I re-read Robert Brenner and Ellen Wood's work on definitions of capitalism, how we could understand agrarian capitalism etc and it turned out that Derek had read exactly the same stuff. And so a conversation started because we realised that disciplines didn't enter into it. We had been reading a common body of theoretical literature which was neither political science nor anthropology but which had helped us to come up with a useable notion of capitalism or understanding how capitalist relations might emerge in agriculture, and that was the basis for the conversation and that's when we realised that actually we could work together, because we think the same way, we're interested in the same stuff, we already have a remarkable amount of reading in common and so that would be the basis, and it worked very well. He's also incredibly brilliant (laughs) and a very generous scholar and it was – it is a joy to think with him because he's super-precise, he just nails it. Maybe that's a poli-sci thing. They are good sometimes at the sort of typologies and I notice you often do that, you often have – well there's five things about crisis and it's like, '1, 2, 3, 4, 5'. It's just about a systematic way of thinking through a problem, that you've actually dissected it and – I remember a paper you did at the Triple A [American Anthropological

Association] on the Social which was very striking because you said, 'There's these reasons why we don't want to give up on the term "the Social" – it's not dead (laughs) and these are the reasons why we want it,' but you listed them and you explored them and I think there's something about that desire to grasp an idea and systematise it which I found very helpful in your work, but I also found it in Derek's work when we started working together. He was the one who would push us to nail it, to say, 'Actually there's these elements. Let's tease them out and –' there may be five or six, it's not the number, it's the fact that you're actually digging in and dissecting a problem.

John: *I'm not sure I've ever really thought of myself as systematic so this is a bit troubling, but there is, it seems to me, a moment in collaboration where you want a dynamic between, 'Well we've got five or six things there,' which is then the springboard to saying, 'Yeah but I don't think number three really fits,' or, 'And there's seven and eight that we ought to get to,' or, on the heady moments 'We should explode that set of categorisations and start over.' So I think the systematic both appeals to me and always feels provisional, so a list gets you into another conversation, but the conversation often disturbs the list. I guess my worry about systematic is that I feel uncomfortable with those people who think that the typology is the end point of their intellectual –*

Tania: Derek's not like that. With him, these are tools for thinking. So the reason we were able to do that project together was common interests in a topic which is probably intrinsically interdisciplinary. We were looking at, 'Well, how do people access or get excluded from land across the whole of South East Asia?' For me it was a strange project because it was the first time I'd ever written about places I hadn't been to and for an anthropologist that's a very weird thing because usually you're drawing from your own field and I have a lot of field work, but I wasn't doing that. I was reading a ton of stuff on Vietnam and Thailand and trying to do something which was deliberately synthetic and comparative, and conceptually strong. But it was new terrain for all of us, so it stopped me just doing my little micro thing – it was fine. So it was the topic and also the spirit in which we wrote the thing, which was a deliberate attempt to answer the big question, 'What's the changing relationship between land and the population across the entire region?' We had a sense that it had been

dealt with in very simplistic terms like land grabbing, or there was a lot of worry about World Bank land titling. But when you look at what are the processes through which people are being excluded from land, those are just tiny parts of it; there are so many other dynamics in play in terms of crop booms and peri-urban development – there were just many other processes. So it was a deliberately synthetic project of a kind which I think one person couldn't have done really, you know? So interdisciplinarity as such didn't enter; none of us were there really wearing disciplinary hats. It's not that I represented anthropology and Derek political science and Phil geography, it was that we all had skills, conceptual strengths and probably a common body of theoretical reading. If one thinks about interdisciplinarity, what enables it is actually that we've all been reading the same people. So that's where theory probably becomes very important, right? If we have a theoretically derived vocabulary that we're all competent in – do you know that experience? Does that work or not?
...

Making concepts work

Tania: In my book that I've just finished on the emergence of what I'm calling 'capitalist relations' in a muddy place, I decided, on very helpful prodding from Donald, to abandon capitalism in favour of capitalist relations, and that was a really helpful intervention he made, yet again, because it solved a lot of problems in my analysis where the thingness of capitalism and its pretence of being a global system – its system-ness even – are all problematic. Part of what I'm arguing about empirically is that here you have people being dispossessed from the land who are not becoming proletarians because there's no jobs, so to perpetuate the thingy-ness of capitalism as a system in which dispossession is followed by incorporation as proletarians is actually to give historical weight to something which is precisely what we need to unravel. So you can't deal with the thingness of capitalism. But capitalist relations as in a specific set of ways of relating to property, profit, competition, derived from papa Marx, is actually a really powerful analytical vocabulary. So the question is, 'What are the things that you need to take as analytical categories and that you can define and use?' as opposed to the things which are -isms, too whole, too clunky. They do too much work and they get in your way and then you can't look any more.

John: *You can't get out of them.*

Tania: No, so I think that was really helpful and it enabled me to do that project with a powerful analytic that was familiar to many people – many people have wrestled with capitalist relations, let's say. So this muddy place, they're going to find it bizarre, but they'll recognise the vocabulary with which I'm approaching it because it's one which has been honed through many attempts to understand. In this case it's about the emergence of capitalist relations, which was a topic for Marx and Lenin and Kautsky and Brenner and many others, so it's a familiar problem which can be defined sufficiently concretely and attached to an analytical vocabulary without carrying a lot of other baggage about what kind of a system or an -ism, let alone a total social formation, this is supposed to be … So that's what I'm trying to do with this and it's tricky, you know I've really wrestled with it, because I think we need these theoretical tools. I couldn't approach a place like this without means and relations of production in my toolkit. I need to know who owns what, what are the relations of property? How do people relate to means of production? Where's the accumulation? How's it being done? These are very Marxist, materialist, and to me indispensable categories.

John: *It's the other side of the ethnographic puzzle question: which is, we can't possibly arrive at objects of urgent interest without a conceptual repertoire. What, you're going to empty your head every time you go to … you would then be an ethnographic tourist, 'Gosh this is interesting.' But there's something about 'what's the dynamic that's put in play?' The conceptual resources get you to look for things, but it seems to me that the way you work, or at least the way you talk about your work, and the way you write about your work, is those resources let you see what is being constructed and configured in a particular thing. So the puzzle is not, 'Oh and here's another space that has become capitalism,' it's how do these relations move into this space? What do they do to it? What does the space do to them? Because they're not the same as 14th-century Bosnia.*

Tania: Exactly, what were people struggling over? In terms of governmentality I would say it was not so much the '-ity' but the governing, which seemed to me a very fruitful idea, if one looked for relations of governing, all the different ways in which one party might be trying to govern the conduct of another, it's a question that I hadn't thought about before I read Foucault, but used as a kind of a nimble analytic – a way of thinking about how people might be forming relations, how relations might be being formed; whether they're programmatic, whether they're … that was just incredibly fertile. It was detaching governing from the government, which is one thing, but also from programmes, which are only one manifestation of attempts to govern, and also seeing governing as an attempt. So there were various things which enabled me to approach that ethnographic work with a set of questions. I was looking at 'Wow! There's a lot of governing about, how's it being done? Who's governing and why are they governing? Why do they think this is something they have to govern?' And so that just became a whole new way of looking at the problem – a way of actually establishing a new kind of enquiry. So it's a relationship to theory which is very much about finding useable and what's the word – nimble –

John: *I like 'nimble'.*

Tania: Nimble, but also it has to have some substance, otherwise you're just back at complexity; there has to be something you're chasing … So in that book I wasn't chasing culture, I was chasing governing and trying to figure out, 'Who's been governing? Why have they been governing? What have they been trying to govern? What are the problems?' (Laughs)

John: *But that seems to me to be what the – I mean it's both what the theoretical resources are that enable that as a set of things to go and look for and it's also what makes the conjuncture of theory and ethnography productive, because it's not, 'Oh what are the governmentalities in place in this space?' because then you –*

Tania: Give them a thingness.

John: *Yeah, you give them a thingness and you catalogue them and a lot of academic work does cataloguing, 'Here's an example of this, here's another example.' But animating the tensions between, 'That's strange, who thought that was governable? Who thought that was an appropriate thing to stick your governmental finger into?' is a problem, a puzzle, and you don't know. The big thing about this is you don't know before you get there and you might know what you want to be looking for but you don't know what you'll find.*

Tania: Yes, so I think that's why I am just totally an anthropologist, because I think that's what we have; that's to say … you know we're licensed to (both laugh) –

John: *You're licensed to thrill!*

Tania: Well, to do theoretical reading and then go see how it works out and then to think about that. I think other disciplines are more rigid in their procedures, their practices. They've got to have hypotheses, they've got to have models, they've got to ... I think we are more free to have a notion – a notion derived from some pretty powerful theoretical work which I've fortunately had time to read. I don't know what it's going to amount to, but can go check it out. And vice versa, because I started doing all that reading on governing because I was running into so much of it. I thought, 'Gosh, there's a lot of people busy here trying to organise things', why? So it came out of a conjuncture and it was also then fed by the theoretical, so it's that sort of back and forth. That, plus some of the other things we've mentioned are what is sort of unique about ethnographic work and what makes it so – in its own way, so productive I would say.

John: *I'm going to stop there with the thought that it's interesting to me that you talk about it as ethnographic work, but I think that there's lots of practitioners who don't do quite the complicated thing that you just described.*

Tania: With their ethnographic work you mean?

John: *Yeah, but it's also why you are – I mean, for me you're one of the people that enlarge my possibilities and ... that's what starts these conversations, right? I have for some time had a sense that there are both people that I read, and people that I talk to, but there are also people that I carry around as that unfortunate phrase, 'Voices in my head' (Tania laughs) who say, 'No, no but look this is interesting!' or, 'Look at that' or, 'Think about that,' 'Do you know I told you ...', and having generous, insistent voices matters. It matters.*

Tania: It does, very much so.

       ...

Questions of conservative rule

Tania: I mean if you've lived through a really remarkable – I mean the strength of Conservative reaction and the effectiveness with which this shifted from a crisis in capitalism to, 'You lazy welfare layabouts and irresponsible young people who need to get on your bikes and –' you know I mean these things don't add up and yet they have been so – I mean they've got away with it; it's a complete transfer of –

John: *I think there is a sense of shock and part of it is that I want to say – because I'm a neo-Gramscian or whatever – that I don't think that this is a moment of massive popular consent. I don't think this is hegemony in the sense of actively persuading people that they endorse all this and they think it's true. So I think we are in a sort of fractured – still in a fractured moment where people think, 'Oh but they would say that' and there's – I mean there's a couple of anthropologists who've written about the politics of resignation which I think is interesting. There's a nice cultural studies man [Jeremy Gilbert] who has written about what he calls 'disaffected consent' which is, 'Yeah we'll go along with it but we don't really – we're not really attached to it.' I have 'passive consent'; I mean there's a whole number of terms for trying to grasp what seems to me to be a really – it sounds old fashioned – a really contradictory moment in terms of the real success is the demobilisation of alternatives and alternative voices. So it might be true as I believe and I think there is empirical evidence to support it, that the public think that government should act, that they should do things well. You know, look at the Greek public, you know? Angry mobs is what you get instead. But the demobilisation is absolutely critical, that it turns into a slightly sad and nostalgic and old-fashioned-sounding set of things.*

Tania: That's how you get demobilised, by being told that you're sad and old fashioned, because you believe in something which is not tenable.

John: *Yeah, and you're unrealistic, you're old fashioned. I mean either you're utopian and much too future oriented or you're old fashioned and stuck in old ways of thinking. So the only way is to work in a society that can't generate enough work, to get work experience for nothing because nobody can afford to employ you, to subsidise capital to employ you and to outsource still more of the welfare state as a source of capital accumulation.*

Tania: What a weird place. ...

The problem of work

Tania: ... We were talking about the panel that I organised with Jim [Ferguson] a couple of years ago, that you participated in. On work, welfare abandonment and such and you know, the more I've thought about it, the more I've come to think that work is a deeply problematic term in all of this. Like work as the norm and the idea that one's worth and value and dignity and claim on distributive resources will all be routed through paid labour at a period in which the horizon of that is receding and is not coming back, right? So this idea that, 'We do austerity now, because once we get the economy growing again, then it'll be back to usual and all you young Spaniards will have jobs,' right? There is no way that that's going to happen and so – anyway in the places where I work in the muddy reaches, the things which are – the catastrophic things which are legitimated environmentally, in terms of land use and so on, on the promise of jobs – the things people will sacrifice for the promise of a job when the numbers show (laughs) that there are no jobs coming, right? I mean, look at the mass farming of soy and wheat and whatever in Brazil, I mean hundreds of thousands of hectares and it's three guys, their tractors and their cook. You know ten people cover it and these are not machines for employing people, so we do have a crisis of work in the name of this – I think it's also fascinating the way that – as you were saying, subsidised capital to provide jobs, the idea of the right to a job, of a claim on a job as a distributive claim, that somehow governments should be involved in make-work projects – making work, which is an old theme in the Third World, like the Government Employment Scheme. But I'm sure it's a mistake because it assumes a normal and it revalues the state of employed-ness as the value in a historical period where that's just not the way it's going. So having you know – being fascinated to read Castells on how this emerged at a certain period in the 19th century, we now have to – we really have to get away from this idea that work is the centre of how you get your share, how you are entitled to a decent life, meaning, value and all the rest of it. Because it seems to me that's actually one of the ways in which this sort of contradictory – what did you call it – concession or passive consent, is being engineered.

John: *It is indeed.*

Tania: It's around a promise of a prosperous future in which everyone will have a good job and a good life; that's not coming … So we're sacrificing now in the name of something which is not coming and I mean, I think in a horrible way we're reproducing it in the universities in the sense of selling students this Bill of Goods which says, 'If you as an undergrad, you get your As and you study hard and then you will actually be able to reproduce the class position of your parents.' And they won't and they can't and those career paths are not there for them. And we're not training them to think critically about that, we're training them to learn how to manoeuvre themselves so that they will be among the ones ... who will get those jobs, and I think it's a huge disservice (laughs) to all those who, however brilliant they are, these young people – I have lots of them and they're fantastic, but their future is going to be really hard and it's going to be even harder if we've continued to route it around the concept that that's the source of value in life.

John: *I'm deeply taken with that argument; it does seem to me that we have got stuck in a terrible place ... and it does seem to me that it's now one of the ... emerging contradictions. So in a world that has moved, it claims, from welfare to workfare, workfare prepares people for jobs that are not going to be there and then blames them for not being competitive enough in finding them. It also ... acts as a way of unhooking the other claims on the share.*

Tania: Yes, exactly. Everyone else is pathologised.

...

2

Larry Grossberg

Larry Grossberg is the Morris Davis Distinguished Professor in the School of Communication at the University of North Carolina, Chapel Hill. An early student at the Centre for Contemporary Cultural Studies at Birmingham, he has been a forceful champion of cultural studies in the US and internationally. He has written about the specificity of cultural studies, developments in contemporary theory, US popular music, youth culture and politics, the changing conditions of children in the US, the rise of new forms of conservatism and capitalism, countercultures, value theory, modernity, the state of progressive oppositional struggles in the US and the rise of populist conservatisms. His most recent book is *Under the Cover of Chaos: Trump and the Battle for the American Right* (2017).

I first met Larry in 1986, at Stuart Hall's urging, when Larry was teaching at the University of Illinois at Champaign-Urbana. A long evening's excitable conversation has unrolled into many others and our shared enthusiasms and body shapes prompted one US friend to observe 'separated at birth ...'.

More information about Larry's work can be found at: https://comm.unc.edu/people/department-faculty/lawrence-grossberg/.

This conversation was recorded in North Carolina on 29 March 2013.

Themes and topics

- Talking through differences
- Taking positions provisionally
- The pains and pleasures of collaboration
- Looking for the popular

Talking through differences

Larry: So here we are in the countryside of Carolina, clear blue sky –

John: *About to do difficult thinking all over again. All right I want to start with one of the characteristic terms that crops up in our conversations. When I say 'moral economy', you ask me, 'Why do you want to use that? What does it do for you?' That's what you said to me the other day and I just think that may be a characteristic starting point for when we talk to one another. And I say I don't know what you want to do with – the unity-multiplicity thing; so we have a set of ways of saying, 'Tell me more, justify what you're doing.' So why do we proceed in this argumentative mode?*

Larry: Is it an argumentative mode? (Both laugh)

John: *Well it depends what you mean by 'argumentative mode'! This is going to go well! Well I think it's – I don't think it's an argumentative – I think it's a starting device that seems to me to say, 'I've heard what you're saying but I need you to reason it, justify it a bit more.'*

Larry: I think it's a way – I mean when we talk, because we don't interact on a regular basis and therefore we sort of pick up where we left off but each of us has moved and it's a way of sort of figuring out what's at stake, what are you trying to do? What are these words trying to do for you? And so when I say – when I ask you, 'What is – you know, moral economy, what is it?' it's trying to figure out why you would turn to that phrase, because I haven't heard you refer to it before. I know that there are people out there, starting with Thompson, who have used it and picked it up, but I'm curious – I sort of know the terrain on which it operates, but I'm not sure what it is that you're trying to get to.

John: *Yeah.*

Larry: And I think the same is true when you say, 'What do you mean by the one and the many?' What you're really asking me is, 'What are you trying to do? What do you think this is going to do for you? What's at stake? Where do you –?' In a sense it's … 'Where do you think you're going to end up?' But it's also 'What are the questions that are underlying the terms that you're using?' Because I think you and I think a lot alike, but we have different questions and styles. I mean it's partly because of my philosophical bent and your more pragmatic bent – but it's also partly because the questions you ask, even the theoretical questions, are not quite the same. I mean we come from the same place, we make the same assumptions, but we are asking sort of different questions – the trajectories are slightly different.

John: *And I think – you're right about that and that's both about what makes the conversation possible – enough shared resources, starting points, puzzles and previous conversations, it has to be said. But also I think that just enough difference to be possibly generative, productive, troubling, moving things a bit. But there is … something important about the time that we have intense conversations, long intense conversations when we see one another, but then they go into suspension and there is something important about not presuming that they just carry on; that nothing has happened in the meantime.*

Larry: Right, I think it's – how do I put this? My interlocutors, the people that I care about – for me it's a very personal relationship as well as an intellectual relationship because I need a level of trust, you know I need to be able to say things and have someone say to me, 'But that's just foolish or meaningless,' and I need to be able to say that. And my – the people that I care about intellectually and personally – are dispersed, you know when I write, I have in mind a very small group of people as my audience unfortunately (both laugh) and it may explain why I write the way I do, but it's as if I'm having a conversation with you and Stuart and Meagan Morris and Ghassan [Hage – and Doreen – added after the conversation because even though Stuart and Doreen are dead, I still write for them] and a few other people that I think share a certain set of assumptions and share a certain kind of political praxis and a certain vision. But we don't – we're not together. I mean it sort of pains me, you know, because when I have an idea, I wish I could sit down with you and say, 'I think this is a step forward but I'm not sure,' and I need someone who isn't so … so embedded in what I'm thinking that they could challenge me. You know, I think in an odd way I think it's the advantage that the Right has, by creating these think-tanks where people bring together the people they want to talk with and they are extraordinarily productive in that sense because they're talking with the people they want to talk with, you know and –

John: *All the time, consistently.*

[0:07:29]

Larry: All the time, constantly, you know, and it's easy enough to say to someone, 'Well would you mind reading this because I think there's something interesting here?' and we can talk about it tomorrow, and you can do that, whereas you know I could say to you, 'Would you mind reading this?' and you probably would but by the time we get together you will have forgotten what you read (laughs). And so I think it's partly the problem of how you have conversations under conditions of spatial and temporal displacement.

John: *Yes, and it does seem to me that produces a very odd rhythm and the alternate forms – so I mean, we do occasionally send one another things we're working on and we usually write (laughs) – usually write back with some response, but that's not quite the immediacy of sitting and saying, 'I'm struggling, you know, I am trying to work this out, I think it's interesting, I don't know where it will end, you know, can I rehearse it? Can I get you to pull it around with the things that you know?' … You know where I come from so I can have a quicker entry to it, it's not like trying to persuade a stranger, but it does mean that I think you're right, that both the – I mean the displacements in both time and space and none of the other techniques quite match up to sitting with a cup of tea or a beer or whatever and saying, 'No, no but that's what I was trying to do. I don't think I expressed it very well but –' and so I think that thing that you started with about trying to work out what's at stake, what are the questions that it might enable you to engage with, becomes a sort of critical point and that's – I mean that's also true about what we've talked about, theory and ideas more generally.*

Larry: Yeah, and there's another kind of displacement and that's a social displacement; that is each of us is talking to other people about these ideas and those people affect the ways we think and talk those ideas, but they aren't together and they aren't necessarily the same people. So both of us probably do talk occasionally with Stuart … but then you have Janet and other people that you talk to, I have a few other people locally that I talk to – although it's not the same – those push us in other directions and so there's a kind of – I'm not quite sure what to call it, but a social displacement because we're not in one conversation, we're in many, and those conversations almost never coincide.

John: *No, indeed.*

Larry: I mean it's almost never the case – it would be an interesting idea and it's my – why I said in a sense it would be interesting now to bring the conversation – our conversationalists together … so I say, 'Look, I want to bring these four or five people to the table,' and you say, 'I want to bring these four or five people,' and then we have a different conversation.

John: *A very different conversation because I mean – because at the moment they're mediated by us. You know you get to hear the things that people are talking to me about as I half-process them and say, 'I've been thinking with Nick about that,' or with Janet about that … but it's true that they are sort of stretched – stretched and reworked conversations. And I mean the interesting thing would be if that imaginative little moment of yours came true and we assembled a big table, interesting group of people –*

Larry: Would the conversation work?

[0:11:31]

John: *– would the conversation work? No indeed.*

Larry: No, because we – Foucault's image of dreaming himself as entering into a conversation that's already going on and that would continue after he leaves, leaves out the fact that it's not easy to enter into a conversation that's already been going on. So you know one of the reasons I asked you about the moral economy was because you know one of the people I have an occasional conversation with is David Ruccio and he keeps saying to me, 'But why do you people want on the one hand to say, "We are against economic reductionism" and on the other hand you describe everything as economies? Do you not think there's a contradiction here?' (Both laugh) Right? Now I didn't before David sort of pointed it out to me, I thought it was a lovely metaphor – things are in movement and circulation and production – productive and you know … but then suddenly David and I are talking and then I say, 'Wow!' Suddenly there's something at stake that I hadn't known was at stake and I suddenly have to ask, 'What – why am I using economies so much?' And then obviously I ask my friends, 'So why do we – what is it that this – why would we imagine moral terrains and discourses on a model of economies?' … But then I say, 'But why do we imagine them on the model of geographies either? Or histories?' And I mean I don't – I think those are the conversations I want to have. I want to say,

'What do we gain and lose by thinking of moral geographies or moral economies or moral histories or ...?'

John: *That does, it seems to me, do what conversations ought to do, which is the gain and loss question, if that's not too economic a form of reasoning, right? (laughs). ... I mean the terms you borrow open up possibilities, so I went to moral economies because of Edward Thompson and because I could hear lots of people talking about 'crisis' through different sorts of moral and moralising registers. So is there a person who – ? Well, there's one person that I know who helps me think about that. And then – so I start playing with it and that question of – it's not being stopped in your tracks, it isn't quite being stopped in your tracks because it's more generous than that. Because it's another loop and it seems to me that's what the good conversations do; they give you a way of thinking about your thinking, rather than stopping you. I mean it's not 'You can't use the concept of moral economies,' it's 'Okay, when that goes in there, what does it open up and what does it stop you [thinking]?' What do you not think with that?*

Larry: And it's ... I think it's made possible, that we can do that with each other, because of a certain similarity and difference. The similarity is that neither one of us is a very consistent thinker (John laughs). I mean neither one of us worries about sort of theoretical and philosophical consistency.

John: *Yes ...*

Taking positions provisionally

Larry: Now there are consistencies I do worry about and when David says, 'Is it not inconsistent to use – ?' I do worry about that. But I mean I might – you might answer it and I might say, 'Okay, so it's another inconsistency.' But in another sense I'm never – I'm not a Derridean, I don't want to be a Derridean, but I want a bit of – like a bit of – that that's useful. So I think the fact that neither one of us and the people I talk to worry about being an X so that someone's saying to me, 'But there is this which says Y and that's not X ...,' and for me, you know, 'Okay'. But the difference between us is also in an odd way productive, because you work by always asking questions and I work by always taking positions, yes? So I work and you ask your question and say, 'So is this an answer?' And then you come along and say, 'Well no, it's not an answer because this and this happens (John laughs) and what about this and this?'

And you work by saying, 'Well so I want to think about how this opens up a field and how that field might be connected to another field …,' and you know, in the end you do take positions. I mean one can't not take positions – one can't write in a sense without taking positions, or maybe one could, but we don't (laughs).

John: We don't, yeah.

[0:17:00]

Larry: But you converse through questions; I converse more by offering a 'Here's an answer, but what's wrong with the answer?' That's what you always give me, that's what the people I converse with – Stuart says, 'You know well that's interesting but what about that?' (laughs), 'What are you going to do with that bit that you've left out over there?' or you know … So I think it works because in a sense many of our conversations start with me saying, 'Well, I'm reading Spinoza and I think it offers me a solution to the problem of counter cultures' right? (Laughs) And then you say, 'Well, what about that?' (John laughs) There's some danger of moralising, you know.

John: *Yeah, and there is I think a really … I do recognise that mode of operating – I mean not just with you, but especially with you which is to say, 'Yeah that's really interesting but –' and so – and it is always a sort of trying to put the 'but' in that is a bit – doesn't deny you but is a bit disruptive of a way of thinking. And I take deep pleasure in that because it seems to me one of the things that you're really good at is offering a, consistent might not be the right word, but a coherent attempt to think through a question and issue and I think I'm messier than that. I think the puzzle is interesting and I don't – I mean I might not know what works but I might limit it to three or four things that work. But … as a way of moving one another around a bit – I mean we're never going to move one another a long way, but doing developmental work that says, 'Well you know that way of thinking – I've not thought about it like that and I'm glad you have and then – and what happens next if we worry about that as well?' And that seems to me to be deeply engaging and is a – and I think in both ways is an act of generosity, that what makes the conversations work is both trust and so on, but it is also recognising that getting your interlocutor's attention, their thoughts,*

their willingness to worry about things with you, is a moment of
immense generosity which is not entirely commonplace in the academy.

Larry: No, I think it's (laughs) rare. I think we – the academy teaches us to work by negating others, rather than helping others … You know, I think you have taught me – I try to use your model which is the, 'Yes that's right but what about – but it's also and, and, and –' in my pedagogy. But not so much in my kind of efforts to move forward intellectually, and I wonder if it isn't – and maybe I'm romanticising your situation, both at the OU [Open University] but also in England a bit … but I think you have more of an ongoing conversation with people at the OU. But also I mean, I see advertisements online for these forums in London and people come – and at the OU – and we don't have that. You know I don't really talk about the kinds of things I talk about with you with anyone. You know, there may be a bit of it with one or two, you know – like I do have one buddy here and occasionally – but he's a Derridean you know, (both laugh) so there's a limit to the conversation. And he's more of a rigorous philosopher than I am. So he does think that it's important to read very carefully and very slowly through the text and I think that's important too, but then I want to play around with it (laughs) and use it and say, 'Oh well, you know it says this and that but I'm really interested in that,' and I – you know I think American academics and it may not be true, maybe – I'm sure it's different at different universities and different campuses; I think we're more isolated than I at least imagine you to be or even, you know, Ghassan Hage or Meagan [Morris] in Sydney. I think there are those conversations that you can have, not the same discussions, but you have discussions with people with whom you share a certain amount of definition of what the intellectual is and how the intellectual works, where here you know, I just sort of play with myself.

…

The pains and pleasures of collaboration

Larry: And in that sense my work has always been collaborative, right? And I don't write individually because it's my careerist choice, I write individually because of the social conditions of production under which I live. You know? I mean one of my students – Sarah, you were talking yesterday – when she said, 'Do you and John ever write together? You two would be amazing collaborators,' and I said, 'Yes we would and it would be a dream come true if we were ever together for a long enough period of time where we could sit down for four weeks and write together,' but you can't do it via email – at least I can't, you know, online – you can't do it by simply, 'Here's a chapter,' you respond, I respond; you have to be together, you have to – that was – I mean that was a lesson at Birmingham was collaborative work means here's a sentence and then you get to say, 'Boy that doesn't work, let's change that word –'

John: *Yes indeed.*

Larry: I can remember the first time I wrote something for a collaborative project, you know it was the 'Cure for Marriage' project and I spent – I stayed up all night writing one page and brought it in and I was so proud, I had done this! And I put it on the table and by the end of the three hours, there was not a single word left of what I had written (laughs) – And I went home crying and then I spoke to Stuart and he said, 'But this is what it is – they're not your words, they're collective words and you move, we move, they move, you bring. It's not that what you wrote isn't there, it's that the product that we have produced is a collective project and not an individual one.'

John: *And – well there are two things from that. One is – I mean that last point, I mean what Birmingham taught me was you write things down to start conversations. They are not the final thought. They start things, they are not the end product. So the working groups that I spent my life in, you know, tapped out on old typewriters, things that would start the next bit of the conversation and ... one of the things it did for me was it taught me that thing about, 'They're not your words. They're not your words, they are part of –' and it made it very strange when I came to the Open University, which has a mode of not collective writing but collective course production, you know the production of course materials. And you could feel the sense of division between people who thought that the draft that they had written was their words and those who thought the draft of what they had written belonged to the course team. And it used to be the case, and I regret its disappearance enormously, that an individually authored chapter would say on it, 'Prepared for the course team by –' right? Not – I don't know, 'The Uses of Nationalism by John [Clarke]' but, 'Prepared for the course team by [John Clarke]'. It defined a subordinate, helpful, productive relationship rather than single authorial authority. And that – but I remember the terrible, terrible, wonderful, strains where you'd say to somebody, 'Well I think you could do that better, more engagingly,' and they'd say, 'But I've written that,' and that retreat to [being] the proprietorial owner of some words and their sequence seems to me to be dismal. But the other thing to go back to is even more important, which is when you say that you write out of, as it were, the collective sensibility, the sequence, the series of quotations, allusions, references, assembled by Larry now I think, 'Yes,' and actually one of the things we do is fetishise joint authorship and that produces some very peculiar effects and stressed effects. So I – like you – I think that one is both motivated out of conversation and is – we are always, however the authorial relationship works – speaking into conversations, right? Imagined audiences, listeners, recipients, and I did once write and it's a phrase that I like, 'I have voices in my head.' And they tell me things and they tell me I should remember stuff that we've talked about, but I –*

Larry: I wouldn't say that too loudly in the United States! (Laughs)

John: *(Laughs) But it has the same unfortunate mental health implications in the United Kingdom, but I can't think of – it's not that the conversation goes in my head, but after we've stopped conversing I carry you around with me. It's like a version of a memory stick. It's not a very good memory but you and some of the other people go around with me and say, 'Come on, John, we did talk about that and you can't talk about that without thinking about that,' you know, 'That's shoddy,' and so it's not – the individual/collective thing is a much more complicated set of relationships. And sometimes I do write with people and sometimes it's wonderful and sometimes it drives me crazy, but I absolutely agree with you that it requires a certain sort of proximity to work. I mean, I've been working with friends and colleagues on a book about citizenship for five, nearly six years and it is animated and lively when we are in the same place, and we go our separate ways and it stalls. It stalls because you can't do the next thing and we have a – we grew a text which has accreted comments – it's got more comments in the margin than it has words in the chapter. But actually ... they are always dislocated; they are not a way of thinking together, they're a way of reminding one another that we don't quite agree about that. But you need to be – you need to be proximate to be able to resolve the disagreements, and so I think in the end we've done an interesting piece of work, but partly at the expense of sort of holding the disagreements apart. And so it's not*

quite what it might have been. But then if you're on three different
continents that might well be the case, you know?

Larry: And I think two ideas crossed my mind as you're speaking
of these things. One is this post-retirement project of yours
at least points in the right direction. The idea of publishing
conversations is an interesting one and we tend to do that
only with the stars. You know, so you get a book of Laclau,
Žižek and Butler and I read it and there are no surprises in
it. I knew what they would say, I mean there were a couple
of points where I say, 'Yes I'm glad you said that there,' but I
know their positions and they don't change much. It's not that
this is a conversation really in the sense in which you know
my pragmatist leanings say, 'Conversations are productive,
conversations change people, you move your positions in
response.' These are not that; these are a discussion between
three people with pretty well fixed positions and in so far as
one knows the positions, it's not all that – it would be more
interesting to have conversations amongst unknowns. You
know, people, I don't know what they think – I don't know
what this is going to end up with, you know? I don't know
where this is going to go and hopefully they don't either. So
they are surprised by their own conversation. Or conversations
among those who are, as you put it 'inside your head', because
those can be just as surprising. You know, you and I have
conversations, I take notes because I'm surprised where – not
only with what you say but sometimes where it takes me and
what I say. 'Oh, I hadn't thought that's where I would end
up,' you know?

John: *Yeah and that does seem to me to be ... a critical bit. It's not a*
guarantee, you know the discovery, surprise moment isn't guaranteed
but the conversational mode does seem to me to have built into it the
desirable possibility that you come out of it thinking, 'God, I really
hadn't thought of that,' or, 'I hadn't thought of it like that,' or, 'I didn't
even know that was at stake,' right? So you know when you told
David's comment to me about thinking about economies, I thought,
'I half knew that, I half knew there was a problem about it,' but
that's a really transformative moment because it stops where the next
thing I want to write should end. It cannot stay there, right? Okay,
well you know at some point I've got to write it but I now know that
if I sit down at the keyboard and start doing it and I get to the end
and I have not done that, I will have you in my head saying, 'You
can't possibly think that's finished! We had that discussion, you can't

possibly have forgotten that already?' And that — that movement, that possibility of movement — not guaranteed but — because we know that cultural studies is without guarantees, but the possibility — being open to the possibility, is what animates the different modes of conversing with friends, colleagues, collaborators, interlocutors that I don't — I said it at the talk on Thursday, I don't think I'm very clever. I don't think I'm an original thinker, I don't think I'm a person who has great thoughts and nor do I particularly aspire to be. But I do think that the things that I bring into conjunction from friends, interlocutors, people who do interesting work, make me, and possibly others, think a bit differently. And it seems to me that the moving bit is the important bit.

Larry: But I think that's what we — I think that's what cultural studies does: we — we assemble things. I mean that's what we do; we bring things together that you might not have thought of bringing together ... And in that process sometimes something better emerges, a better understanding. Yes, you could argue that it's A but if you bring A and B together then something new suddenly appears about both A and B. I think your description of sort of writing as opening of a conversation is crucial and completely antithetical to everything that the academy stands for, you know? Because — so if you read a book, there are two ways of responding to a book. One way is to say, 'What's wrong with it?' and the other way is to say, 'How do I continue it?' and so I mean when I teach *Policing the Crisis* and people say, 'Oh, X is missing, they didn't do Y, this is inadequate,' and my comment is, ... 'Well yes, so continue it. It's not that they failed, it's that they started a process and they didn't think this was the end of the conversation but they thought the questions mattered enough that it was worth saying something, however contingently and hesitatingly, to start the conversation going,' which has continued in their work and in other work and in that sense it's a success. The point isn't, you know, to criticise a work, as to say, 'Oh, I think this is an interesting opening and I want to take this and I want to continue it. I may not want to take all of it or I may —' you know, you don't have to say, 'This is wrong,' you have to say, 'I'm not going to pick up that bit, I'm going to continue this bit or I'm going to put this bit in conversation with this bit of what I'm doing.' But we — you know it's very hard to do that. And it also — the other thing I wanted to say is my contradiction (John laughs), the contradiction I cannot ever get out of, is a pedagogical one. Because I think to enter the conversation you need to know something.

[1:06:33]

...

Looking for the popular

Larry: Before we finish, I want to raise question, because for cultural studies what we do often does connect to a bigger problem or question, which is, 'Where is the popular?'

John: *Yes. All right, I will let you pose that one.*

Larry: Okay because there's this wonderful line in Stuart[1] – I could say there's one wonderful line in my work but it seems to me ... you know –

John: *You can have it for this.*

Larry: You know I'm reluctant because, of course, Stuart serves a certain function for us and I'm sometimes a bit nervous about making Stuart into the icon.

John: *The authoriser.*

Larry: As if you know kind of the founder of a discourse, although for us personally he was ... So he has this wonderful line on – in the end of 'Deconstructing the Popular' where he says, 'Popular culture is one of those places where a socialist resistance or alternative might be organised and if it is not, I don't give a damn about it.' And I want to know – I mean I certainly no longer believe that popular culture is really serving that role – and I think Stuart's turn to the high arts is partly about that – of a certain loss of hope. Notice I didn't say 'faith' – 'hope' in the popular culture. But I want to know where the popular is today? The popular isn't quite the same as common sense and it isn't quite the same as popular culture. And I don't know – I mean – and I think somehow the popular is crucial to cultural studies, yes?

---

[1]   The line is in Stuart Hall's 1981 essay 'Notes on deconstructing "the popular"', in Ralph Samuel (ed), *People's history and socialist theory*, Routledge and Kegan Paul, 227–239.

[2:27:15]

John: *I think so too.*

Larry: But I don't know where it is any more! (Both laugh)

John: *And that's one of those nightmare questions because ... I don't think anybody does. I mean I don't have a piece of work or a piece of analysis where I think, 'Yeah actually that would be a really good starting point,' because I don't know – it's partly that I don't know anybody who poses the question, because we are weird (laughs) and that –*

Larry: Speak for yourself! (Laughs)

John: *– that's certainly significant. It's part of a shared inheritance. I think you're right about the distinction, not absolute but separating, teasing out the popular and popular culture. For me it has another puzzle which is one of the ways in which I always inherit it was the national popular, right? And now I don't know where the national bit of it is either (both laugh). And that's partly because of transatlantic and other forms of disruption. It's partly that the national looks like not the reliable domain that we thought it was in all sorts of ways, partly the dismantling of the United Kingdom says if you talk about the national popular, you might have some real geographical cultural troubles. And then there's the popular. Yes damn! And that would – and there is a question about where. Not the forms, the sites, the modes in which that might be – the ways in which people live their, not imagine their relation to their real condition, but live their relation to those real conditions of existence that Althusser talks about as if it was easy to find. But live their subordinations, live their marginalisations, live their miseries, live their contradictions; they live them and not just imagine them.*

Larry: And they live them – see and that's always for me the point at which I say, 'Yes and that is not only ideological but affective' ... The popular is about what Williams was calling the 'structure of feeling' – and I don't know where that is. And I think we suffered – or we were enabled by – a certain illusion at a certain moment in post-war culture where there were national media, BBC, in the United States the three networks, certain national radio programmes, we were enabled by an illusion that this was the starting point for us to talk about the 'national popular'. And maybe it was real (laughs) I mean it had its real effects – but it's gone now. It's gone – music, radio, television, film ... writing, I mean in no – I cannot find a discursive place to say, 'Well here –' and my friends horrify me by saying, 'It is the technology itself'.

John: *Yeah.*

Larry: And I think – well I can't do anything with that (both laugh). If that is right, we can't do anything with that. What would it mean to enter onto the popular and struggle over it? What would it mean if it's the technology itself? So it may be right, but if it is I have to pretend it's not anyway (John laughs) and so I don't know where one goes any more.

John: *Well I agree with you, and when you said, 'My friends tell me ...' I thought you were going to say something else. And one of the things is – is the sort of randomness with which people pick a site, a genre, a form, a – you know a practice and say, 'There ...', you know? And I want to say, 'Yeah, I know, but only 20 people do that!' or whatever. And so I think there is both the sort of disruption of that – at least the imagined national popular that you were talking about, and there is the proliferation of points and so do we think that we have to think a popular that is itself the multiplicity that you were talking about? You know – that – and I'm with you that if the answer is the technology ... it's too late for me. I can't – and I know people who have done interesting things about the transformative and affective consequences of those technologies, but those are in their articulations with cultural relations, structures of feelings – I mean it isn't – it is about the articulation of the technologies into particular configurations and please let it not be the technologies! We can't have spent all those years avoiding that for it to turn around and bite us now.*

Larry: Yes ... I think my answer to them is, 'You're confusing what I might call the logic of commensuration of choice with the field of choice.' So the technology is what organises an overabundance of possibilities. So when I give my students – which I no longer do, because I do not understand where the popular is, but when I ask my students the desert island question, 'What five books? What five records? What five films would you bring?' their answer was always, 'Well could I bring my iPod?' (Both laugh) 'Can I bring my Kindle?'

John: *Yeah – it'll all be there.*

Larry: Because it will all be there and I would say, 'No' and they would say, 'But what do you – what does that mean?'

John: *What sort of question is that? (Both laugh)*

Larry: What sort of question is that? But I wonder – it seems to me that religion is one of the sites of the popular in the United

States. It seems to me – and I've suggested this, although I'm very hesitant, that in an odd way the economic relations themselves have become a site of affective investment. But I – but both of those are deeply depressing.

...

John: *Well, but I think – I mean there is a question about the conjuncture, which is, 'Do we have to think about the popular as a radically decentred field?' That just as the concept of the people loses increasingly, so the concept of the popular names an impossible set of connections, so that all we can do is think of tracing the bits, and I don't just mean digital bits.*

Larry: No (laughs) – because we cannot – I mean the conjuncture cannot be so fragmented that one cannot see the articulations. Now I think it is possible to say that the problem – you know, to use that image again of fusion, it is possible to say that we don't understand how the bits – where and how they are fused at particular moments. We can't find those articulations. But I don't think cultural studies can ever rest by simply saying –

John: *There's a lot of stuff out there.*

Larry: – it's only multiplicity; the conjuncture is so fractured, so fragmented that that's all there is, because I mean that isn't – it wouldn't be cultural studies, it would be something else, right? It has to be more – it may be that the articulations, the fusions have not been made yet strongly enough to create a crisis, to create a hegemonic position. It may be that we don't see them; we can't find them yet. But we cannot give up the idea that they are somehow at play, that articulations are somehow at play, that they are not free-floating bits.

John: *Yeah, I agree, and if that doesn't define the project for our declining years I don't know what does! (Both laugh). I'm stopping.*

Larry: Okay!

3

Wendy Brown

Wendy Brown is the Class of 1936 First Professor of Political Science at the University of California, Berkeley. Her work has drawn on feminism and Foucault to inflect political theory in order to critically interrogate formations of power, political identity, citizenship and political subjectivity in contemporary liberal democracies. Her publications range from *States of Injury: Power and Freedom in Late Modernity* (1995) to *Undoing the Demos: Neoliberalism's Stealth Revolution* (2015).

I met Wendy in 2004 at a conference on Contemporary Governance and the Question of the Social at the University of Alberta. I remember being enthralled by how seriously she engaged with questioners and their questions following her talk there. We have managed to find occasions to meet and talk more since then.

More details can be found at her university web page: http://polisci. berkeley.edu/people/person/wendy-brown.

This conversation was recorded in San Francisco on 2 April 2013.

Themes and topics

- Talking theory
- The seductions of theory
- Between theory and politics
- A moment of ambivalence

Talking theory

[0:00:00]

John: *So I want to start with one particular thing, I think, which is the conversations we've had over several years have always been grounded in particular problems. So I don't think we've ever started, I don't know, an abstract, intellectual, philosophical –*

Wendy: With a thinker or a problem that was a purely theoretical problem, yeah.

John: *Yeah, so – and I don't know whether that's me dragging you in to my sense of the murkiness of things or whether that's how you think too?*

Wendy: I think that's definitely how I think too. I'm actually very poor at simply sustaining a theoretical argument with its entailments and its implications for more than about 30 seconds. I'm very poor at it! I mean it's why when I teach, when I teach like the history of political theory and sections, you know, I do an early modern course and a high modern course and so forth, I have to use copious notes and it's not because I don't know the thinkers, it's precisely because I cannot sustain that kind of an argument. Whereas if we give ourselves a problem; whether it's a big problem like post-Thatcherism, or a very particular thing like what just happened in the thing called the 'Sequester' in the US? Is that a form of austerity politics snuck in? You and I will be talking about Foucault's College Lectures in no time, but I can't just rehearse those lectures and have no interest in doing so.

John: *Well that seems to me to be the interesting – (both laugh) it's one of the reasons I think I can have the conversations with you, which is I don't think I've ever wanted to write theory in a – you know, the definitive way of analysing whatever.*

Wendy: What does that mean to you, 'writing theory'?

John: *Well it means abstracting the ways – the conceptual apparatuses from the contexts in which they make active sense for me. But to write a theory – for me to write a theory of the welfare state, right – (both laugh) would mistake, I mean it would be a problem because I'm not even sure the object's there to write my theory about, but the theory would ascend that terrible ladder of abstraction.*

Wendy: Okay so let's talk about this for a minute because it's fascinating to me for many reasons ... the groundedness of theoretical work in neoliberalism in particular, that seemed so essential that as soon as we started talking about that object at some big level I become suspicious and I simply just think it's wrong. I just – it's universalising, it fixes concepts, it's inevitably essentialising – no matter, I don't care who – how cautious you are about all of that, I just think that it's one of the reasons I think we both love Foucault and Stuart Hall.

[0:05:34]

John: *Both –*

Wendy: (Laughs) Because both – they start with a problem or a formation or a 'conjuncture' as we like to say, but not with a high theoretical concept. And that's not an anti-theoretical claim I think; that's a recognition about a particular kind of theory and uses of theory that engages us.

John: *No and I – the animation with which you said that seems to me to be absolutely what ought to be exciting about doing, I don't know … I find myself and I'm not happy with it, using the word 'analysis', right? Because it marks out something which is not the drift downwards merely to describe the empirical object better, you know? Though I think the field I work in is very prone to doing that. And not the abstracted theorisation, but that sort of tense thing, where if your concepts, if your – the theoretical resources that you can mobilise are going to do anything for you, they're going to have to work and it seems to me it's the work that's the interesting bit, in which you might know better about the thing and the theory might move to the actually –*

Wendy: Explain that one again with … so you might know better about the thing, but then the theory itself also becomes what? Informed or elaborated by the problem –

John: *Yeah, by the stress of having to deal with a problem. And I think – you know, I mean I think – I mean that's certainly Stuart's view of what theory should be and I think – and I might disagree with you about this; I think on his good days that's what Foucault does and I think there are moments where – and I really no longer know whether I think it's Foucault or whether I think it's Anglophone Foucauldians who abstract things that become a bit too general, a bit too disconnected, a bit too all-knowing. And I don't know, there are moments where I read Foucault and I think, 'It would have done you good to –'. There's a point in* Discipline and Punish *where he says, 'Yes but I'm not at all interested in the witch's brew of what went on in prisons,' right? And I want to say, 'Yeah but there might be something in there that would make a difference.' And he says something about – one of the sets of lectures about, 'I'm interested in the knowledge of government; I'm not interested in the mess that goes on when you do it.'*

Wendy: Okay but let me argue with you for a moment there because –

John: *Good.*

Wendy: – I think in both cases, Foucault is trying to say, 'I'm interested in Object X, not Object Y.' He's not saying, 'I'm not interested in objects at all,' so in *Discipline and Punish* he's I think trying to say – I haven't read the text for years now and it's a shame because I used to teach it all the time and that kept it fresh for me, but not now – but I think in *Discipline and Punish* he's trying to say, 'Look I'm interested in the disciplinary dimension of the prison, not in all the rest of the detail.' And you're right, if you were trying to do a study of the messiness of disciplinary power and why it wasn't totalising and why it wasn't the whole story, you would have to be interested in that whole mess. But he's trying to extract something from it. So for better or worse, I think he still is interested in the object. It's far better than what you'd call the 'Anglophone Foucauldians' and I'm not going to just implicate your people (John laughs) – let's call all the Foucauldians who make a move to just wield the concepts. I think that would horrify Foucault.

John: *Yeah.*

Wendy: Because I think his concepts come from genealogies. You know that's why you have a study of sexuality and prisons and discipline and madness and health and, what am I forgetting? Knowledge itself. So even in that other example you offered, the – you know his interest in the knowledge of government rather than its gritty processes, I think he's trying to say, 'I'm trying to get at this thing that will illuminate something about our time and how governing works,' but it's – he does not seem to me to fly to that high theoretical plane.

[0:10:46]

John: *… I think that's certainly true and that's why I hesitated about what happens as it were in mobilising –*

Wendy: But I do think some Foucauldians do and it's painful.

John: *It is – it's painful, but I also know that there are real temptations –*

Wendy: Which we also turn to.

John: *– to pull bigger generalities out, to see the whole, whereas I think you're right that Foucault does have the notion of having to discover the object that will illuminate a field.*

The seductions of theory

Wendy: So here's something that we've never talked about … To be sympathetic for a moment to those high theoretical moments, I don't know if you ever went through this, but when I was young … college … first discovering theory, the headiness of it was unbelievable, right up there with sex and drugs and –

John: *Even Rock 'n' Roll.*

Wendy: – even Rock 'n' Roll. It was unbelievable. Once you got the idea of like the Labour Theory of Value, let alone ideological state apparatuses (laughs) – it was –

John: *Yeah!*

Wendy: So the … and we should pause for a minute and ask about that headiness because there is something in the power of the – of the explanatory – of the category or the argument that seems to illuminate the world. Of course, it leads you astray in the same way that sex, drugs and Rock and Roll do, right? (Both laugh)

John: *Nice imagery!*

Wendy: I mean – but we should (laughs) –

John: *But it's true!*

Wendy: It's a moment of thinking, 'The world is complete!' … 'I've got it all,' and the power and the erotics of it and so I – I want us to be sympathetic to that side not only of our colleagues but ourselves where we're drawn to that and not just be, as it were, kind of, you know, the Mackinnonites of the theory world (both laugh). So I don't know you well enough to know if you also had that moment. Because I think of you as a very grounded guy –

John: *Of course I am, but that doesn't mean not knowing the moment.*

Wendy: Right, because we met in older age (laughs).

John: *Yeah but – you know the encounter with cultural studies at Birmingham –*

Wendy: That would be it.

John: *– was it, you know. I mean I was reading stuff that was thrilling, exciting, animating, right? Brought us to life, and you know I – from my Capital reading group through to, you know, the grisly encounters with Althusser, Gramsci – and I mean Gramsci is interesting of* *course because he's – especially in that period we were reading him alongside Althusser and you get a very different sense of what I think Althusser calls 'theoretical work', but it's certainly not what Gramsci calls it. So that – so cultural studies I think had that sort of double movement which is the excitement of theory and you know – and the joys of sitting round arguing at an abstracted theoretical level.*

Wendy: Very abstracted theoretical level, yes!

[0:14:18]

John: *And I have this abiding memory of being at a party in those years with – someone came up to me in the – I was going to say kitchen but it's actually where the drinks were of course and said to me, 'I know you! You're John Clarke, you're one of those heavy theoreticians,' and the series of ambivalent responses to this (both laugh) were terrible, which is denial, 'Oh but yes, I am really,' and then, 'You're not just talking about how fat I am are you?' There's a problem about 'heavy' in this context. So when we were both not drunk I had another conversation with her which was – which inflected it back of course through questions of gender, right? 'Cos at that point – this is what, early 1970s in Birmingham – theory was what 'Big Boys' did.*

Wendy: Absolutely.

John: *And indeed one of my ambivalent relationships to the continuing work of theory is that it largely turns out to be Big Boys who still think they own the stuff.*

Wendy: Absolutely and it was precisely also why I was drawn to it and I was aware of that, that part of the erotics of it for me was – was being one of the boys without being 'one of the boys' and that was really exciting. ... And at the same time... I guess I want to try to get at something else about it, it – it emancipated you from the world. Even as it promised an explanation of the world, you could sit with somebody and just knock the concepts around in this thrilling kind of a way. So yes it was what the Big Boys did but it was also a way of – I don't know how to put it – it wasn't just that it was thrilling; it seemed like an access to power, an enormous access to power and I guess that's – you know, because it seemed like it was on top of all the rest of the knowledge, but also it opened up the world. There's one more thing about it I have to say and this is our difference. Because my formation is in the history of political thought, which is in some ways nothing but these big theory heads! (Both laugh) All dudes, every last one of them white, big, European –

John: *(Laughs) Heavy.*

Wendy: – I was also drawn to the sheer … I guess I'm going to say aesthetics of it, you know? Plato, Hobbes, Rousseau, the magnificence of building a theoretical architecture in which a world could be conveyed. I think I was drawn to it in the same way that scholars of literature are drawn to the way that a literary text holds a world. And that for me complicates where we begin.

John: *Yeah.*

Wendy: Because we begin by agreeing, 'Absolutely, you've got to start with the object, you know, let's talk about – that's where we trust theoretical moves these days,' and yet I also have that – and I can't defend it politically, I can only defend it at the level of – I want to say desire or taste or you know, what speaks to me, that I still get breathless when I read Hobbes. I don't get breathless when I read Hobbes because I'm excited that he's offering a world that I want, but because of the … intricacy and magnificence of the theoretical universe that he builds. And I don't think in the end it's helpful! (Both laugh) But I can't repudiate – well I shouldn't say that. I think it's helpful to understand a world that he was mapping through him, because it's an extraordinary map; neither true nor false, just extraordinary. But I can't defend it just because it's an extraordinary map, it's also like somebody who's drawn to a Rembrandt or to Proust or something else. And I don't think you have that part, I think that's where we differ a little, but I think your own thinking is dependent on those who do have it, because that's partly whom you learn from. That's my sense of you.

[0:19:14]

John: *Yeah, and that's certainly true and I – I mean I don't think that I quite have that aestheticised sense. I mean I quite – I will read and enjoy theory, but only at the level that I might read and enjoy a really long 19th-century novel (Wendy laughs) of no particular distinction. Right?*

Wendy: Equally perverse!

John: *So the map of the world – you know maps of the world are lovely and some of them are beautifully done and I'm still – I'm, in a really dull sense, I think I probably don't get at their mappiness ... for the joys —*

Wendy: Yeah right.

John: *— and that's almost certainly a sense of loss and I think it's also about different trajectories. So I am not — I mean quite emphatically — not the product of a disciplinary formation, which means I've never, never acquired a whole historicised apparatus of theory and how to think with those theories. So you know I bump into stuff literally. I turn the corner and it turns out that somebody, Wendy say, has written about stuff that I think, 'How did I know that?' right?*

Wendy: And then you're into that world, yeah.

John: *But that's different as it were from learning the, the ... learning the disciplinary formation and at the same time be disciplined by it. And I mean my sense of strain with disciplines is partly that — they bring you up in a very particular way.*

Wendy: They do bring you up. You didn't even come through the sort of Marx, Weber, Durkheim formation did you? Not even — (laughs)

John: *Not even that! So you know I know it because I went to — oh at least three first-year lectures in my morass of an undergraduate degree; one on Marx, 'Dead, wrong', Weber, 'Dead but interesting', Durkheim, 'Dead but French', right? (Laughs) And that pretty much wrapped up the history of sociological thought for me. So I — you know, and one of the things that cultural studies did was take me back into different —*

Wendy: Yes right.

John: *— different inheritances, but through a very different route. So I mean I was in the* Capital *reading group alongside reading Levi-Strauss on totemism, alongside, you know, literary criticism and social history. I mean so I — none of them had a sort of position of command.*

Wendy: Yeah that makes sense.

John: *I mean, Levi-Strauss probably didn't, but we ended up with 'Bricolage', which is a nice word and still does things for me and I — I did last week describe myself as I think 'promiscuous' in those terms. I — actually what I described myself as was a 'slut' in conceptual apparatus, because I don't think except that Gramsci provides a sort of point of return and orientation, but Gramsci isn't quite a theorist.*

Wendy: How is that? I mean only — I ask — I'm curious in part because Gramsci is one thinker whom I imbibe through other theorists who are important to me but have never been informed by directly. So — yeah it's just — it's just a missing piece there.

John: *I mean for me it has a sort of … has a definitive articulating role. One is I went to Birmingham at the point where Birmingham was discovering Gramsci, and you know that was the – led by Stuart, it was the discovery of an apparatus that would allow you to do cultural studies while not giving up on the discoveries of Marxism, while not collapsing into crude political economy and hegemony and articulation, allow you questions of the national popular and more, allow you a way of orienting yourself in it. And I guess it's continued – well I don't know – there's different accounts of why it's continued for me. One is I'm lazy, one is there's a really – several snotty critiques of Birmingham and cultural studies and Gramsci which call it 'Gramsci Lite', right? It doesn't – it slides so far away from political economy that it's not the real thing.*

Wendy: I see, it's just cultural.

John: *Yeah, 'merely cultural' in that interesting phrase.[1] And – but it still works for me, and partly because I think – and this is to go back to what theory does, which is it provides a set of orientations. It doesn't quite tell me what I'm going to find when I get there and that – that gap, that little gap, and so it's not that I only use Gramsci or that Gramsci is the only thing in my head, but it remains a sort of set of terms, orientations, dispositions that I carry around with me. I mean –*

Wendy: I think that's often true of the things that literally blow the positivist world open for any of us, that whatever that was, that remains the ground of our thinking, and I suppose to go back to our – before we move on to another topic, to go back to the sort of what theory has offered us, I mean for me it – it is and remains the way to cut through an empiricist positivist *Weltanschauung* – and I know it's not the only way. I mean, I have learned from Nietzsche and Foucault that genealogy is another way. I know from some of my friends who are historians, really good historians, that that's another way. I think it's possible, through anthropology … minus its colonial formation and apparatus (John laughs) that that can be another way. So I think there are other ways, but for me the really – the vitalism in theory is, apart from all the erotics and the headiness that we talked about at the beginning, it is precisely about taking a factoid or a given-ness or a formation and being able to undo it as given. And – or as naturalistic,

---

[1]   An ironic reference to Judith Butler's 1998 essay 'Merely Cultural', *New Left Review*, 227: 33–45.

or as unhistorical or anything else and it's theory that always allows me to do that, and it's partly because I don't have a historical, a head for facts, so I don't have a good way to undo the present historically. So – but I do accept that it's not the only way, but it's –

John: *No but it's – I mean one of the things that I really like about your work is, I mean that mapping of the possible lines of disruption, is not dissimilar to mine. I mean, I have slightly more engagement with anthropologists – but that's because I think the really good historians are possibly more rare.*

Wendy: Today they are; I think that's right.

John: *There are a lot of interesting pieces of historiography, but the really good historians who can dislocate and understand why they're dislocating and treat the thing that they're working on as a way of, you know, reconstituting ...*

Wendy: You don't get many Hobsbawms ...

John: *No you don't. I mean you get some, and when I bump into them I am uplifted and inspired. Those are great moments. But it's true about – I suspect it's true about all the practices that might be ... the good and exciting ones are the ones that tread that delicate line between the richness of the empirical, archive or ethnography or whatever, and understand that that's simultaneously an engagement with difficult, unfinished theoretical resources, that you know – that the exciting historians are those which know that you can't just have the archive or the anthropologists, you can't just have the ethnography; I mean they forgo that innocence.*

[0:28:42]

Between theory and politics

Wendy: I completely agree and I think that not only do they know you can't just have the archive or the ethnography or the social study, but that on the other hand, you can't just have the theoretical concepts, that it's in the dialectical transformations between them that the most interesting stuff happens. So the way that I would also develop that as a critique of certain tendencies with theory is that my greatest intellectual resentments I suppose are toward those who ... for whom theory becomes a – either (a) a substitute for knowing the world or (b) a ... how am I going to put it? A set of political positions.

John: *Ah, say more!*

Wendy: So where somebody takes a notion like ... like I could borrow one from my own lexicon, 'wounded attachments', or 'performativity', or 'human capital', or ... let's come up with some others, or 'ideological state apparatuses', and those things get wielded as if they are political positions rather than notions that were developed in order to try to apprehend something about our world, without particular political entailments. I mean the author might have had some political entailments but I think that one of the things that happens on the Left too often is that theoretical categories or pieces of theoretical arguments get wielded like weapons rather than like candles to light a room.

John: *Mmm, what a telling differentiation (Wendy laughs). No I do think that's powerful because I think that it's both true and, I like the candle end obviously, but I think it's interesting about how in some modes, theory does that work of fusion of knowledge and politics.*

Wendy: Oh that's interesting, yeah.

John: *What is it that's that rather than anything else that allows you to say, 'This is true, right and is like the only way – the necessary way and leads to these political consequences'? What is it about the – I don't know, it does seem to me there's something at the level, about its level of abstraction that allows that more than other things. I mean, if you took an ethnography –*

Wendy: I suppose that's right – yeah, right – it's harder –

John: *They might have a sort of disposition to be nice to some of the people in it and to hate others.*

Wendy: Or to rescue them or to –

John: *Yes, you know I mean, I have a love/hate, deeply ambivalent relationship with anthropology, because I think they are professionally nice people and it's a professional deformity that's somehow built into the mode ... but I'll get distracted by that. But there's something about the capacity of a certain sort of theoretical work to side-step those questions and to insist that the politics is formed directly into the thought, and I think then there's other – I mean we've got a long conversation to have about activism and politics and the academy, which I know are salient questions and – but the theory thing is I think an interesting moment for that.*

Wendy: I think it's just a mistake, and what I mean is (John laughs) I think it's a mistake on the part of students of theory, and I committed this mistake myself over and over and over in early decades; it's a mistake to think the theory is the politics – you know Stuart once said, 'What theory does is make meanings slide,' and of course that's not all it does, but if we start there, if what it does is open up and open up meaning, then it is such a patent mistake to then turn it into politics, because as he put it in that same lecture, 'Politics is about arresting signification,' it's about – it is precisely about trying to make meaning fixed and hegemonic. So to convert theory into political positioning is really to – to lose the theory for the politics. I understand the impulse, I had it, we've all had it; I don't have it any more. I mean at this point, while I certainly go to theory to try to open things up, that impulse to try to use it as a political weapon is I think really pretty much gone, but maybe you know with – maybe that's a hormonal issue! (Both laugh).

John: *I think we need a better explanation than that.*

Wendy: We probably do but I mean, it's really interesting to think back about the moments when we thought – well let's go to Marx for a second, so Marx says in the beginning of *Capital,* I think it's in the preface to one of the German editions, maybe the fourth German edition – he talks about the role of abstraction and he doesn't use the word 'theory', he uses the German term for abstraction and he says, 'We can't do without it because – because the world is not manifest, because things are not clear, because we don't even have the tools of the chemist or the biologist, you know chemical reagents and other things and so we need abstraction to reveal the secrets of Capital; we won't get there any other way.' And my reading of that is that he's trying to – trying to invoke the importance of a certain kind of remove from empirics and details, though starting from them, but an effort to back up and away from them in order to be able to understand them. It's not backing up and away from them in order to take political positions on them. He never says that, he never says that what abstraction will do is give us politics or a revolution; it's precisely about revelation, and many people are worried about the notion of revelation. Marx and we could have that discussion but I – I think that it's a certain revolutionary impatience on our part that wants the abstraction or the theory to move directly into the political positioning and to make the revealed truth of this world yield automatically a certain kind of political positioning on it.

John: Yes and the – I mean to back up to – I recognise the personal history you offer and I am absolutely sure that you know in a number of respects I was a – this is not a projection on you, this is me being an arrogant, hateful, sanctimonious 'heavy theorist' –

Wendy: 'Heavy theorist', exactly, or what we used to call 'theory heads'!

John: – who knew that if you knew that, everything followed. But I think though Birmingham seduced me with theory, I think the good sense of Birmingham was always that the two things do not fuse. I mean we had lots of horrible rows and arguments, but not just the good sense of Birmingham but the good sense of Stuart is that both are important, right? You wouldn't be doing cultural studies and you certainly wouldn't be doing it here in this way –

Wendy: Right, if you didn't have political stakes, yeah.

John: – yeah if – and if you didn't think that those political questions were not significant orienting, you know, got you started on stuff.

Wendy: Right, right.

John: You wouldn't think that the knowledge you generated was directly unmediatedly a political programme or a political set of instructions –

Wendy: Exactly.

John: – for the next politics kit. So I think that – I think that tension is always at stake and I mean, I think it's always at stake even for those who don't think that academic work is political, they just don't quite know the stakes. But that rush to make the connection seems to me to be wrong headed and I am going to sound slightly sanctimonious still; I think unproductive is the scary thing, which is the people that I can think of who know that have probably brought about less political consequences than my Trotskyite friends who sell papers at what used to be factory gates (Wendy laughs). And actually because I am feeling sanctimonious, I wish some of those who tell me theoretically that the class struggle is all we need would go and sell some papers, right? Because it makes me angry, because I think it's a way of being big and a big boy usually ... that does difficult things.

Wendy: I agree, we haven't – we didn't seize upon that one invitation you offered to think about the masculinism of this, but there is something – and I never quite fully, I used to think about it a lot, you know, what the masculinism of what we called 'theory heads' as opposed to 'theory heavies' (both laugh) was ... and I don't have anything I think particularly insightful to say about it right now. It's ... it has something to do with being able to – I'm going to put it this way, it certainly feeds an illusion of mastering the universe and –

[0:39:46]

Wendy: – but I don't know if that's true, say, for physicists or mathematicians. I mean that's – I actually just don't know because obviously they also are participating in the – in a parlance, and are drawn to a study that will allow you to master the universe; this is how it really works. I somehow suspect that it's not as masculinist in – I don't know why, but in the natural sciences. It might be.

John: *We need a research grant.*

Wendy: We do! (Both laugh)

John: *But I think something about the forms which mastery takes would be interesting, but to go back to the Left social theorists.*

Wendy: I mean what is it about it? I don't know the answer. I don't know why the Left social theory thing is so heavy in its boyness. It is so heavy in its boyness.

John: *Yeah, and it is always announcing. I mean, one of the things that … got me thrilled when I first saw you talk in public was your ability to tell a theorised coherent analytic story and then to respond to people's questions about it, as though they were serious. I remember saying to somebody, 'Look, you can see her thinking' with somebody, and I think the announcing mode is different to that, which is you've made the announcement, people should be grateful that you've made the announcement and if they've not heard it you are going to repeat it again. Because there isn't anything else, there's an announcement. That's the way things are, it's like …*

Wendy: There's no teaching, there's no connecting.

  …

A moment of ambivalence

Wendy: I do think that often when people come into a Left analysis or a Left orbit, the – the assumption, no I wonder if this is still true – I don't know, it's not so much that it's going to be easy, but that it won't be – it's finally where you can abandon – all contradictions may be abandoned at this gate, here ye enter, (John laughs) you know, and that you won't be troubled any more by – by ideological incoherence.

John: *Yes.*

Wendy: And it's wrong.

John: *Yes, no I was at a − I was at an anthropology conference and responding to a very wonderful speaker [Susana Narotzky] who was talking about an ethnography of Spanish industrial settings and she used I thought one of the words that I now love, and she used it interestingly and the word was 'ambivalence'. And so I put my hand up and started to ask her the question about ambivalence and a friend of mine, a much tougher, rigorous, Marxist analyst, walked behind me and hit me on the back of the head (Wendy laughs) shouting, 'Will you just give up with the ambivalence thing?' to which I said, 'I can't! Right?' Look it might be my problem, but it defines what David Scott calls the 'problem space' for me, which is actually if I can't be ambivalent, I don't know what I'm going to be, because I have deeply, deeply personal and analytical and political ambivalences.[2] They combine in me to make me anxious in a −*

Wendy: But in a fruitful way − I mean a really fruitful way.

John: *Oh, I'd like to think it was fruitful, but I recognise that my friend was absolutely frustrated by my inability to get on message and −*

Wendy: That's too bad because you know, to me even Marx can be read through the lens of ambivalence. I mean − and what I mean is, I'm sure you do this as well, when you teach *The Communist Manifesto*, one thing that you can show students is how extraordinary his admiration for capital is. I mean just − he's wowed by it, I mean it's unbelievable what it's accomplished in, as he puts it, 'its scarce 100 years'. And on the other hand it's this dastardly thing that is producing all kinds of formations that he wants to criticise. But on yet a third hand, it's digging − it's producing its own grave diggers, and on a fourth hand, it needs us to rise up, and you know − and you can just read − I'm not saying these are contradictions, I'm actually saying its ambivalence.

John: *I think that's right.*

Wendy: I don't think he would like the idea that he was ambivalent, because I think there's part of that guy that was convinced of his programmatic Manifesto-like, you know, dimension. But I think ambivalence is the most interesting part of it. And not just because it's theoretically entertaining, but because it grasps the complexity of the world.

---

[2] This story occurs again in a later conversation with Jeff Maskovsky. I have only a limited number of stories …

[1:00:15]

John: *And well — and it seems to me that what it does is insist — can ambivalence insist? It's a way of saying … 'You know there's that and there's that and that, I know you don't want to look at that, but it might be important'; and I'm in the middle of writing something at the moment and it's going to end with trying to think about popular responses to imagined economies as in part deeply ambivalent. And the ambivalence is itself constitutive not of politics, because I don't think that's true, but certainly of political possibilities. But you'd have to think about them as ambivalence because they're not dispositions, you know. They're not dispositions to be against everything; they are moving, you know, they are flickering in and out and people are quite capable of consenting and dissenting in the same bed.*

Wendy: That's right, you know what that just made me think of is back in the *Manifesto*, just thinking about the way that Marx says, you know, all the hallowed occupations and all the hallowed relations have now been submitted to a cash nexus and you have to ask yourself, 'So does he want them to be hallowed again? Does he want the family to be sacrosanct again? Or is he just trying to bring out the way that capital has kind of made these things — burst them asunder or made them vulgar or crude? Or is he in fact — to go back to your term — deeply ambivalent about the damage done, the disruption achieved, the flattening, the submission of humanity, the reduction of it to its basic relation? Or is there a little sentimentality about feudalism and its associations?' (Both laugh) And if you can't read him that way, you actually miss the richness of the historical story, but also the trouble with the politics; what is it we want?

4

Anu (Aradhana) Sharma

Anu Sharma is an Associate Professor of Anthropology at Wesleyan University. Her work explores questions of the state, democratic governance, citizenship, social movements, non-governmental organisations [NGOs], gender and activism. Her fieldwork in India has examined initiatives from women's empowerment programmes intended to transform gender relations, to transparency and anti-corruption legislation empowering people to question the state. The first of these provided the basis for a book, *Logics of Empowerment: Development, Gender and Governance in Neoliberal India* (2008). She also edited (with Akhil Gupta) a fascinating reader titled *The Anthropology of the State* (2006).

I first met Anu in 2007 as part of a workshop in Paris on 'Questions of Citizenship'. She was recommended as a participant by one of my colleagues – Kathy Coll – in a project based in Paris examining the issue of citizenship. The recommendation was a good one: Anu brought much to the workshop, and meeting her provided the foundation for intermittent exchanges, encounters and conversations, including this one.

More details can be found at her university web page: www.wesleyan. edu/academics/faculty/asharma/profile.html.

This conversation was recorded in Chicago on 20 November 2013.

Themes and topics

- Thinking with multiple resources
- Subjects behaving badly
- What is an NGO?
- Having troubling thoughts

Thinking with multiple resources

[0:00:00]

John: *So it's always difficult to know where to start, but part of what I've got out of knowing you is that sense of an ability to think multiply, so ... when you're thinking about – when you're writing about empowerment, it was for me one of the sort of magic moments of seeing, you know, feminism, Gandhian approaches, neoliberalism as multiple resources. So why do you think like that?*

Anu: I think that partly has to do with my training, because I started off in – very much in a political economy mode, and went from there to a more mainstream international development economics mode and then entered anthropology via that route and was always more attracted to sort of political anthropology; I knew I was going to be doing that, so that my training in political economy was not – was important to me. And yet sort of anthropology brought a whole new dimension to it, I thought. And so I think I still think in all of those ways, not mainstream economics so much, but you know, the sort of neoliberal side of it is coming from – very much from my training in political economy. I've always been a feminist studies, gender studies person, even though that wasn't my – what in America are called 'majors'. But that was very much a sub-focus and so ... the sort of feminist framework is coming from there. And then anthro also introduced me to some subaltern studies and historiography. I mean you can't – when you're doing subaltern [and postcolonial] studies you can't escape sort of – because much of it is about colonial histories and mobilisation in that time. So the sort of Gandhian stuff and that is coming from there and I can't separate those out in myself (laughs) – yeah.

John: *Yeah, and I think that – I mean but that's one of the both joys and difficulties, it seems to me, is that once those things are present, they are – they are difficult to separate out. But isn't there a lot of pressure to clarify? (Anu laughs) To find the prime mover in all of this? To tidy things away?*

Anu: I think there is, because you know there are moments when people will ask you, 'Well what's anthropological about this?' Right? Or, 'What's – yeah, what's particularly anthropological about it?' Because it's interesting that you bring up that chapter in my book where I'm – there's no ethnography really. It's mostly analytical stuff and ... you know, and that's where I think anthropology is capacious enough as a field, as a discipline, that you can basically sort of wiggle your way out of that question (laughs) and say that this is a discipline that precisely allows me that interdisciplinarity and makes room for it, and you know, I am talking ultimately about subjectivity and governmentality and forms of subjects that are being produced and how these apparently incongruous frameworks actually come together in these strange ways, which helps – I mean it opens up conversations with people like Wendy Brown, for instance, who's been a huge influence, who's coming from political theory. But I can talk that talk, I think, given my training in anthropology perhaps.

John: *Yeah, well, and it does seem to me that's one of the interesting things, is the – John Jackson somewhere talks about conceptual 'wriggle room'[1] and it does seem to me that one of the things that you have and that I think cultural studies did for me was to enable me to do that wriggling and to not get stuck, and I guess one of the – I mean one of the thrills about listening to you, reading you, is about the not-getting-stuck bit. Right? So subjectivity? Yes. Political theory, governmentality? Yes, but you don't end up becoming a person who writes about Governmentality with a capital 'G' … So who are you?*

Anu: (Laughs) Or Neoliberalism with a capital 'N'. Who am I? (Pauses) A feminist anthropologist really – and who does political anthropology, so those kind of parts come together and sometimes I get pegged in interesting ways that I want to avoid like, 'The person who does neoliberal governmentality' … and I had an interesting experience writing this piece that just came out in *POLAR*, where I studiously avoided writing about neoliberal governmentality. I was writing about state transparency and I situated it in this new regime of neoliberalism, but I sort of said – I wanted to make a different kind of argument about writing and orality and state power. So I situated it in the context of neoliberalism but I sort of moved on. But I got pulled right back, 'No, this is all about neoliberalism.' So even within anthropology, and these are political anthropologists, legal anthropologists, there is a kind of move to sometimes pin people down in these trendy

---

[1]   In fact, the term he uses is 'wiggle room', and he uses it in both *Harlemworld: Doing race and class in contemporary America*, University of Chicago Press, 2001 and *Real black: Adventures in racial sincerity*, University of Chicago Press, 2005. I prefer the wriggle, though.

ways that, even if I were to try to avoid doing it, I can't. And these are supposed to be anonymous reviews, so I couldn't even say, '[Folks], been there, done that. I've written about neoliberal governmentality, I'm trying to do something else' – you know, but yeah, I mean there are ways in which you get pulled and pigeon-holed, but there are ways in which I try to kind of – I do try to avoid it in my own way.

[0:07:21]

John: *And I mean, I think you do, and I think what's interesting in that example is that the pigeon-holing to be resisted is often a double one, which is there's a disciplinary pigeon-holing which is, 'Well are you – ?' People keep saying to me, 'Are you really a sociologist?' and I want to say, 'No, no, don't make me be a sociologist or any of those other things.' But the other one is the sort of big concepts of the moment, 'Are you a political economist? Are you a Foucauldian? Are you a – ?' I mean I don't know – I have a sense of how dismal it must be to be in one place all the time.*

Anu: (Laughs) Yeah.

Subjects behaving badly

John: *So … that being the case, one of the things that seems to me to make the wriggle room work for you is not just being an anthropologist but is about taking seriously the way people live their relationships to these big things. So you know the work on empowerment, you might have that non-ethnographic bit at the start, but it's got the wonderful ethnographic bits later on where, instructed as governmentalised subjects not to behave badly at the public event, those women do. … And that seems to me to be important; why do your people behave badly when everybody else's behave like the subjects of governmentality?*

Anu: (Laughs) I actually don't think people do, and you know I think there is a way in which sometimes scholarship can reify these forms of discipline and regulation, which is not to say that people aren't regulated or disciplined, but that it's not the be-all-and-end-all of their lives, and in different contexts they sort of challenge those forms of regulation as well. And in some ways – and I think this is where I am – I would call myself a Foucauldian but my Marx is also very important to me, you know, and my – and my subaltern [and postcolonial] studies people are also very important to me because none of these frameworks by themselves sort of capture the richness of social life, which is what I'm trained to study, and the materiality of it that sometimes is lacking in Foucault is very much brought into focus by Marxist frameworks. And thinking as a scholar of the state or processes of rule – institutions of rule (both laugh), you know, I mean I think that's one of the ways in which I can also – I also have wriggle room because I can talk to political theorists, I can talk to ethnographers, I can do that, but I can certainly talk to feminists, who've done brilliant work on the state. But the – the thing about the Indian context also John, it's always – the postcolonial state has been very centralised, but it's not been as totalising and as perhaps, maybe, some of the states in Europe where a lot of the scholarship on governmentality and the state has come out of, or the US, that there are people really that are at the edges of rule and margins of rule who have never quite been captured by statist programmes or ideologists in the same way. Which is not to say that the state is not present in their lives; we've – different people face the state all the time, but they also escape its logics, you know?

John: *Yes …*

[0:11:54]

Anu: And particularly when you're talking about the margins, it's – they – the women that I wrote about in that book, face power and oppression through means other than the state as well … So this idea that the state can regulate these women very easily … it's not so easy actually. So it partly makes – I mean it has to do with that context. I mean the state has never been a very strong welfare state to begin with. So that element of there's always something else going on that's beyond regulation. Which is not to say – I mean some of these very women were also forcibly sterilised – well not forcibly, but you know in quotes, they were told that they would be given 'X, Y or Z' in exchange for being sterilised so that they didn't produce too many kids. But they knew exactly what was going on and they criticised it all the time, so it's also not like they didn't understand, were simply being regulated and that's the end of the story.

John: *I mean for me that's one of the great things I get out of some anthropologists, and you in particular, which is that – I mean that multiple sense of consciousness, that you know you are inside things and yet you may also reflect on them.*

Anu: Exactly.

John: *I mean one of the phrases I go back to publicly a lot is, 'I have no reason to think that people elsewhere are any dumber than I am.'*

Anu: That's right, that's right.

John: *I don't think I have any reason to think they're any smarter than I am either, but I certainly – I mean that sense that people might know perfectly well what's being done and have a carefully constructed relationship to it, which is both enrolled in it and yet not simply its outcome; not simply its product. So where does that imagination come from for you? What gets you to think such a complicated thought? It's not just ethnography because I've read ethnographies in which people look like the victims of their circumstances or forms of rule ...? Is it feminism? Is it subaltern studies? I mean because it's not political economy and it's not particularly European Anglophone Foucauldianism and there's not a lot of active practising subjects going on in there most of the time.*

Anu: I think actually feminism definitely, subaltern studies absolutely, although the sort of gender analysis in that is kind of not there (both laugh) you know until Gayatri Spivak sort of raised that issue and others did, but I also think cultural studies actually; Stuart Hall was a big influence. I remember reading Gilroy and Hall during [the] first year of my PhD programme and it opened up a whole new world for me in terms of thinking about everyday life and everyday forms of resistance. Clearly Jim Scott's work, you know, which also dovetails very nicely with the work of subaltern studies people. So I think cultural studies there and this idea of thinking beyond this notion of false consciousness and being duped and spheres of critique and forms of criticism that happen on an everyday basis for me. I think that's where some of it is coming from.

John: *Well good (both laugh). Because clearly it's one of the lines of continuity for me but I don't always bump into it elsewhere, so that's – but I want to drag you into a slightly more difficult conversation. No, it might follow on from that actually, because it's about the different piece that you did – a piece for* Citizenship Studies *in which you talk about the vocabularies through which people represent themselves, their needs and their expectations, including old-fashioned concepts of entitlement.*

Anu: Yes.

John: *And so I – and one of the things that I thought was wonderful about that was that it ... Okay I need to push myself back a bit, which is, 'Oh that's so old-fashioned, that's just people using out-of-date words,' but actually there's a moment where Raymond Williams talks about the 'residual', posing questions that cannot be answered in the discourse of the present. He doesn't use the word 'discourse' but that sense, and it seemed to me that actually what you did was a – intentionally or otherwise, a very Williams-ish moment of saying, 'Look, this enables them, this vocabulary enables them to talk desires and possibilities definitely.' Tell me about why you got to that bit?*

[0:17:42]

Anu: Yeah, you know it's so interesting because that word *mai baap* for instance, 'You [are] my mother and father and as a caring parent you have to care for me in that mode', it's something I ran into all the time. So the people on the ground, the women that I was working with. But then the officials would turn it around and would call it the '*mai baap* syndrome', which is problematic –

John: *Ah! People suffer from syndromes.*

Anu: I know, right, it's something that needs to be – they need to be disabused of and cured of and so, you know I have – one of my dearest friends is a historian, is an Indian historian, so I had a long conversation with her about this and – and I wasn't thinking in terms of Raymond Williams but after I wrote that, I read this piece by Jim Ferguson who's been a huge influence in my intellectual life. If I were to mention three people, he would be one of them. He wrote this piece in his book on Africa called 'Demoralising Economies' where he talks about how the sort of neoliberal discourse on the economy and on belonging and on citizenship, you know, relationships between states and citizens, is a very demoralised – morality is kind of taken out of it; it's a technical discourse. And he talks about people thinking through on the ground, responding through notions of witchcraft, responding to this demoralised discourse through referencing these older ideas about people who eat other people, you know, or who get fat and those are the sort of ways in which people make sense of what is going on and talk back to this technical discourse —

John: *Mmm, yes.*

Anu: — through those terms. It's kind of a — you know, a moral economy to deal with the present — the economy of the present, and to give it meaning where it's completely senseless in a certain sense. So maybe one of the ways in which I would revisit that piece is to kind of think about this — they are harking back to a different moral economy which is not non-hierarchical at all, but which is — which allows people to use certain languages to make claims on those in power or with power.

John: *Yeah, God, that's great, and you should, along with all the other things that you were going to do obviously! (Both laugh) One of which we should talk about some more, which is about — we were talking before we started this about the work you're doing at the moment in particular around the shifting boundaries and categories around NGOs movements, politics. States, etc. Do you want to just remind me about where that came from and why it matters?*

What is an NGO?

Anu: Yes, and one more thing about the last question that you asked, you know, so if what I'm partly talking about is this construction of a juridical subject under — through, you know, these programmes of empowerment, rights-making subject. And there is a sense in which that discourse on rights, it both has a sense of morality but it's not necessarily the sense of morality that discourses of belonging have that people talk about in a different way. So what I saw them doing there by using these old kind of terms is really kind of putting a different kind of morality into that rights-bearing citizenship. So they are citizens with rights and they see themselves as that, but how are they recoding that form of juridical subjectivity is ... So this project which — it's, as I was telling you, my ethnographic ground keeps shifting on me, I decided to work on the urban social life of the Right to Information law in India, 'RTI' as it's called. And it was passed in 2005, which is around when most former British colonies actually enacted these laws including Scotland, and I believe England was 2004. So it happened around the same time for a lot of the Commonwealth or the former British colonial world. And the – so I ... and how it was first talked about in India when it was passed was that finally India is independent, this is India's arrival into postcoloniality. Because even though we were independent, we were being ruled by a state that was using colonial means to govern, especially the Official Secrets Act, which kept the state, although democratic, unaccountable etc etc. So this is the second independence, and we've finally arrived in a postcolonial democratic moment. So that rhetoric and those words really sort of intrigued me and I said, 'Okay, well what does this one law mean for – what is it doing in terms of people's perceptions of the state? Citizenship? What is it doing to activism and notions of democracy and justice and whatever?' So I went to Delhi thinking I would work with two NGOs. I mean I decided to work with two NGOs who work with urban – with slum dwellers basically, because I was interested in thinking about how people at the margins are – what does this mean to them? How is it changing their daily lives? And so one of the NGOs is this NGO called Parivarthan, which means 'change' in Hindi. It was started by a former bureaucrat who gave up his job in the Indian Revenue Services, a senior commissioner-level job, because he was just sick of corruption in his own department and he initially just took leave of absence and started a stall outside literally his own building and said, 'If you have trouble, if you're not getting your tax returns or whatever, come and talk to me' (both laugh). And he started discovering more and more issues, and then he got the Magsasay Award and he used a part of those funds to start this NGO. He – and later, after leave of absence, he actually quit the government and started doing this full time. Now this NGO is not only led by a former bureaucrat, it also came out of a people's movement for the right to information. So this movement spawned a whole bunch of NGOs working all over India who are helping people who are basically popularising the use of this law and helping people understand it, use it, get benefits through it. And this movement was also led by a group – it perhaps, it's not a NGO but MKSS,[2] which is also led by a former bureaucrat. So you have a movement, led by a former bureaucrat, that gives rise to NGOs, one of which

---

[2] The Mazdoor Kisan Shakti Sangathan (Association for the Empowerment of Labourers and Farmers) is an Indian grass-roots organisation.

	is also led by a former bureaucrat that I work with. Where is this? Where does the state end and – ?
John:	*God, I love the notion of renegade bureaucrats, I think it's really nice.*

[0:25:55]

Anu:	Yeah, and I met many of them, and then the leader of this NGO, his name is Arvind Kerjiwal, he's a big public figure. He decided that the RTI law was really good in terms of exposing corruption and things not getting done the way they should, but that it had no mechanism for punishing errant officials and, you know. And if you read my piece, one of the things I show is that – one of the things I argue is that the RTI law gets the work done, but it doesn't give you information, actually. So if you are – if you're entitled to something, let's say food, and you file an RTI application and say, 'I did not get my rations, who was supposed to give me these rations?' and whatnot. They won't give you the information, they'll just give you your rations, (both laugh) right? So you never actually know – still know the decision-making process or why – where the, you know, the obstacle is. And so he felt that it had sort of plateaued, the RTI law was being used well, people's work was getting done, but the principle of transparency? Not quite.
John:	*Yeah.*
Anu:	So he started a movement called the India Against Corruption [IAC] movement, which is very much – and they wanted to pass a new anti-corruption law. A much more – a stronger – what they called a 'stronger' law, and there were all kinds of issues with the movement in terms of a bunch of people feeling that they were the voice of the people and the people really want this and what they were proposing was a very centralised agency to deal with corruption. But on the other hand, they were also talking about decentralisation and including people. So there were problems with that discourse and I think those were much discussed. But for two years this movement went on and they really – you know it was called the 'Indian Spring', they really got a lot of middle-class people interested in their project out of the homes. And also lower middle-class, and so they went through a series of hunger strikes and the government made promises but then

reneged and so they declared a 'Last Fast' in July of 2012 and this was going to be a fast until death. Yes, as declared. Well a few days into the fast the government basically completely ignored them. So they decided that they weren't going to die (both laugh) and they declared an end to their indefinite hunger strike and announced on 2 August of last year, of 2012, that they were going to form a party and provide a political alternative to the People of India. Because they basically felt that they'd reached a point where unless they were inside government, they could not pass this kind of law. And so they've – on Gandhi's birthday, birth anniversary last year, 2 October, they announced their party. Because they were using a lot of Gandhian tactics, a lot of Gandhian rhetoric of self-rule, of decentralised governance and it's called the Aam Aadmi Party, AAP, which means the Common Man Party (laughs) because that was their whole slogan, 'We are common man, we're ordinary citizens and this is what we want', and that was written on their caps that they used to wear.

John: *As opposed to conventional politics ... which have excluded and ignored.*

[0:29:42]

Anu: Exactly, and there were a whole bunch of – they did a whole bunch of media programmes after this and one of the things that the leaders of the social movement who were now a party, not all of them went the party way. Some kind of broke away and – but those who formed the party kept saying that this is not a party – it was almost like a party in denial, 'We're not really a political party' – yeah!

John: *(Laughs) Extremely interesting!*

Anu: Yeah and, 'This is really a social revolution, come join the revolution and we're just fighting through different means. We're still the same. So nothing has effectively changed but everything has changed,' and so you know – so I'm just trying to get a sense of – get a hold on these shifts. Social movement gives rise to an NGO which gives rise to another social movement which then becomes a political party, and how do you map politics onto this? Because some of the very interesting discussions were that this move that the IAC had made from being a social movement to a political party really did not bode well for social movements in the country because it sent the message that if you really want to do – make change, you have to be in the government and not pressure the government from the outside. So you know, where social movements are doing the good kind of politics of dissent from the outside that, you know, as a party you would be forced to do dirty politics and play power politics, so it would be a different kind of politics. NGOs of course are apolitical apparently or anti-political, so that's a whole –

John: *Somewhere above or below politics.*

Anu: Exactly, so – so it just sort of drew these strange lines between institutions that are all part of the project of rule if you think about it, are all connected through these regimes of governmental practices, and yet how politics was getting mapped on and how it was being talked about was very intriguing and strange at the same time. So I want to look at this.

    …

Having troubling thoughts

John: *Okay I'm going to make it, for my purposes, end up somewhere else because … you along with some other anthropologists, and I know that I shouldn't think of them as a coherent whole (Anu laughs) but have been – what's the nice way of putting this? Profoundly influential in reshaping my world, and one of the ways that that works is by the world, or at least its different constitutive elements, because I think I'm a relatively naïve product of British scholarship and, you know – and that includes British cultural studies, I mean it's not an entirely innocent formation. And then even more so by going into a field of social policy which has I think, in British terms, always assumed that Britain is the leading example of a welfare state, against which you can see how all these other strange places fall short. But actually your work, like several others, says, "Oh come on!' Right? 'The world is not in fact constituted in quite that spatial pattern.' And I'll give two particular examples. One is when I … read you on NGOs I think, 'Ah! Okay that explains not what you're looking at but stuff that I'm working on,' right? So it's not – they might not be called NGOs in – though they increasingly are in the UK, but they'll be called 'civil society organisations' or 'voluntary bodies' or – and I think – I read you and I think (gasps), 'Okay look that shape-shifting thing, I can see that!' So there's a, as it were, a set of conceptual moves that are in the periphery (laughs) from that wonderful imperial standpoint, which come back to haunt me. But the other is that the – that good anthropology has done that provincialising Europe and provincialising Britain, provincialising England in the way that one might have hoped and I … I will never be an anthropologist; I will never have the patience to do ethnography. But there is something about the reimagining, both of the world and the relations through which it is constituted, including large geopolitical colonial, postcolonial relations. But also the specific set of practices which cannot be read, as it were, from an Anglo-centric Euro-centric version which says, 'Oh and I wonder if they'll catch up.' Because actually a lot of the work that you and others have done around NGOs looks to me the other way round.*

[0:47:15]

Anu: You know one of the things – and this was quite a moment in my own education, because I entered anthropology not really knowing much about it. I was interested in thinking about questions of poverty and development and I had considered economics programmes, a PhD (laughs) in economics and I was –

John: *Congratulations! (Laughs)*

Anu: I even got in! And I was asked to take, you know, test my maths skills, calculus, which would be fine. I'm not scared of that stuff and I had enough of a background in that to do that, but on principle I didn't want to do it, because I didn't want to ask those kind of questions about the issues that I was interested in. And so I wanted to really sort of understand what all of these things mean on the ground, the people, and so anthropology became the way for me to do it. But as I entered it, I also entered it with the feel that anthropologists do these micro-studies in these various places and you learn a lot about that, but then that's, it kind of [limited]. And I remember I think it was Akhil [Gupta] actually who sort of said, 'No but that's a very strange way of thinking about anthropology. Because it's about what those micro – what the particular tells you about … the general and where they connect. How can that particular shed light on the general?' … 'And how does the general shape [and take shape in] that particular too?' So it is … a much messier thing that anthropologists are doing. So you don't want to think about anthropology as simply doing these local, you know (laughs) studies, and so for me that's been – that's really, even as I think about the travels of neoliberalism elsewhere, there is this universal discourse of neoliberalism. What light can these specific examples shed on that and trouble it?

John: *Now: okay, the word 'trouble' seems to me to be the critical bit because I've seen a lot of anthropology which does, 'Here's a particular example of the general,' and it's interesting that it's not quite like the general, but I think – I mean when I know the people and I talk to them, I say, "Yeah. Okay and what do we know about the general after you've been there?' Right? 'If it's an instance of neoliberalism and it comes out funny, do we need a concept of neoliberalism after, or something else?' But it seems to me that – and you know that I'm an enthusiast about some anthropology but my frustration is also that the troubling – the work of critical interrogation of the general is cut short sometimes. And that's terrible. I mean, why would you want to know about? I mean it's not that – no I can't say that (laughs) – that the particular is always interesting, but for anybody else, they want to know how they might think again after an encounter with the particular.*

Anu: Right, right.

John: *Please tell me! And that's why it seems to me Akhil [Gupta][3] is one of the odd ends of anthropology because he and I have always had those conversations because he thinks that, whereas I know some anthropologists that I've not had conversations with because that's not part of the world they – they borrow the theory, but they don't make the particular speak back.*

[0:51:15]

Anu: Yeah, so the particular becomes an example of the general simply and –

John: *Yeah, and it may say it's more complicated than you thought, but it's only complicated.*

Anu: Yeah, and that that next step of troubling, that general – the narrative, yeah I – I agree with you [I think anthropologists like Lila Abu-Lughod, Syvlia Yanagisako and Anna Tsing, among others, do this very well]. And I think for me personally, it's

---

[3]   Akhil Gupta is currently Professor of Anthropology at the University of California at Los Angeles – and has been another recurrent conversationalist since I was introduced to him at a cultural studies conference by Larry Grossberg. Anu Sharma did her PhD work with him when he was at Stanford University.

that second part, that second step, that is really important and those are the kinds of ideas and works that influence me and that I – you know, that have been most useful. Because – and there too, for instance Wendy Brown's work on the state, on the US welfare state, absolutely brilliant, speaks to me at so many different levels. But at the same time the Indian state cannot be subsumed under that – so as a feminist who takes a lot from those frameworks and studies of the US welfare state, what do I take and what do I not take? And not get bogged down by? That somehow the Indian state also fits this example, because it doesn't. It's not a classic example of a de-welfarising state. In fact if anything, post-liberalisation India has enacted more and more welfare measures; a social insurance scheme, a guaranteed work scheme, a right to food, and they've only expanded it. So you know, it's not your classic de-welfarised state.

John: *Yes, and part of – I mean part of my trouble in the social policy field is that people who ought to know better, I think, talk about the end of the welfare state, the dismantling of the welfare state, and I think, 'Actually I mean …' even in Europe people still receive large amounts of welfare and states still spend large amounts of money on such things, though the things might be different and might be organised for different purposes. So I'm troubled as it were in the field where people – but part of it is – is no I don't think it's crossed anybody's mind that India and the Indian state might be doing welfare but not like the Swedes do it, or that in Latin America, Latin American states are doing different versions of certain family support and –*

Anu: Absolutely.

John: *– okay well, did we not want to know that? And it is in my complicated relationship I think with anthropology, which is I at least want to borrow other people's stories and turn round and say, 'Oh! By the way – what are you going to do about the fact that when you say the "end of the welfare state" that there's all these other things going on which are not socialist, social democratic, statist things that we'd recognise? But they aren't the end of the welfare –' how do you – ?*

Anu: That's right.

John: *And that seems to me to be troubling, I mean to be doing the work of troubling.*

Anu: Exactly, exactly, and I mean, you know it's – I think we sometimes in theory tend to reify things that are much more complicated on the ground and I think that's where somebody like J.K. Gibson Graham – their work is I think very interesting in precisely getting us to think about not replicating certain kinds of totalising ideas and practices in our own work, and you know even yesterday there was this whole discussion about NGOs as people building off Didier Fassin's work and sort of talking about NGOs about the kind of moral core, and particularly NGOs doing humanitarian work and this moral consensus – representing a sort of moral consensus and how some people felt that therefore working with NGOs really posed ethical problems for them when it came to criticising these NGOs; that they couldn't critique them because these were the moral core or they represented the moral consensus. And I was like, 'Well I think – not a problem for me!' (Laughs)

John: Yeah.

[0:55:48]

Anu: And maybe it's because I don't necessarily work with humanitarian NGOs, but – but you know by not sort of thinking critically and approaching these institutions critically, are we not reifying that idea of moral consensus which may not exist at all? Or –

John: *Or if it does, it's one of those classically complicated, compromised, contradictory formations and it – and you know this isn't just me being nice to you, honestly, but I think that one of the things your work consistently does is resist the reification, right? It's to resist the one-dimensional-thingness of things, and it's a source of joy – (Anu laughs) No I mean it, you see? It's a source of joy and a resource to think with, because I ... because wherever I'm operating at any time, people think the thingness in its singularity. So people talk about welfare states, 'Yeah well I'm sorry, they don't exist'; states and welfare get combined in particular 'thingly' ways, but you wouldn't reach out and touch one. And I'm not sure that if I was to write down a shortlist of NGOs that I've encountered, that I could think that they were a unified, singular, political, ethical, organisational formation (laughs) –*

Anu: Absolutely not.

John: *– and any one of them – and I'm just thinking about when you were in your beautiful piece on NGOs, it is the shape-shifting character of things that is such a key to political tactics, possibilities and movements –*

Anu: Absolutely, absolutely.

John: *Okay, I think that's more interesting than whether NGOs have a singular wonderful characteristic?*

Anu: Are they a thing?

John: *God no! Please spare me from that.*

Anu: So my whole point in yesterday's plenary, in my five minutes, was to make a case against NGO studies – tentatively, which is not to say that these institutions, therefore these institutional boundaries are meaningless – absolutely not. But how are they discursively produced, in what instances? And to what political effect? ... Rather than thinking of them as a priori given. When – even in that meeting we had, you know, 150 people working on very different kinds of NGOs, right? You have international organisations, Transparency International, somebody working on TI, somebody like me working on an NGO that became something else entirely – [a social movement and then a political party].

John: *Yeah.*

Anu: – you know, other people working on little religious charities. So, like you know, it's such a wide field and I was trying to get people to think more in terms of a governmentality frame and regimes of practices that connect and shape these institutions as separate nodes perhaps.

John: *Yes, I'm glad to hear it (both laugh) – no, because I think I mean the only possibility of doing proper grounded, theorised yet critical work is to understand that it's those things in motion being produced, borrowing all sorts of auras from – I mean like states borrow auras from the existence of states.*

Anu: Absolutely.

John: *NGOs borrow – and it matters in all sorts of ways that they call themselves 'NGOs' and not something else and – and, but that's about practices and tactics and sometimes they work and sometimes they do achieve pertinent effects and sometimes they disappear without a trace. All of those things look like a field of studies; the idea that you're going out to pursue – I don't know, well partly it's like when we were doing the citizenship studies book, the idea that there is a thing called 'citizenship' and what you can do is catalogue its infinite varieties seems to me, (laughs) at least, a dismal prospect for intellectual work. Actually it is in motion, contested, in dispute ... borrowed for complicated reasons, bent to other things. Why is that not – ? I mean – but you know that.*

[1:00:40]

Anu: Yeah.

John: *And part of the joy about having these conversations is that you know that! (Anu laughs) And every now and then I think, 'And there aren't quite enough of us.'*

     ...

5

Jeff Maskovsky

Jeff Maskovsky is a Professor of Anthropology who works at works at Queens College and the Graduate Center, CUNY (City University of New York). His research and writing focus on urban poverty, grassroots activism and political economic change in the US. His publications include *New Poverty Studies: The Ethnography of Power, Politics and Impoverished People in the United States* (2001, co-edited with Judith Goode) and *Beyond Populism: Angry Politics and the Twilight of Neoliberalism* (forthcoming, co-edited with Sophie Bjork-James).

I first met Jeff at a meeting of the American Anthropological Association (AAA) in Washington, DC in 2001. I had found the conference a largely disappointing experience and this was the last panel I was attending, on US welfare politics. Suddenly, I had found my point of connection: Jeff and a panel that included Judith Goode, Catherine Kingfisher, Ida Susser and the late Sandi Morgen engaged in discussions and issues that felt important and engaging. I rushed up to the panellists after it concluded and tried very hard to make friends. As a result, they became my new support network for anthropology events and introduced me to SANA (the Society for the Anthropology of North America), which became my first anthropology affiliation. We have remained in touch ever since and I became a regular AAA attender. Jeff has also invited me to participate in a range of wonderful things since then, including the workshops he organised with Sophie Bjork-James on 'Angry Publics, New Politics' in 2017.

It is important to know that Jeff's reaction in the editing process for this conversation was both helpful and demanding, since he suggested that I should add more comments and clarifications of my own. The results are below.

Further information can be found at: www.gc.cuny.edu/page-elements/academics-research-centers-initiatives/doctoral-programs/psychology/faculty-bios/jeff-maskovsky.

This conversation was recorded in Chicago on 21 November 2013.

Themes and topics
- Paradoxes in popular politics
- On political trajectories
- Politics, certainty and ambivalence

Paradoxes in popular politics[1]

Jeff: … [One of the many things we have talked about together over
            the years is the challenge of thinking conjuncturally in these
            uncertain times. And for me our conservations and your work
            have been invaluable to me; they have helped me to think
            through difficult cases, especially those that might seem on the
            surface to be easy to understand but that are more complicated
            than they seem. For example,] I think there's an interesting
            issue that we in New York City and perhaps you at Open
            University have to contend with … [that major urban areas
            are now, in this moment of rising authoritarianism, somehow
            now being talked about as] centres of cosmopolitanism, and
            if there is this uncomfortable right-wing stuff happening it's
            happening elsewhere … It's not us, it's somewhere else. But
            if you look at New York City – and my colleague, Jackie
            Brown, at the Graduate Center, she's working on this, she's
            [making the point that] New York has this horrible history
            of repression and racism and parochialism … [I find it very
            unsatisfying to hear analyses suggesting that urbanites who
            respond to elitist technocratic rule] are just stuck in their
            militant particularisms … They're that. That's part of it, but
            they [can] think more than one thing at the same time, you
            know (laughs). [So popular politics, at least in the United
            States, is simultaneously about a growing recognition of the
            failures of technocratic rule to guarantee welfare and health
            and safety for everyone, but it's also rooted sometimes, and
            by some people, in long-standing sentiments that are deeply
            problematic, even as those people seek to defend themselves
            against the challenges they face from above, so to speak.]

John: *Jeff, Jeff, … I do think that may be one of the defining sentences.
            That actually the terrible thing is lots of people can think
            more than one thing. They might even think as many complicated
            thoughts as we do.*

Jeff: Exactly. I mean, like, you can think, 'Leave me alone and
            let me have my liberty,' and you can also think, like, 'I don't

---

[1]   These extracts follow on from a discussion of Jeff's paper for a panel on popular
      politics at the conference we were both attending. He had offered a typically
      fascinating analysis of popular resistance to the then Mayor of New York's
      technocratic public health measure aimed at banning the sale of giant-size soda
      (pop) bottles.

want to be the subject of your stupid, like, project to, kind of, control me.' And those things are not exactly the same thought, you know.

John: *Indeed. And the ways they rub together might also be productive of other possibilities, discomfort does that sometimes, sometimes it just makes people angry, but that might also matter. And I do think that it is about being able to attend to the particular without assuming that it tells a whole story, but it interrupts the telling of big stories without …*

Jeff: So I want to know, since this is a conversation, where and how you see yourself coming to that position. Was it always there, because –

John: *Oh, no.*

[00:17:32]

Jeff: Because, you know, I was thinking about, like, the various moments at which I read your work, which start very early in my career and then, kind of, I put it away. And then when I first started my career at CUNY I was in an urban studies programme, which I'm still in, and they were like, 'Oh, you're the anthropologist, we don't know what to do with you, you teach urban subcultures.' And so I was, you know, so what that meant to them was like, 'You'll teach the Chicago School, you know, the deviant studies kind of subcultural studies.' And so I was like, 'Oh, no, I can't do that.' So then I went back to … Birmingham School stuff and I read it again, you know, from an urban studies perspective. And then, of course, I got to know you and then we've had this … dialogue going on and, you know, I realised that in my own mind it's not clear to me where the John of today, who I know, meets the Johns of the past whom I've known [through his work]. Because I see continuity but I also see some, you know, I think I see some, well, I see some interesting departures but I also see some restraint on your part. I think so, I see some fealty to the original project that I don't see in some other people who have moved on, but I also see some [departures], you know, what I would consider to be healthy and useful and interesting …

John: *Dear God, it's a long career.*

Jeff: So where, how do you periodise it in your own mind? I've never asked you that.

John: *That's a really tough question because I'm not sure ... I think there are overlays, and I think there is some fealty to the original projects but that's partly, I think, the, I don't know what you'd call it, the good sense of Stuart Hall, right, remains a, sort of, fairly easy but demanding touchstone [always committed to ways of thinking better] ... [In response to Jeff's persistence: the Birmingham Centre picked me up as a not untypical radical student of the late 1960s and early 1970s and connected aspects of radical sociology to varieties of Marxism – and lots of other things. The subcultures work we did was very class centred (as many have pointed out), but subsequently cultural studies opened up contested questions of both race and gender – contestations that others have subsequently put time and effort into making me take seriously. Entering social policy via cultural studies made for interesting, and often frustrating, conversations, before I found ways of bringing them together – to my satisfaction, if no one else's. Latterly, I think I have had a revitalised interest in cultural studies questions of agency, contingency and conjunctural analysis.]*

Jeff: [Stuart's approach] is in some ways unsurpassed, right, and we haven't ever really [needed to invent a new paradigm, except for the sake of academic fashion] ... We could say we have, but we haven't really got past it.

John: *And there's a film going around in the UK at the moment about Stuart called* The Stuart Hall Project *[by John Akomfrah], and it's breath taking and alarming, and it's alarming because we haven't got past that, right, and that's striking. So I ... if I have a mission, do I have a mission? That's sounds a terrible thought, it is to say, to take up some of those things ... [the] baseline is theory matters for what it does for you and enables you to do, I mean, not to be a theorist, right? So I guess I'm less disposed to rigorous theory than I would have been when I was in my mid-20s, I'm more promiscuous about what to borrow from. [For example, recent work that explores ideas of assemblage alongside articulation in* Making Policy Move.[2]*] And ... a friend of mine once asked me, 'Are you a Foucauldian?' ... And I said, 'Well, I'm not, I don't think I am a Foucauldian, but it seems to me that ...'*

Jeff: We're all Foucauldians now (laughs).

John: *Because after Foucault you can't not think without him being there, right? And so that's okay, and I don't, and I guess part of it is that I don't think that I am obliged to be pure in that systematic, having*

---

[2]   Clarke, J., Bainton, D. Lenvai, N. and Stubbs, P. (2015) *Making Policy Move: Towards a politics of translation and assemblage*, Bristol: Policy Press.

a systematically, rigorously worked-out theoretical position is not the most important thing in my life.

Jeff: All right. So that's, to me, not a surprising thing to hear from you, given what I've read, given what you've said, given what we've talked about. What the interesting thing about it is, to me, that I want to hear more about from you, as I cleverly commandeered the interviewer position from –

John: *Cunning.*

[00:21:41]

Jeff: ... So... what's the good part of [theory] for you? [And what are the political implications of using theory for you?] This is the part that's a little bit hazy to me about you, I've always, kind of, wondered, okay, he's not a Trot, you know, and he's not even like a covert Trot which we see over and over and over again in my line of work, you know.

John: *Yes, we do.*

On political trajectories

Jeff: ... Another part, and I'll pick it up. We had Tim Mitchell come, who I think is a wonderful thinker, a very interesting guy, ... he came and talked about the carbon democracy book. And, you know, he's such a nimble, interesting thinker and that's such an interesting great book, and yet [his politics, when all is said and done, is clearly animated by the question of how to mobilise the] industrial working class. [I don't think he's got] a particularly romantic view of the industrial working class ... I don't know when, or if it ever existed. It is still present in that book in surprising ways. And [it is still] present in his thinking about what the political is or was during the 20th century, and how it might be changing into a, kind of, managerial middle-class thing [in the age of oil]. But ... I don't see that presence in [your work] ... I think that's interesting because I have a sense of where it is for me in a certain kind of bottom-line dangerous way, which I think I'm more, a little bit more explicit about, which is just like I have this weird fantasy of, like, of this, kind of, like, the poorest of the poor and some parts of the middle class, kind of ... coming together in some sort of formation. I see that, I see everybody in between as, kind of, a problem, you know (laughs)? You know, fractions of the middle class and fractions of the poor, usually the bottom, kind of coming together. I am very distrustful of a lot of the layers that [are] in between there.

John: *The respectable layers.*

Jeff: Yes, the respectable layers ... But I also don't want to, kind of, wallow in abjection either, as this route to politics, but like, you know, I don't do that. But I think that's, for me, this, it's the political space I've been in in my own life ... And so that's the touchstone for me ... And so I can give specific examples of where that played out, it played out in '80s politics [during the AIDS crisis]. It played out in how ... middle-class gay men were confronted with ... poor blacks who became very political in their [own] ways, much to the dismay often of some of those white gay men. ... [Many people made politics in] that difficult space ... and I don't want to erase it. [It was extremely difficult for people to manage race and class divisions and differences while also trying to work together in a movement.] But I do think there were a lot of other people, the in-between people, who were like, 'We're out ... We're out of this whole fucking thing.'

John: *It's nothing to do with us (laughs).*

Jeff: Right, from the beginning, like, they were out. So anyway, so my question is for you [is what political moment defined you?]. I mean, by the way, maybe there isn't one, but I want to see what you say.

John: *And I, I mean, it's a series of 'hmm, yes but' moments, which is a very classic Clarke position. So I don't have, I don't think I have, a romance about the industrial working class because that's the one I grew up with and it's difficult to hang on to that romance if they're on your street, you know, they're your next-door neighbour, and all of that. So you know that they're a bit, I mean, good, good-hearted people, [and] bastards, you know, I mean, a whole set of contradictory things.*

Jeff: Definitely, they're not any one thing, right.

John: *No, indeed. And you know, my father was a very active trade unionist and voted Conservative all his life. [That meant that I understood] that working-class politics was a contradictory formation [even] before I went away to university and discovered the words. So all of that's true, but I am a product of the discovery of all the things that I'm not, is actually what I am. I went to university in '68, just after it had all happened, right, that's bad timing.*

[00:26:18]

Jeff: Or good timing, depending what way you look about it.

John: *But you know, I caught the tail-end of a very English version of student politics. In the year afterwards, I was a founder member of my university's women's liberation group.*

Jeff: Okay, that's interesting, that's something we have in common, feminism, … feminism was very influential to me …

John: *Absolutely. And, you know, it is, I think, one of the decisive moments for me, I mean, not that they kept me in the group for very long, but –*

Jeff: But it's also like being a political space that's not necessarily your 'own', and learning to inhabit it and just being okay with that.

John: *Yes. And I'm very clear … that I was brought up by feminists in all sorts of ways, I mean, not without problems, not without. And then there's all the other things that I'm not, all right, so there are sexual politics, right, where, you know … Somebody yesterday paid me the enormous compliment of asking me what my partner did, but using the word 'he' about them. And I thought, that's nice and then explained it …*

Jeff: No one can, the codes are also unclear, that's funny.

John: *He said, 'And it's because you ask queer questions.' And I took that as an enormous compliment because it seems to me that actually, whatever else you make of it, queering, those figurings of who people are, is important –*

Jeff: You're pretty queer queer though.

John: *Yeah, I am.*

Jeff: I mean, you were queer on that wave well before the movement.

John: *I was a pre-poststructuralist, right, and so it's all those … And then one of the things that Birmingham, and especially the work around* Policing the Crisis, *did was to say, 'Come on, you can't understand this space and who you are in it without thinking through race,' you know, badly or not, you can't do it without. And, I mean, that's one of Stuart's other gifts to me, and so I'm formed by the politics of what I'm not in, I think, so I've no idea what it's about except all those people will eventually rise and leave me behind (laughs). But that's all right.*

Jeff: Or carry you along with them …

John: *So I'm a, sort of, unfinished thing, I can't, I almost made it to Trotskyism and failed, you know, I have long, miserable, difficult*

*relationships with British Labourism and social democracy, you
know, I'm in the position of saying publicly, regularly, I don't believe
that 1978 was the high point of human civilisation, and Margaret
Thatcher and Tony Blair, if only we'd not had them, we'd have been
all right. Because I was on the 'wrong side' in 1978 [rather than
being part of the Labour movement], I was the person attacking
Labourist social democratic institutions for their exclusions, and, you
know, so I'm not having that one. So I'm a bit available (laughs).
[I think this argument about political nostalgia is an important
one – the complicated politics that made me created a distance from,
and scepticism about, social democratic notions of universalism and
progress – underscored by working in the field of social policy.]*

[00:29:46]

Politics, certainty and ambivalence

Jeff: I have something I think we share in common, it's a lot of being, I think it's a lot of being in politics but not of it a lot of the time, you know? And finding that to be a productive space to be, it's a, kind of, disavowal of a certain kind of citizenship, right?

John: *Yes, I mean, it's a disavowal of a certain type of certainty too. And I –*

Jeff: Yeah, which citizenship often requires (laughs).

John: *Yes, it requires you to sign up, as do most of the political mobilisations. And I have two moments that I remember, one is of being at a meeting of political economy anthropologists, and one of them insisting that we needed to get back to questions of revolutionary discipline. And I immediately said –*

Jeff: For whom?

John: *Yeah, well, that's a different question, but mine was, 'I'm not in favour of this because I will be the first one that you put up against the wall and shoot. I will fail to live up to the demands of revolutionary discipline.' And I know that on Saturday there's a session about Neil Smith [the geographer who died in 2012], who I love deeply, but I will never forget Neil hitting me on the back of the head [at a conference] and saying, 'Would you stop using the word ambivalent?' I think part of my response to Neil was always, 'No, I reserve the right to be ambivalent,' and it is the way of occupying that space, which says, you know, I think this matters, but it may not be the*

only thing that matters.[3] [So the apparent purity of 'class struggle'
always provokes a 'yes, but …' reaction in me.]

Jeff: Well, the irony is, the best of Neil, in my mind, was the
           part that was in some way intellectually animated by those
           ambivalences and you could see it in his work here and there
           … I think you weren't the only person who got smacked in
           the back of the head on that front, but –

John: *(Laughs) I don't know whether to be pleased or disappointed by that*
           news, but I know what you mean.

Jeff: – I think I've always been ambivalent, I don't really know what
           it would be like to be certain, I've never been certain. I mean,
           like, I can't, I mean, I remember the height, I remember, this is
           my, this is a funny, funny story, this is my moment of absolute,
           this is my great moment of the revelation of uncertainty, for
           me. I was in an ACT UP[4] meeting in New York City, in
           1990, so it had been, 1990, 1991, it had been going along
           for some time then, and this was a time when, you know,
           this radical activist formation had been, with hundreds and
           hundreds of people were in these meetings which would
           happen weekly. And I went for weeks, you know, I went in
           New York weekly for years, and then in Philadelphia I went
           for many, many years, five years, six years, I mean, I was and
           remained involved after that. But at this one meeting it was
           a, kind of like, this very hybrid complicated political space,
           the question came up, 'Why is Madonna not giving us more
           money to stop the AIDS crisis?' And it became a very sincere
           argument of incredible anger at Madonna for failing to, you
           know, live up to her obligation to the queer community
           that was suffering. I mean, all of this is completely true, my
           reaction to that is, like, just complete disbelief that anyone
           could think that Madonna would feel any obligations to
           anybody but Madonna, you know? And … I just remember
           thinking, like, it implies a certain kind of certainty that people,
           you know, that people have connections and affiliations and
           ideologies that map coherently. And I just thought, like, I

---

[3] This story about Neil Smith's frustration with my enthusiasm for ambivalence
     also appears in the conversation with Wendy Brown. It was clearly a significant
     moment for me.

[4] ACT UP (the AIDS Coalition to Unleash Power) emerged in New York in
     March, 1987 and became an international organisation dedicated to direct action
     and advocacy by People With Aids.

mean, I think Madonna wasn't coherent, she could have given a lot of money, who the hell knew, you know? I mean, she might have given a lot of money but maybe, I mean, but she was up for grabs, just like anybody else, at that particular moment. And they were very angry at her because they sensed that she was up for grabs and that she didn't –

[00:34:47]

John: *And that she failed to feel that, yeah.*

Jeff: And she failed ... In the end, in retrospect all the AIDS activists have commented on how they were so uncertain, this was a very bleak time in AIDS activism because the early victories had succeeded and then everyone kept dying again. You know, and it wasn't until later, in the late '90s, that people actually started living and all of these great reclamations of health began ... But I do remember, like, being in these meetings and just not having the reaction that everybody else was having, I couldn't get angry at [Madonna]. But I also, you know, I wasn't indifferent to suffering or to the anger, I wasn't reacting to it by saying, 'I'm unsympathetic to you, you idiot, because you're angry,' but I just couldn't muster it on my own. I couldn't be angry at Madonna, although I was very sympathetic to the people who were ... I mean, I was as outraged about the AIDS crisis as anybody, but I wasn't, I couldn't, I didn't know who the target was, I was never certain and I never, kind of, deluded myself into, I didn't need to say I'm certain about this in order to act.

John: *Now, I think that's a really significant point, which is I often feel as though I am summoned to act out of certainty. You know, two weeks ago I was on a trade union picket line, right?*

Jeff: Why not?

John: *Why not? And do I believe that trade unionism will bring about, do I even believe that trade unionism will increase people's salaries? I mean, it's not going to increase mine because I won't be there. Actually I think all the historic evidence around academic salaries, it's probably not really ... but do I need to –*

Jeff: And the histories of academics, which in terms of unions actually acting in any sort of way, formal or not, in protecting their own interests as a collective group is completely, you know (laughs), debateable, you know.

John: *I remember the first meeting of the what used to be Association of University Teachers that I went to when I got to Open University, and it included inviting the vice-chancellor of the university to come and explain his strategy for coping with the financial crisis, and then giving him a round of applause. And I just thought, I used to think I was not in a very good trade union when I was in the polytechnic sector, and I get here and I think this is … My father didn't join trade unions for this. On the other hand, I have no problem about turning up on picket lines and acting, because I don't need to be –*

Jeff: It doesn't need to be a pure politics for you to, it doesn't need to be the pure, the pure cause to make it worth [participating in].

John: *No, I don't, and I don't have to be, I don't know what that terrible phrase was, a conviction politician, to act. If it's, if that's what we've got available –*

Jeff: So, are people who think like you or me on this, kind of, with a comfort with uncertainty, then are we just doomed to be, kind of, these peripheral Zelig-like figures who inhabit or, like, haunt everybody else's movements? Or is that it, or do we, or is there something else?

John: *I think I'm too old to answer that question, you see, I think I am doomed … [to be a supporter, not a leader.]*

Jeff: Well, I mean, okay, so say it's not you, not you personally then in that sense, but like is the, you know what I mean.

[00:39:04]

John: *Can we be a movement of ambivalence (laughs)? And –*

Jeff: A movement of that, yeah, a movement of ambivalence.

John: *Yeah. And I think you could, but I think it might not happen (laughs).*

Jeff: Well, maybe in fact, maybe it's one thing to do a thing about is that all movements are movements by ambivalence one way or the other, whether they like it or not. [And whether they admit it or not.]

John: *Well, and one of the things that would be interesting then would be to rethink politics as the performance of certainty.*

Jeff: And the lack thereof, yeah.

John: *… And that's why politics, doing politics, turns out to be so hard because for half the day of every day of every year you have to look as though you believe, I mean, that's worse than being religious …*

Jeff: All my long-term activist interlocutors, the ones that have actually sustained themselves the longest, are ambivalent, they don't know what's ... I mean, they have certain skills that they know will work to do certain kinds of things.

John: *Oh, that's certainly true.*

Jeff: They know how to do, they know how to do certain things, they know how to make a campaign and how to get a certain kind of group of people into a meeting. They have, like, certain ... ways, tactics that they have, and skills, political skills that they've perfected. But they don't necessarily have a sense of how all of that's necessarily going to play out in any new case (laughs).

John: *Yeah, yeah. But I think that's interesting because I think the alternative to that is that, is a position which flip-flops between zealousness and cynicism, right? So you either believe and you are driven by a certainty and a belief, and when it doesn't happen you turn into a cynic betrayed by the moment, the people, the failures of history, or whatever. Or you find that little, I'm going to, actually I'm going to call it a zone of comfort of ambivalence in which when it all goes wrong, that afternoon you don't think that's the end of history, that's the end of it. I mean, the number of times I've been in, actually even with you, in anthropology conferences and people have complained about the failure of the working class to turn up, and such like. And I think it's a bit like Madonna, why would you think that the working class is going to turn up, have they not got better things to do, or at least alternative things to do? What made you think that they were about to fall in line? You know, my public persona on that one is, why would anybody join a Clarke-ist movement?*

Jeff: So would those, those who were certain would say about us is that we are a reflection of the uncertainty of the times, of the base, in the, you know, they would say that we are just, not even a clever refraction, but just a reflection of a certain kind of, you know, flexibilised, uncertain –

John: *Flabbiness (over-speaking)*

[00:42:21]

Jeff: Flabbiness of, so ... So where do you go from that?

John: *Well, of course I go in two different directions, the nature of ambivalence, one is to say, well, you would say that, right, of course you would, you know, a politics of certainty is always going to find a way of dismissing the ambivalent or uncertain or, you know, unfinished. But the other is to say, well, in the end I'm not sure that — see delicate ambivalent phrasing? I'm not sure that this moment is retrievable by the organisation of a mass political disciplined vanguardist movement. And by the way, if these are any of the people that I know who are certain, they shouldn't be allowed anywhere near a vanguard position for anything, right? Partly, and I'll draw a distinction, partly because I think I get shouted at by people who occupy significant positions in academia and don't do any of the activism. I take it much easier from people who are actually going out and doing organising of something or other. So even my friends who are Trotskyites I have some time for because they put the time and effort in. The ones who are, I think, shout loudest about the class struggle and advancing it, don't seem me to even go and sell newspapers, and I think that's a bitter and cynical view of mine.*

[00:44:20]

Jeff: No, I think I see those points, but I think I also see, I also see, you know, it's very difficult for me to know this but I'm not certain of the certainties of the past either, if you (laughs) — You know, I think this is not my point, I mean, many people have made this point but, you know, I'm not so sure that, you know, at the height of trade unionism or Fordism, or whatever the bit, even with all the political failures or whatever, I'm not so certain that those weren't massively uncertain times for large numbers of people in terms of political outcomes. You know, even supposedly these moments where we weren't, like, with five people trying to form a revolution in some place or another, but where they were actually dealing with some sort of known, kind of, reformisms that nonetheless needed some sort of mass politics behind them. You know, even those moments seemed terribly unsettled, there's a way to read them that way, you know …

John: *Yeah, and the temptation now is to read them back through their accomplishments, not through their attempts to make things come true.*

Jeff: Right.

John: *So in one of the classic social policy stories that I tell a lot in such moments, is from around 1880, 1885, the organised Labour movement in Britain demanded the right to work. In about 1907 it got, not the right to work, but labour exchanges, right? So, you know, a critical moment, a critical thing that brought people together delivered, not intentionally, nobody wanted labour exchanges except Winston Churchill, nobody wanted labour exchanges, certainly the working class didn't. It wanted the right to work. But the historical accomplishment was unemployment insurance and labour exchanges, and that seems to me unfortunate. Now we don't even have unemployment insurance and labour exchanges (laughs). So, I mean, it is to say that I think, reading backwards into those struggles is risky because I doubt if I had been, you know, a trade union organiser in 1887 I'd have ... [led a struggle for labour exchanges] –*

Jeff: ... Well, this is also I think true of the civil rights movement in the United States where there's this incredible dynamism in conflictual terrain within this movement and with its articulated movements that's going on for a century or more, you know ... I think there are so many different registers of uncertainty that have to be accounted for when (laughs), when one, kind of, talks about politics, that it's tricky terrain, which is why it's so much easier to start from a position of, it's not even certainty, maybe certainty is not the right ... It's actually, I think, starting from a position of, well, if it's, I guess it's a certain kind of convincing that one does to oneself, but I'm not, I don't know, maybe there's another word for it than certainty, I'm not ... I guess it's faith is really what it is, there's a distinction between certainty to me and faith which seems to me to be, one seems to be rooted in knowledge, the other one seems to be rooted in something else.

John: *The jump, and we are faithless, and that's an interesting little trouble.*

Jeff: I mean, and this poor guy who had such faith in Madonna, you know, I mean, good for him, (laughs) but I could never have that, I could never believe, I could never believe, I could never believe, you know, so that's the thing, I could never believe any of this.

John: *Well, I want to a tell a better, nicer version, I think, than where we might be getting to, which is one of the things about that little sequence of things, things of politics of people that I was not. About gender, about sexuality, about race is, yeah, but if you'd started in 1965, 1966, you wouldn't have known that those were going to be politics, right? And so if you'd have wanted to do politics you'd have been into the Labour movement in some form or another, you might have been in Campaign for Nuclear Disarmament, you know, but you wouldn't have been ... [expecting the questions about gender and oppression or racialised hierarchies]. It's not, it's not that they're not there, but it …*

Jeff: I do feel though, having had a certain kind of moment in my life where, like you, you were, kind of, in the right place at the right time, but not quite.

John: *Yes (laughs).*

Jeff: You see what I mean?

John: *Yes, I do.*

Jeff: … But I do wonder what it would be like to just experience something along those lines, sometime (laughs), you know, like before the end, you know?

John: *As an insider, properly.*

Jeff: Yeah, well, you know, I do think that that would really be … I mean, I wonder how, you know, it takes all kinds, you know, and there will always be people like us who came after or next to, and who would, you know, have what we have to say. But, you know, there is, I guess, I can't say, I mean, I'm mostly afraid of that kind of faith, I mostly see it as pernicious … But I also see it as, kind of, I guess it's also, it's something I envy as long as I don't actually have to try to put it on. It's the suit in the window, as long as it's in the window I really love it, but as long as I don't actually have to put it on and realise that it's tight and it doesn't look good (laughs). You know what I mean, like?

John: *I just can't get out of it.*

Jeff: And I can't get out of it, exactly, and I'm going to have to wear it for the rest of my life, you know. I mean, so, you know, in other words, I guess I have a certain level of identification with that, like to be it even though I can't be it. Like there's moments where I, like, I think I'm a little bit more permissive of that, there are good colleagues that I have who are unreconstructed in this way and from whom I hide my true levels of, kind of, ambivalence and uncertainty, for whom, it comes out but I'm much more modulated about it, I'm much more careful. Whereas there are people who I just feel like, fuck off, you are so certain and it's so dangerous, and it's doing all this kind of stuff that I can't stand, that [I try to intervene and if that doesn't work, oppose them] … But then there are other people who feel equally as certain but their mode through the world is different somehow. [There are people who have taken certain positions that they hold for a really long time. I don't think they are completely certain all of the time, but I admire their projects and I would never try to target them with a critique of certainty.]

John: *It is about how total the totalising project is, right, which is, and that seems to me the point of, I mean, I have a, I think I have a number of distinctions, I mean, I think there are people doing all sorts of political work where I think, 'Thank God you do that,' right? And if you asked me I might even, I don't know, stuff some envelopes or send some emails or, you know, I'll do those things, but I'd be best a, sort of, foot soldier or, it's a horrible metaphor, I'd be a drone.*

Jeff: A body at the right place at the right time to absorb the shock, you know.

John: *Yes. Do you want somebody to make it look like a bigger number, that's fine? And then there are people where I think, yes okay, it's like my Trotskyite comrades, I'm, 'Go on, do it but, you know, please, even though we might use some of the same words, you know, I can talk about capitalism too, but we're not actually the same.' And that matters. And then there are people who I think occupy that, a political position, not necessarily that one, in a totalising and moralising way, and that's the point at which I want to say, 'Actually, no, I'm really, I'm really not going down that road.' And I'm willing to have an argument about it, all right, that's a public matter as far as I'm concerned, which is if you think that's what we should all be doing, you know, I need to tell you that I think that's probably wrong.*

...

6

Paul Stubbs

Paul Stubbs is a Senior Research Fellow at the Institute of Economics, Zagreb, where he works on issues of poverty, inequality and social exclusion, social welfare reform, the translation of travelling policies and the shifting articulations of politics and policy. He has written on social policy and regional development, social inequalities, social activism and the post-Yugoslav period – and much else. He is variously an activist, a consultant, an ethnographer and researcher.

I first met Paul when he invited me to take part in one of a series of workshops in Croatia whose title combined a set of keywords in unsettling ways, including neoliberalism, governance and the sovereign frontier. I went, despite doubts about my knowledge and competence to engage in these issues in that space, but I have never regretted it. I found a friend for life in this strangely, but excitingly, displaced Liverpudlian and we have subsequently managed to find many things on which to collaborate, including a book with Noémi Lendvai and David Bainton: *Making Policy Move: Towards a Politics of Translation and Assemblage* (2015). The dynamics of this collaboration form one of the topics for this conversation.

More details can be found at: www.eizg.hr/about-us/employees/ researchers/paul-stubbs-phd/220.

This conversation was recorded in Chicago on 22 November 2013.

Themes and topics

- Being dragged out of place
- Who studies policy?
- Making up things – and places
- The work of agency
- The threat of being found out

Being dragged out of place

[0:00:00]

John: *Where should we start?*

Paul: I don't know.

John: *We should start with the fact that one of the ways in which you've made me think was to drag me out of place and to get me out of both a very British cultural studies and a very English social policy. So why did you do that when I was relaxed and comfortable?*

Paul: Yeah, I mean, I dragged you out of place because if it was good enough for me it's good enough for you! Because I do think that precisely that issue of being forced to move or looking at things from somewhere else is the most privileged thing that I've had. Do you know what I mean? That I actually did no work on global social policy until I was living in Croatia and, I mean, I think that British cultural studies and English social policy, and an English radical social work, was [for] me, and it felt like it was the most liberating and the most universalist, and the most cosmopolitan and the, you know, absolutely French and Italian and blah, blah, and Freire and all, but it wasn't. Because it was very much struggling in a place that I had always been in and therefore took for granted in weird class, gender, racialised kind of terms. And it's only when you get away from that that you can then begin to, what's the word, usefully pose questions that are about space in ways that are not merely about geography and about, you know, the nature of centres and edges and cores and peripheries, and all of this stuff. But, I mean, I also think the biographical thing is extraordinary. I mean, we didn't manage to meet until, what, 19..., 2000-and ...

John: *Four? Five? Six?*

Paul: So I was already – 45, yeah, 45, 46.

John: *And I was even older.*

Paul: And I'd known your work and had admired that work but seen it very much in a, in that cultural studies, social policy mode. And then there was, you know, and I remember it well at editorial board meetings of *Global Social Policy*, so very early on, probably in Helsinki or somewhere where we had a conference, and I was the book review editor. And Nicola Yeates gave me the book, and I got it back to my room and I opened the acknowledgements or the preface which begins to talk about anthropology. And suddenly it was like this was the voice that I'd been waiting for, this was the ... Because Noémi [Lendvai] was different, through Noémi, but Noémi was a, you know, I was the external examiner, she was doing, partly, work on a place I knew, she was coming to certain anthropological positions. But here was John who was steeped in these things also doing that. And that thing I wrote for Berlin which has never been published, which might end up, bits of it, you know, I was having huge problems with Bob Deacon at the time over precisely this anthropological turn, in a way. And problems with some of the other people in global social policy because this was a, kind of, post-nation-state, anti-social justice, kind of position that I was articulating, supposedly. And so just those first three pages just did it for me and it was like, 'Oh my God, it is possible to worry about everything, to see nothing as fixed, but actually still to have a politics.'

John: *Yeah. Well, I, (laughs) yeah, we need to go into that in more detail then.*

Paul: And I think the book was very much, I don't think the book was about the frustration with cultural studies, but the frustration with social policy, the empiricalness, the narrowness, the Englishness.

[00:05:34]

John: *Yes, all of, and especially – about the presumption that things are fixed, that if you say 'welfare state' you know what it is, which seems to me to be one of the most disastrous moments in an academic field. You know, if you bump into a welfare state you know what it is ... good luck with the bumping thing.*

Paul: Well, and then it's sectors, isn't it, education and housing and social protection, and it's too important to be just those things.

John: *Yeah, absolutely. And, you know, and so part of the fascination for me is, I mean, I once described, rather miserably, my life project being to convert social policy to cultural studies. And I know that I've failed, but that's not the most ... But it is in whether, where anthropology performs, some anthropology, performs an enabling role, because there are weird people there too.*

Paul: No, well, I don't think we're ever going to stop anywhere. Do you remember my intervention once, in the middle of my most interesting in Latourian, kind of, translation stuff, saying, 'I'm too old to have heroes,' that it is against Stuart Hall's idea. These are just, these are things you wrestle with and neither of us are ever going to be a Foucault scholar, a Latour scholar, and that seems to me to be the most ridiculous waste of time precisely because you don't bring unusual suspects together in order to have an edgy conversation. I think it'll be close enough to it, you know, but my Butler-Goffman [combination], I mean, I would need a lot more time but I probably wouldn't get much further than I've got already with it. Do you know what I mean? I think there's something about that's what we do and we are more sparky.

John: *What does it enable you to do that you're worried about now? And so I think it is not scholarly in that systematic, you know, I am going to pursue this for the rest of my life mode. … And indeed almost entirely in a 'Please God, no' version, because the notion that I'd be stuck with whatever it was that I'd got, if it was the* Daily Telegraph *reporting riots, whatever, you know, this week. If that was my work, as it were, I'd retire, just no help at all. But the sense of a more … both playful and exploitative relationship to theory seems to me to be what's partly at stake, which is, I'm perfectly willing to, I don't know, I'm sure somewhere I've used the word taking people's ideas out for a walk, and because they let you see things. But you don't necessarily have to, I mean, you can give them back afterwards.*

Paul: No, it's interesting because there's a lot of academic work out that, not all of which we've read, and it is interesting because I do remember you, what's her name, the ethnographer, Hodgson, no, the woman, Dorothy – Dorothy Smith.

John: Institutional Ethnography *[Dorothy Smith's book]*.

Paul: Yes. She's the last person I remember you mentioning who had moved, really moved. Do you know, something, you found something in that work that shifted you off that current axis in a bigger way than other stuff.

John: *I think that's true.*

Paul: And I'm thinking who was the last one who did that to me (laughs)? Janet Newman, I mean, because I'm reading *Spaces of Power* and I love it. I'm actually frustrated a little bit because I know where she's going to go next with it. I feel like I've been on that journey too, you know, the neoliberal stuff, but the methodology, do you know, and I just think that there's, yeah, there's no need to dwell. But the danger then is being seen as not having served one's time and, do you know, and

I'm still, I think, grateful for and suffering from that one year of Althusserian Marxism that I had, do you know.

[00:10:17]

John: *Yeah (laughs), mine lasted slightly longer than a year ... But, but nevertheless, grateful for and suffering from, but grateful for is part of that ... There are things that it enabled me to think then and still to think, that nobody else did. And when I read Gibson-Graham, that most unlikely of Althusserian Marxists, right, they talk about what they take from, I mean, they don't do Althusserianism, but they take a set of conceptual tropes and make them work for them. And that seems to me to be right, you know.*[1]

Paul: No, I agree.

John: *And knowing that they're Althusserian is not a reason for not thinking with them, you know, I mean, it's not a, they don't just belong in a bracketed bad moment of Marxist structuralism.*

Who studies policy?

Paul: No, but, I mean, I don't want to picture us as victims because we're not, but I think that the kind of, you know, two thoughts here about things that have happened or things that I feel, I wonder if you feel the same, certainly for the first one, the second one might be interesting as well. But, you know, amongst anthropologists the fact that we do social policy means that we're really weird, do you know what I mean? Thank God for the policy bit, and I guess for you the North American bit because that also has social policy people. But it's felt like, you know, 'Why are you doing this when you should be doing governmentality or borders or the body or ...'

John: *Some hot topic.*

Paul: Yeah, exactly.

John: *And whatever else you might say about social policy, it has never been a hot topic.*

Paul: No, and try in social policy communities to throw anthropology in, not in a big A, but as a, kind of, meanings, interpersonal, agency ... [you get] bafflement.

---

[1] A reference to J.K. Gibson-Graham's book *The end of capitalism (as we knew it)*, University of Minnesota Press, 2006.

John: Indeed, no, bafflement. And I'm going to, there's a connection to this that's important I think, but I do think that, that I agree with you. I mean, it's not being victims but it is occupying strange spaces on the edge of everybody else's worlds, and the moment that connects it back to Dorothy Smith is being invited to go to a conference, postgraduate student conference in Denmark on the anthropology of welfare. And I turn up and do my maundery stuff, and Dorothy Smith turns up and does one of the keynotes. And I both, I knew the book and liked it, but actually what she did was do a version of who I'd like to be if I ever grew up. Right? I mean, she performed brilliantly for how to think, in this particular ethnographic mode, about a world of welfare and states and bureaucracies and relations of power. And she did it without waving a conceptual apparatus at us, right? ... Just talked about doing it.

[00:13:34]

Paul: No, indeed, indeed.

John: And saved that for the questions. So I was about to ask her a question about, well, you know, 'It's interesting that you say that, but doesn't it have a particular view about language? And what about Bakhtin?' thinking, you know, I know about Bakhtin, I'm clever ... And in the answer to the question before I was about to get mine in, she said, 'Well, and of course, you know, there are these different tributaries to this way of thinking about language and ethnography and the constitution of the world which run from, you know, Foucault, and discourse to Bakhtin and, you know, polyvocal, poly, you know, heteroglossia.' And I thought, I'm glad I didn't get my question in first because I've have looked like a complete prat then. And there's something, I think about, and she was doing it in a way that enabled and supported and pulled along in a very gentle way PhD students interested in this field of stuff that they couldn't get their head round. And I thought, actually, and so the Dorothy Smith thing is doubled, it's the book and the work that she's done.

Paul: Yes, but the ability to, yeah, to walk through it, yeah.

John: But it's the lesson of how to carry people with you in that, or as Stuart would have said, 'How to articulate, you know, what you know and what people want to know and make those connections.'

Paul: Yeah, yeah. No, I mean, you know, I mean, there are, this is not about dilettantism for either of us, there are threads, there are some constants, but those constants are fixed points around which one starts to try and experiment with different positions, of view and vocality, and of method, and all this. And I actually think, you know, dragging you out of your, dragging you out of that comfort zone, John, I can't remember how many times I've, kind of, used, misused, plagiarised, borrowed, taken for granted your point that South East Europe is an emergent space in which the boundaries of authority, power, governance are not fixed, but neither are they anywhere. And therefore it is a privileged site into exactly those forms in this, you know, and I couldn't see that because I was in that so much, you know. No, the second thing was, I mean, I just, because I do think there's another thing that I do that you don't do, which is, it's not the consultancy virgin stuff, but it's this, kind of, NGO activism, this kind of, you know, that mode of being in the world and stuff. But it bothers me, I mean, and they're good people, some of them are my friends. There's this NGO trying to be a think-tank on, kind of, democracy, transparency, but they had a workshop, a week's workshop on interpretative policy, qualitative policy analysis, to get away from just writing these policy papers. There was me struggling with auto-ethnography, with critical policy studies, with all kinds of stuff, and all the questions were about ethics and ontology actually, but the ontology was from three or four people who are seen as the avant-garde of critical policy studies in Croatia. And guess what? It's Laclau and Mouffe or Norman Fairclough, and it is so straight and so dah-dah-dah, and I was traumatised for half a day, and I sat there and I thought, 'I'm not going to say anything,' there was a bit of Bourdieu thrown in and I said, 'What about field?' And they don't like that, it's not meaty, it's not precise enough about field. But then it was like, 'Okay, okay, I've been worrying about this for 30 years so I don't expect you to answer this, but I'm hoping we can have a conversation about it. Is there anything outside of discourse?' And they both went, 'No, absolutely not, there is nothing, there is nothing that is not discourse.' And, okay, fine, I'm out ... I can't do this.

John: *Yeah, yeah, I can't be there.*

Paul: And yet, you know, we write discourses and practices, don't we?

John: *Yeah, we do.*

Paul: Constantly ...

[00:18:18]

John: *Because we started with the problem, I mean, what is there outside discourse?*

Paul: No, indeed. Because it can't, I mean, it can all be discourse, but then discourse is a bit different from others ... In terms of their effects, at least, you know.

John: *It's the sign of discourse of being kneed in the groin by the state, right?*

Paul: Yes, (laughs) indeed.

John: *That's not entirely discursive though it might have discursive effect. And I just think that, (sighs) I don't know what it is that we suffer from, I think it's a sensibility and it seems to me it's stacked up with different things. One is a, sort of, strange history of bits of critical thoughts that we found interesting for some purpose at some time.*

Paul: Yes, and we're already out of time and place anyway, or already weirdly positioned in relation to other things, yes.

John: *And it is, it's something that came up in the conversation with Anu [Sharma] that I recorded the other day, which is the refusal to take any object as singular and fixed, right? So when people say, 'Well, it's ', I'm reading a book at the moment which says, 'Well', it takes a very anthropological imagination view of the state and it says, 'Well, you know, it's the state effect, it's all these things.' And then turns to something called governance as though it's an object.*

Paul: Yes, does it in the same way as they say you can't possibly do that with the state.

John: *And you want to say (laughs), 'No, no, don't do that, please don't do that.'*

Paul: No, but you know why they do it, and we do it, and I will accuse you of doing it tomorrow, because everybody in that panel tomorrow has an essentialist category, because if you didn't have it you couldn't write the paper.

John: *Your one standing point, just temporarily it is.*

Paul: Yeah. And as long as that's not the same standing point over a long period of time ... And then becomes prior to the lived relations in which it is embedded, then it's a problem, then it's not a problem as long as it – escapes out of that.

John: *As long as it could always be, you know, what, if, he remembers his Derrida. If you understand that it's always under the sign of erasure, the thing itself, even if you want it for now, cannot be the thing.*

Paul: No, and it's our equivalent, it's our soft equivalent of the dependent and the independent variable, actually, I'm afraid, you know, that's all we're doing is saying it's all, it's all in flux. But just to get a handle on the flux you have to hold on to one thing, you know, I don't want to do physics envy and chemistry envy and all this. But it is actually, although if I'm going to be harsh to each of us and people like us, we tend to hold the same things for granted, politics, liberalism, technocracy, those ..., and I think that's why I got interested in the consultant stuff. Let's not have them as the wicked men in suits who we don't interrogate at all, do you know, and that –

[00:21:47]

John: *Yeah, they're just the evil carriers.*
Paul: Yeah, and they might be, I mean, it might be true at one level but it's not interesting.
John: *But it's like Anu's NGOs, of course there'll be something at some point, somewhere, but the idea that you would then turn that into the categoric statement of what they were, ditto consultants. And that revelatory moment for me, when I was the only person in the room who was not, who had not been a consultant, was – okay, so that's not a class of people who are consultants, it's the people who are –*
Paul: Absolutely not, it's a loop.
John: *– doing studies, doing PhDs, you know, and doing consultancy and criticising consultancy and all of that. So, I mean, being taken out of place, I want to come back to it ... And that was a different sort of being taken out of place, that was being taken into a milieu in which people were much more complicated than me. I mean, in terms of elements, the things that they had to pull together.*
Paul: Yes, having the identity assemblages had to engage with something that was called consultancy, which is never the same thing, but it's called that therefore it is the same thing, you know, at least discursively.

Making up things – and places

John: *But the being taken out of place, I think, I mean, one of the things you hinted at, which I think it really did, was to say, 'Here's weird.' South East Europe, strange bloody place this turns out to be, if it's a place at all. So the United Kingdom then? ... And I mean, it's turning, it is, you know, it's Chakrabarty's provincialising wherever it is that you started with it, right, which is, bloody hell, you know,*

> *now that I start looking at the United Kingdom, people are making it up all over the place, you know?*[2]

Paul: Yes, indeed.

John: *Borders are shifty, you know, authorities have been recomposed in interestingly diverse ways and, my word …*

Paul: Yes, so those paradoxes, or you would say contradictions of, you know, take, perverse confluences that lots of things coming from different places, but that constant making up of new stuff. And you know, when I, the first response to your chapter where I was saying, you know, it's moved, we've moved from *Yes Minister*, via *The Office*, to *London 2020* [he meant 2012], in terms of managerialism. Or we've probably gone beyond *London 2020* [2012] now. But you know, that was, sustainability's in there, empowerment is in there, all of the things that we struggled for or with, and I think, you know … And it's why I'm going to look forward to writing the last chapter [of *Making Policy Move*] with you because I think I do have to go back to Freire in this, and partly I have to back to Freire because there's a praxis in Freire, there's an ethics in Freire, and there's a move between the political as we would want to see it, and the institutionalised, which is fascinating. And you can't be anywhere with Brazilians, South Africans, you know, the new interesting institutional configurations of a radical politics without seeing that, because it is Freire, it's not just Freire but it is him too.[3]

[00:25:29]

John: *But it is that configuration of things that you can't, bits that you can't leave out of trying to think about a field, a whatever.*

Paul: And you know, the space I move in didn't have Freire, it had Soros, and I think that makes a big difference and this is, you know, qualitatively, which isn't actually even about normative judgement, it just is about who took the space.[4]

---

[2]   A reference to Dipesh Chakrabarty's *Provincializing Europe: Postcolonial thought and historical difference*, Princeton University Press, 2000.

[3]   During the meetings on our book, we had recurring conversations about the significance – and complexity – of Paolo Freire's work, especially *Pedagogy of the Oppressed*, Continuum, 1970.

[4]   George Soros, the Hungarian-born investor and philanthropist, whose investments in creating the Open Society Foundations in the former Soviet bloc have become controversial, especially among the current authoritarian regime in Hungary.

John: *Yes, yes. And one of the panels that I was at yesterday had somebody telling me about how things took place and that meant space and time, and I thought, you see, the trouble with you anthropologists is you don't read anybody else, right? So there is, and taking place is not quite the same as taking space – it's not quite the same as occupying. And I mean, I [have been] supervising a wonderful PhD student who is doing work on West Bank settlement in Palestine Israel, and it has made it almost impossible for me now to use the words 'occupy' or 'settlement' – in the spirit in which I would have used them before.*

    ...

The work of agency

John: *But one of the things about the translation orientation and the questions of agency that we've ended up with, and I'm not sure whether I think now we make enough of it, but it's certainly for me one of the things it feels like is about work. I mean, it's about the expenditure of effort ... So agency's all right but it always sounds a bit flibberty-gibberty, you know, easy, but work sounds a bit grungier.*

Paul: No, it's, and I think it is that, and it is interesting because I did, you know, Stuart would use work and it would always have inverted commas, wouldn't it? ... Because he didn't want it to mean raw labour power, it's not, it's not essentialistic, it's not economistic Marxism. But even when I used it I had to put play in because they are supposedly opposites, and yet everything is, there is work to be done and there is play to be done, there is play to be performed, because it's never finished and then contradictory. It is always both and lots of other things.

John: *Yes, indeed. And that seems to me to be the, I don't know what to do with it when I've got it, but it seems to me that the notion of, sort of, easy, systemic, structural reproduction, whatever else, you know, it misses how much bloody trouble people go to to keep things going, or to make them go slightly differently, or any of those things.*

Paul: Yeah, yeah, yeah. And it's never, you know, and that's why actually conjunctural stuff is also hard to do because you never quite know. You know, I mean, one of the things I will say tomorrow is where are you all in terms of whether this is new or not, because actually the call for the panel says new, new, new, new, which is just a way of getting on the programme, you know, being accepted.

John: *It's a bit of work.*

Paul: And we all know that that's bullshit, but actually, you know, your paper [for the panel] will go, can go loads further, about, hang on, we've seen all this before but it doesn't matter that we've seen it before, it's different now by definition because this is now and not then. And so there's, kind of, this time stuff is very complicated and it's this idea of non-linearities of space and time are somehow, the borrowing, the homologies, which is why you're living, you know, your point about living history rather than going in the archives because archives are not archives, are they? You know, it's my interactions with the archives and so on, you know, these things are never ...

John: *Indeed. But one of the things about doing, I mean, this is, when we did the, we did a launch event in Sheffield for the new edition of —*

[01:12:03]

Paul: *Policing the Crisis.*

John: *Which was fun and weird in all sorts of ways. But there were two things that mattered, one is that Chas and I had an enormous disagreement about the hegemony question in the current moment. But the other was a quite serious discussion of the changing conditions of intellectual work, in the sense that the possibilities of* Policing the Crisis's *wonderful conjunctural analysis had something to do with the fact it was five people, right? It wasn't an act of individual scholarship to investigate the present moment because none of us would have done it.*

Paul: No, I mean, and there as a lot of that about, I mean, it wasn't, do you know, I think *Policing the Crisis* was clearly the best of that whole bunch. But Glasgow Media Group, do you know, there was the London Edinburgh Weekend Return [Group], and so these were not just ... These were two things, right? They were academic collaborations but they were rooted in the real, they were both taking from the present and acting upon it and trying to do more than understanding boxes terms. And I think that's a kind of, you know, I wouldn't, it's silly to, you know, it's nothing like that, but those seminars in Croatia were my attempt to do something like, you know, both those things, collaborations between some people who I knew and some people I didn't know, and some people I hoped might find something, but also [linking] theory and practice.

[01:13:56]

John: *Yes, and it seems to me that that, I mean, that that's one of the things that Marxism has, I don't know what to call them, delightful, I mean, you know ... Moments in which those sorts of things were enabled, encouraged, made possible, didn't necessarily materialise in the form – who knew that* Policing the Crisis *was going to be* Policing the Crisis? *People never know what the material end point is going to be.*

Paul: Sure, sure.

John: *But I'm struck by the ways in which we try and imagine possibilities of collaboration, even in much more strained, dispersed, difficult circumstances.*

Paul: Because it is dispersed, in a sense, yeah. No, and I mean, you know, the translation book will be finished, but I have a feeling that, do you know what I mean, that the moment wasn't ... It's probably always what happens with written work is that actually it takes so long that the productive moment came too late in the process, in a sense. That the, do you know what I mean, that the peak of the possibilities, I mean, it's complicated stuff this because these are really important things we're talking about, these are real relations, do you know, it's probably the hardest ... I mean, people might argue long-term emotional relationships, sexual relationships are more complicated, I'm sure they are, they're in a different register, right. But writing something with other people, both collaboratively and separately and across distances and using technology, and all kinds of things were, you know, things get thrown in and out, and it ...

John: *Yes. And, you know, and certainly for, I mean, the citizenship book which preceded it, the impossibility of holding everything that matters to anybody, at any one moment, into this project is, like, impossible, you know, so ...*

Paul: No, no, not even coming close, you know. And knowing that you're not going to come close, so, you know.

[01:16:13]

John: *Yeah, and knowing that, you know, it's got, it crosses lives and those lives are stuffed full, and part of what made* Policing *possible was the fact that we gave up, actually most of us gave up PhDs ... But used the resources that supported those to ...*

Paul: And now you can't do that, no.

John: *You can't do that, Noémi [Lendvai] can't do that, Dave [Bainton] can't do that, I couldn't, I'm on the point of retirement, [which] will enable me to do whatever I want, that's my fantasy even though I know it's not true. But, but, and it was the same about the citizenship book, which is every time we, you know, it only moved when we could get together and look one another in the eye. Because, not because we were bad people, not because we didn't care about it, but because as soon as you're on your own there's all the other stuff that demands your attention and effort.*

Paul: Yes, indeed. I was saying something a bit different from that, I think, which is that the moment you agree to collaborate it's already too late, because you wouldn't have agreed, you know what I mean, you've already passed that moment where the …

John: *That point in which, where you can recognise it all.*

Paul: You know, it all comes together in some kind of weird way, you know.

John: *So we're now just trying to hold it together for when we have to …*

Paul: I think so, no, that's right, it's boundary, it really is just, kind of, containing so that it doesn't become an imploding … What is it, TV sets don't explode, they implode? … It just leaves a mess, right, or a hole.

John: *Melt.*

Paul: Right, yeah, so there's a hole. But, yeah, and do you know, I'm both profoundly liberated by the fact that I work in a place where the new managerialism is still kept at bay, to the point that I can be the neoliberal, in a sense, to raise standards and stuff. So it must be weird, but there is no, not just resources, but understanding, commitments, possibilities of those real collaborations … And I had more of those in the '90s, you know, working with ethnologists who were interested in everyday practices in war and with anti-war campaigners, and that kind of stuff, do you know? But this has been, you know, this has been, this remains incredibly productive, I think, and … What was I going to say? Work, work is a relevant issue because I do think we then need, you know, so much like plotting what the, because it is a privileged position … And the more you see what's happening the more it is, and an extraordinarily anachronistically privileged position.

John: *Yes, God, I know. I mean, from my dad's deep suspicion that they pay me money to talk, right, to having, even if it's increasingly squeezed space and time to think, right? And in my case, however much I might grumble about the managerialisation in the university, you know, to the extent that I can persuade people that this is a good idea, I get to do good ideas, right? I mean, those are strange things.*

[01:19:43]

The threat of being found out

Paul: Yeah. And I mean, you know, most of the things I really want to do won't cost much money in the future, actually, but they do involve time and that's ... I mean, it is weird that dilettantism, which is not a concept that either of us have used, has actually framed –

John: *Much of this, much of this, indeed.*

Paul: – much of this. And I guess it is, why we both perform is because there's still the nagging doubt, just as you come to retirement, that one day we're going to get found out, right? That this is not real work, or we're not real workers. There is real work but we're not real workers.

John: *We're not it.*

Paul: We're not it (laughs).

John: *I did, I bumped into Leticia Sabsay[5] in the corridor a month or so ago, she said, 'So, you know, the retirement thing, are you going be all right?' And I said, 'Well, basically I'm hoping to get to the end of December without anybody having found me out.' ... She said, 'Found out what?' And I said, 'That I'm not a proper academic.' Because in all sorts of ways I think I'm not scholarly, I have not pursued a life dedicated to a subject that is my own, you know, I accept invitations to talk about –*

Paul: Things you know nothing about.

John: *– things I know nothing about. You know, I've done this thing recently on complaints about medicine, the last chapter for a book, because some interesting people, mostly historians, were doing a weekend workshop about complaints about medicine, and they're people who know stuff, right? They've been in the archive and things, and they were trying to find somebody who would do the last word at the*

---

[5] Leticia Sabsay was then a Research Associate in the Oecumene (Citizenship After Orientalism) programme at the Open University. She is currently an Assistant Professor of Gender and Contemporary Culture in the Gender Institute at the London School of Economics.

weekend, and they talked to a friend of mine who's a historian in Birmingham, he said, and I checked this with him, he said, 'Well, you should ask John Clarke, he'll talk about anything.'[6]

Paul: Yes, because he'll be funny, yeah, no, I know.

John: *And, you know, and I think it's another site of ambivalence. I don't want to be a real academic, right? I don't want to be – I don't want to be that scholarly person, you know, pursuing something to the grave in finer and finer detail, endlessly reflecting on … Because I love what I've done, right?*

Paul: No, indeed, indeed.

John: *But also it feels a bit strange sometimes.*

[01:22:23]

Paul: But I do think ambivalence is crucial to this, and it is like, you know, I'll probably behave tomorrow in the way that you didn't want me to behave, do you know what I mean? But it's almost like I feel I owe, you know, privileged position to be able to read those four papers, and wanting then to be able to do something that isn't, do you know what I … We don't like boring, but there's smug at the other end, and we don't like that either, actually. And we, we probably can come across as smug in some ways because we connect these things very quickly and we fix people into … Do you know what I mean?

John: *No, I do, I do, …*

Paul: Plus, we don't write enough about, we don't reflect on exactly these things.

        …

---

[6]   See the collection by Jonathan Reinarz and Rebecca Wynter (eds), *Complaints, Controversies and Grievances in Medicine: Historical and social science perspectives*, Routledge, 2014. The historian in question was Matthew Hilton.

7

Allan Cochrane

Allan Cochrane is an Emeritus Professor of Urban Studies at the Open University (OU). His research and writing have explored the ways in which the spaces of politics and policy are made up in practice in ways that reflect relations of power within and beyond the state. It is in this broader context that my research has focused on a series of mainly urban sites through which it is possible to consider the workings of power, the possibilities of politics and changing forms of policy intervention. His publications include the co-authored *The Lived Experience of Multiculture: The New Social and Spatial Relations of Diversity* (2018) and *The University in Its Place: Social and Cultural Perspectives on the Regional Role of Universities* (2018), as well as the sole-authored *Understanding Urban Policy: A Critical Approach* (2007).

I first met Allan at a meeting in 1976 to discuss the viability of a Midlands branch of the Conference of Socialist Economists (not viable ...) held at Catherine and Stuart Hall's house in Moseley. It was four years later that I moved to the Open University and came to share a very happy and productive large office with Allan, John Allen and Sue Himmelweit (who both feature in this conversation). He and I worked together on courses, on a research project and in contributing to the development and management of the department and the wider faculty. He has remained a good friend who has also enriched my social life over the years (and my cultural life from his music collection).

Further details can be found at: www.open.ac.uk/people/adc5.

This conversation was recorded in London on 28 March 2017.

Themes and topics

- The Open University as a space for critical thinking
- Opening up possibilities
- Disciplines and interdisciplinary thinking

The Open University as a space for critical thinking

John: *Let's start with a reminiscence. So, we both ended up at – turned up at the Open University –*

Allan: We did, in the beginning of the 1980s.

John: *Do you have any sense of what made it an interesting place for doing critical thinking?*

Allan: I think one of the things that happened was that somehow people got brought together at that moment in the Faculty of Social Sciences. And I think partly it was done deliberately, actively, by the person who was then dean; partly it was accidental and it related to the production of one particular course and it brought people together around that [D102: Introduction to the Social Sciences]. When I arrived actually, which was in 1979, the most remarkable thing that happened to me was I went to see the dean … on the day I arrived, and as I was going in to see him for my meeting, Stuart Hall who'd just arrived at the same time on the same day was walking out and I thought, 'This is going to be a good place to be.' I'd only met – at that time I'd only met Stuart once before as you know, I think, because you were there too, but I knew that this was an important sign of some good things that were likely to be going on in the university or in the faculty. The other thing that was there … had to do with the way in which the university itself was growing up at the time. So, it had gone through a period really of having to survive and having to think and having to make its own way and one of the things that it had ended up quite fundamentally oriented towards was the notion of interdisciplinary social sciences and also critical social sciences. Before we got there, for example, there was an important course, I think, a course which helped to frame some of the debates that we came into which was called 'Patterns of Inequality', and it was an attempt to bring together different disciplines, literally to think through what the title suggests, the way in which there were different patterns of inequality globally, locally generated and maintained in all sorts of different ways. I think the fact that they'd brought that together helped to frame what then happened with the new Level 1 course that you worked on, which I think was a very exciting course that brought together some amazing people one way or another. I was working on a different course which was about urban studies [D202: Urban

Change and Conflict], which was an attempt to do much the same sort of thing and again brought together some quite remarkable people, many of whom I've continued to see, some of whom I've continued to collaborate with over the years. We were trying to open up different ways of thinking about – at that time, I think they were trying to think about different ways of thinking about urban geography, and I had no idea what geography was at the time – I was appointed as an interdisciplinary member of staff, which I always thought was a wonderful thing to be, to get a job as. So, yes, so what was coming together … was a moment in the life of the Open University and probably in the life of the faculty which was a moment of coming out of a period of struggle in the sense of trying to define itself, into a moment of a bit more confidence where they were able to bring people together and actively try to construct a space in which people could think collectively and differently and in all sorts of ways. I suppose one of the things that was right there from the start was a commitment to working together, so teams were always important [even if] teams didn't always work very well …

John: … but with the working together thing, and I'll go back to interdisciplinarity in a bit, but the team thing seemed to me to be one of the great gifts of the OU from my point of view, because it's true it didn't always work well; there were some people who resisted any of the possibilities and disciplines of working collaboratively, but it just felt like one of the ways in which two things were made possible for me. One was the weird thing about how you teach when you can't see anybody; having that as a shared process of trying to work it out was wonderful, but the other one was about precisely the point at which – the moment where you get stuck trying to do something, whatever it might be – and if you're on your own, getting stuck doing something is one of the more dismal bits of doing writing, and so I still remember working on – I think it was probably D211 [Social Policy and Social Welfare] – and getting stuck on the first chapter, and you were the person who took it off me and said, 'Don't worry, this'll get done' (both laugh). That was a bit of a dramatic process but in other respects, the circulation and the accumulation of comments and wisdom and occasional stupidities from other people seemed to me to be one of the big lessons about how you might do intellectual life and work, really.

[0:06:21]

Allan: Yes, I think that's true … there are two experiences that we might want to share; one I'll share with you and one that we shared at the time actually. I had the same problem – it sounds like the same sort of problem. I was trying to write something for the D209 State and Society [course] and I just couldn't do it; I would write, it would get longer and longer and it was about something I thought I knew. It was supposedly about thinking through the way in which states formed themselves in the 19th century … and as I wrote, it either got longer and longer and unmanageable or it just stopped and it was dreadfully difficult and a colleague, Grahame Thompson, actually took me aside and said, 'I'll help you – we'll go through this together and I'll help you get it done.' He doesn't remember this when I've spoken to him since, but he actually made an incredibly helpful intervention which meant that it got me going … You and I, I will remind you, once had to rescue a chapter that somebody who was trying to write was failing, was stuck and actually, because we were doing it collectively, we ended up having to write it again and, in a sense, take it back to him. It ended up being published in his name, written in his name, but we – that was part of the doing the stuff together; it was because we were a team that we were able to do that and to take that into account. But I think those were extreme examples; the more positive ones were about how much one learned from others. You're right about learning about how to do the sorts of teaching, I think. When I first started I had one of the most irritating people in the world, who was an advisor from the Institute of Educational Technology who was taking me through everything that I had to do and actually I hated it, I hated it so much! (Both laugh) In retrospect, it was amazingly helpful. It forced me to think – partly it forced me to say, 'No, I want to do it this way, not that way,' but it also, on other occasions, forced me to accept that actually that was quite right, how else – I needed to think about it, because I had to be – I had to learn how to teach in that way and I could only do that collectively but also, I could only – it's funny, talking about interdisciplinarity, that I could only learn to think in that way by talking to other people and by other people telling me what was important and what wasn't. I was learning; throughout the first course I worked on, I was learning both to write, not just write but teach in other ways, TV – in those days we had TV programmes, how to think through the way in which that worked, and we had audio – we had everything. The poor students were drowning in material that we sent them in those days and – but we – I learned so much; I learned so much from the people I was working with who were mainly geographers. They weren't all geographers – Patrick Dunleavy made a huge contribution, although he was there as a consultant by the time I was there, because I'd got his job [after he left for the London School of Economics] – but [the geographers – like] Linda McDowell and Chris Hamnett [taught me so much about different ways of thinking about the world]. It … was a remarkable experience, and of course the other thing that happened was we had summer schools for students in those days, and I'm not sure whether residential school was a good thing or a bad thing in the end, but one of the things I do remember right from the early days was teaching with you as a double act on a crime and society module – and it was the most amazing experience of learning, both from you but also how to teach and listening to the people who were talking back to us. It was the most exhilarating period for me and a remarkable experience. Institutionally it was amazing, it was just the right moment, I think, when things were happening and there was a degree of confidence, but also a degree of wanting to do things differently and I was learning. I suppose others were learning too; we were all learning. Of course, the other thing is I suspect we all, all of us, despite the fact that I'm saying we're all learning and all this sort of thing and it was all true that we were, but we were also an arrogant bunch; we also thought that we knew a lot about a lot of things and –

John: *Oh yes we did!*

Allan: – it was wonderful to think that even in that context there were people that we were getting stuff from and moments when we were insecure. There's no doubt about it, you find yourself – partly because you were stretching yourself because, unlike mainstream institutions, you were being expected to teach not just what you might be expert in but something which was cognate, something which might – you might have been interested in.

John: *Might just!*

[0:11:57]

Allan: And that was always a challenge, so you were always reliant on others and you were always listening and you were always – you had to be confident; you did actually have to be confident. I think some of the people – there were probably some people who fell by the wayside because they lacked that confidence.

John: *Yes, and I think – there were some people whose confidence was not necessarily quite so productive. I do remember colleagues whose second draft was exactly the same as their first draft, despite the 30 pages of comments, and the third draft was the [same] … So, I do remember all those things as well, but I do think your description of that moment is absolutely right and compelling and part of it was about what the – both the context of the OU but also the context of the course teams enabled me/us to do, and some of that was about discovering how to do things, and I remember when – the first course team I worked on, we wanted to teach Level 1 students theory in the social sciences and everybody gathered around us and said, 'You cannot do this, you cannot teach entry students theory,' and we said, 'No, we think you can teach them theory if you teach it well enough,' and I think we – we did such a good job of it that they thought they knew everything by the time they exited from it and that there were only Marx and Weber in the modern world and that would do everything. But I think it was the collective confidence of that and the collective willingness to experiment and to trust one another to do it well was, I think, gripping. … I'm not even sure that by the time I retired, that I knew how to teach at a distance; I … think I was still trying to make it up, but what was great about it was the willingness to – generally – to play at that as a process in which you started again the next time you got to a new course and it wasn't that you just redid it, it's that you started [again] … and one of the things you said there was the – not just teaching the things you know. I think one of the great gifts of the OU to me was that it let me – invited me to and let me do, a series of weird … I ended up writing about a collection of very strange things, from the US welfare state to the crime novel and probably more that I can't remember, so there's something about that open intellectual horizon of that, collectively, that was gripping.*

Opening up possibilities

Allan: So partly it was the environment of the Open University but partly it was the people who had been brought together. Somehow we came from different backgrounds where we were trying to do those things before. You and Stuart obviously from cultural studies, I'd been working on a community development project; there were a whole range of different things that came together. Doreen Massey coming in from her work on regions and so on at CES [the Centre for Environmental Studies]. It was an interesting – it was a moment when people – it wasn't just the Open University, it was also the people that were around the Open University, how we were trying to think. Yes, so I think there was something quite significant – significant about the people. They're the people that I work closely with – people like you and John Allen who I ended up working closely with over 20 years, really, at different times, but also of course we had – we did have Stuart Hall and we did have Doreen Massey at that time and that was a very productive time and a very inspirational moment to have them as well. But I think what's interesting for me is how it all goes on and feeds into a continuing series of courses, research projects, writing projects that we got involved in at different times and in different ways. If somebody had said to me, 'No, you're going to be writing about regions and urban policy and stuff,' well maybe I'd have believed them, but in some ways it's very odd that I ended up doing that or even the stuff that we ended up doing about managerialism and [that you and Janet Newman developed much further. I had already written about local government, but that's not quite the same].

John: *Well, even if you had written stuff about local government, there was something about things kept opening up –*

Allan: Yes, different ways of thinking.

John: *Things to think about and ways of thinking and it's – that's for me one of the things that I got out of being there which is that double movement which is new things to think about, but new ways of thinking, partly because it was usually working with new people who brought new things to that process. So, the managerialism stuff; there was you, there was Eugene, but I was doing it because I'd been working with Janet and, and ... so all those –*

[0:18:08]

Allan: I think the physical proximity – the Open University and the faculty in particular were important sites in which we could have these sorts of discussions, but I think the other thing that you've hinted to there, you alluded to there, was the way in which a lot of us were also – either were or were going to work with other people outside, and it was something that became a trait, that we didn't see ourselves just as being individuals, we saw ourselves as being able to contribute more to a collective endeavour, both inside the OU and beyond it actually, it was a …

John: *Well, I think that reflects something of what you were saying about who the people were who came in that moment, because they came both, as it were, bearing networks and the OU didn't disconnect us from the things that we had been before, but it also I think was partly a politics of 'cultural things' about working collaboratively and those networks, whether it was Doreen at CES or Stuart, wherever he was, but people came with a disposition to working with other people, which I think is not by any means the generic case of the British university in any of those periods really, and so it – I do have that sense like you, that we flourished in a place that was almost perfectly designed to enable us to flourish. But I want to go back to the leadership and the interdisciplinarity thing because I think both Stuart and Doreen were both, as it were, individually profoundly productive, they were wonderful collaborators, they provided a particular model of doing intellectual leadership which was not the hegemonic star but about trying to create the spaces and ways in which other people might think with them and, as you know, they were the two people who were on my 12 original critical dialogue discussions who aren't there now and I –*

     …

Disciplines and interdisciplinary thinking

Allan: Yes, well I think you're right, they're very different actually in terms of how they did things and the ways in which they sought to involve people. I think they – there is a sense in which they – I never thought they quite got the – they weren't quite able to – the Open University actually didn't provide them as much as it should have done, with the space in which they could do what they wanted; Stuart never really managed to reshape sociology and Doreen kind of did in geography, but Doreen was always slightly disconnected really from those sorts of things. So, I think it is interesting that they managed both to make us think and to inspire us and to lead us or provide leadership of a particular sort, which without ever being given those roles perhaps sufficiently clearly – but maybe that was one of the good things, I don't know. They were very important – they were so important in terms of helping us to think through what we were doing and how we might engage with different sorts of ideas and they've continued to – they continue to inspire in that way, I think. ... For me, the working together, sometimes across disciplinary boundaries, sometimes within slightly odd disciplines, we – and what was really important and I think that some of the ways in which in a sense we came together and others around – with us, I don't mean 'around us' but as part of that grouping, we were trying to move to change to think about ways in which we might – . First of all, we were a grouping called 'Interdisciplinary Social Sciences' and we became 'Applied Social Sciences', then we became 'Social Policy' and in a sense, we were always slightly on the edges of the disciplinary framework within the faculty and then the way we were, that was okay, that was definitely okay, and first it was fine because we were just all working. We were associated with particular courses and we worked on those to do what we wanted to do, working in – generally in interdisciplinary postings because that was what we were supposed to do. But there was an interesting tension emerging between discipline and interdisciplinarity within the faculty and we ended up trying to construct something which made us – gave us the status of a discipline without quite being one and it didn't entirely work out because we ended up with a 'Social Policy' label, which I think was always problematic, but we were trying to revisit issues of social policy in ways which were not really social policy; they were about understanding social change, ... it's why 'Applied Social Sciences' was always quite a good title because we were about thinking through how people lived their lives, but also how that related to, if you like, everyday life in a wider sociological sense or – there was something significant about how we were trying to negotiate all that. For me, one of the really interesting things is how I see myself – I've ended up in Geography; now I'm retired, I'm in the Geography Department, but I was never in Geography while I was at the Open University. I still am at the Open University but I'm retired, but as an employed person at the OU, I was never in the Geography Department, I was in a grouping that had no name, then I was in Social Sciences and Applied Social Sciences and Social Policy.

[0:25:25]

John: *And, let's not forget Social Policy and Criminology.*

Allan: And then Social Policy and Criminology as it became, that's true and I in fact have been – I think I was head of each of those things at various points or another, all four of them. But, what was interesting was that what that allowed me was a degree of flexibility and fluidity, so I worked on interdisciplinary courses, I worked on social policy courses, I worked on geography courses. I don't think I actually ever worked on a criminology course, unlike you with your crime novel, [but] I worked on a range of courses and it's interesting because disciplines began to settle much more throughout the period that we were there. But there were still spaces for us to operate and collaborate, but it became slightly less open, slightly more framed by disciplinary concerns, for a whole number of reasons, partly because the – externally things have changed as well, there was a – if you look at some of the things that happened throughout the '80s and '90s into the 2000s. ... So it was interesting I think in that respect that we – it was possible to work across – and that was partly because of course the disciplines themselves, certainly while we were there, were much more fluid, or at least until – they were much more fluid for a long time and it was possible to get excited about the way in which geographical thinking might reflect social policy, and that's my feeling about urban studies or urban policy, but it might also be possible to inflect the ways in which geography really had to think about cultural issues and cultural studies, and those were things that were much more there – all those things were happening at the Open University and with the people we were working with, but also – actually also outside ...

        ...

John: *There's about three things that I need to ... one of which is I do think the things about continuing to be obsessed by some ways of thinking that come to apply to different fields, topics and relationships is really important, because one of the things that did that for me was a discovery of at least some bits of anthropology where I found people who were interested in some of the same things I was, in a way that people in Social Policy formally rarely were; some friends, but not as an intellectual formation. So, that was − I recognised the affinity bit of that, and the other is the persistence of ways of thinking, so I'm ... in the last two years, I've found myself going back to cultural studies things and saying, 'Actually, the question about how we think conjuncturally which we started in the mid-1970s is now more important than it's ever been,' and I'm sure that with more complicated thoughts that we ought to be doing about it and so on and we might talk more about that later, but I − so there's something about new objects, new connections and some things that keep you going, but there's a little moment in what you were just talking about where you did a ... just a − it was a passing moment with a smile attached to it ... in which you said, 'And being a Marxist, of course, we knew everything wherever we were working,' and that just reminds me. It's true, but [also] it's an ironic relationship that you and I have shared to knowing everything and being Marxist over the last − oh dear God − coming up for 40 years, and I think it's an important one because it's been one of the sites where we have both been able to draw on different sorts of thorough grounding in Marxism and Marxist categories and modes of thinking and yet not found ourselves entirely contained by them. I don't know whether it's a generational moment because I have really strange encounters with students at Central European University who tell me about Marxism and are then somehow surprised that I might have read* Capital *and I can remember and cite − quote bits of* Capital *to them and they look at me as if to say, 'So, are you a Marxist?' to which my answer is, 'Not really,' though I know a lot of Marxism. So, there's something important historically, generationally, intellectually; I've just come back from a workshop where I sit around bad-temperedly saying, 'I do think people ought to use the idea of contradictions more systematically than they do these days,' and it was there in what you were saying − I think it's one of the things that was important for both our works in thinking about, as it were, policy studies, social policy, policy and politics, everyday lives and states, and so there's a configuration of things there that I think enabled us to work in and on social policy as a field, in a rather difficult and critical way.*

Allan: I think that's fair. My feeling − I think having worked through various varieties of Marxism and getting excited about them and still being excited about them ... one thing I still get excited by, it may be a strength, it may also be a weakness – but one of the things is that when you ask about disciplinary homes, it becomes less important, because actually I suspect that at my core of my being is still a belief that I can have a holistic understanding of the world in some sense. I wouldn't generally articulate it like that, but I think part of me thinks that breaking things up into – I have ambivalent views about disciplines, that breaking things up in-to disciplines creates its own problems. On the other hand, you see that's perhaps not quite what I mean – on the other hand, what I think is that actually coming at things within disciplines, in the same sorts of ways, can be very helpful and very productive and sometimes disciplines provide you with boundaries which frame questions in ways that are helpful, but I wouldn't like to think of myself as being trapped in a disciplinary frame. So you're right, so we can think about putting some of those things together in a social policy context, we were trying to – it's interesting, if you think about conjunctural politics, in a way it's about trying to put things together in ways that help you to understand what's going on, about how people live their lives and how change is possible or not possible or likely or not likely, and all of that is part of what you're trying to do. And you do that in whatever discipline and … these days I would not say, 'Actually I think I can capture all this holistically, I can make all this unified,' I haven't got a unified theory that's going to work, but I can't deny that in the background was that, and that helped to frame the way in which I then could approach a range of things. I think I now take a more Simmelian position, which is an essayist position, that it's possible to have lots of different ways of thinking about similar questions, which never quite answers all the questions. Each of them may answer a particular question but that doesn't mean it can answer the whole question, but it's interesting to have lots of different attempts to do it that overlap or don't overlap … so I think that's probably where I would position myself now … Broadly, that's how I would position myself; I would position myself in thinking in those ways, so I don't think I'm going to find – I think once upon a time I probably thought there was a definite answer which I was going to find; I don't think that any more. I think there may be a series of semi-definitive answers to a number of questions which I may be able to find and which point in a similar direction, but yes, but it doesn't mean the whole thing is clear cut.

[0:49:42]

John: *I think I share a lot of that and one of which is – is the ambivalent relationship to the disciplinary framing of knowledge where I think one of the things that I liked about cultural studies and one of the things that I liked about our version of social policy was that they allowed you to think about everything, or the possibility of thinking about anything, without being told that you couldn't think about that. So, I have my …*

Allan: That's true of geography.

John: *– and I think it is – at least geography as she was practised at the Open University – which was I think rightly called 'the new cultural studies' at one point, and it had the open horizon. But – and increasingly it's become my bad-tempered view that if you think economists know about the economic, there's something wrong with the category of the 'economic' as well as economists and ditto what political scientists know about politics, probably not, and sociologists know about – there's a problem and – and – and, so I – and I think that Marxism is one of the ways that says, 'Yes, well actually you need to be able to think that everything is at least connected' in – even if we haven't quite worked out how, the nature of all those connections. So, I think all of that's really important and it's why I guess … I think I write essays but I'm not sure that I think I'm an essayist, but at the moment the question of the conjuncture is about trying to write a demand that people – God, what do I want to say? That people take account of things being more than one thing at once. One of the things that I am hugely depressed by, about the – this is 2017, so the thing that I am most depressed by, is people who tell me that they know the moment that we are in, that it is an age of rage, the era of populism, the moment of nationalism or whatever, that there is something, a singular moment that tells us where we are, and it does seem to me that the only thing that I can do in response to that is to say, 'Oh, and that and that and that and that' … and that's I think the thinnest version of conjunctural analysis, is to be able to hold things up and say, 'Even if I don't know everything, I know that there is more than one thing going on.'*

Allan: Yes, I think that's probably what I'm trying to say. When I – it may not be essay-ism at all, but I suppose my problem is – right, it's not clear for me if you then think you are actually going to be able to bring them all together in something or not – yes … sorry, I'm just trying to get my head around where it leaves me. I don't want to say that they're all just independent, you see, because I do think that things come together, cluster, overlap, become over-determined even. I think all that happens, and that actually what I want to do is to think about how that happens in practice, yes, but … that doesn't mean that there is some overarching reality or truth; it's actually the process by which these things come together that is what one's trying to capture, yes that's what it is.

John: *And, for me, the bit that I find hardest, both to think and even harder to write down, is that it is in the process of coming together, these things take on a particular character, so there may be populism in the present, but actually the present is not populism, it's populism in the form articulated – as articulated with/by nationalism, racism – but it's not nationalism or racism in the abstract, it's them as inflected by the moment of coming together with populism, with globalism, with – so, it's not you find any of the pure things, it's the messy connections between them all and then what happens, but – and it's not going to be on tape, but all of that required me to wave my hands pathetically and I don't know how to write it down … the other bit that makes me think it's not just a question of being old – but that when Stuart led our attempt, after the event, to do this in* Policing the Crisis, *there were five of us working on it; not entirely full time but – and the notion that the heroic scholar might do a wonderful, definitive conjunctural analysis on their own, in which they knew not just about what was happening in the United Kingdom but the relational constitution of the United Kingdom in its complex relations with it, all those other spaces and places. I don't even know about the bit of the United Kingdom I live in, whichever bit it might be.*

[0:55:56]

Allan: Well, nobody does … Collaboration is something that [has always been necessary for me]. Do I think it's possible to have a lone scholar who's bringing stuff together? It might be, there might be somebody, somewhere, who's able to do that but I think that – I think even such a person could only exist and thrive because of her or his coming together with others and being able to actually debate and engage and be part of wider sets of collaborative structures and engagements. So, I think that to me is the – it's weird, the model, it's – the academic model in which you have sole-authored this and sole-authored that, is weird. It's not that person A or person B hasn't – doesn't play a lead role or hasn't got a predominant position in any particular piece of work. That may well be the case but it's actually almost impossible to imagine somebody simply doing it, without having been inflected by, reflecting, working with a series of others, and I've found it – I've always found it very productive to work with others. That's reflected partly on the extent to which I have written jointly with others, but even the stuff that's not been written jointly with others is so obviously part of a collective endeavour. I may have been the person who wrote it down but it's come out of a whole series of debates and discussions. The other thing is, you know when people always write things like, 'This is the result of me talking to all sorts of people but of course the end result is all my own fault; I'm to blame for anything that's wrong,' I think that's probably true, although sometimes others are to blame for what's wrong, actually.

John: *They've told you the wrong thing.*

Allan: They've told me the wrong thing, or if I'm part of the wrong movement at the wrong time in the wrong intellectual shift, but obviously you, as an individual academic thinker, intellectual, have a responsibility which is your own responsibility about how you articulate what you want to say, how you have honesty about what you're trying to say and how you're trying to say it. But that doesn't mean that you are doing it as a person on their own, you're doing it very much as part of a broader network, broader set of relationships, broader collaborative framework, I think normally – almost always and I think, actually the interesting thing is the contradiction or the tension which –

John: *I think it's the tension –*

Allan: Well, let me explain why I think it's – it might work because it's the way in which the funding regimes work at the moment, because the reason – I might go as far as to say contradiction, but let me not do that – is that on the one hand, there's a huge emphasis, a massive emphasis on collaborative activity, mega projects which bring together big teams in the social sciences to do all sorts of things. On the other hand, there is a huge pressure to identify key thinkers, key leaders, individuals … Similarly, there's a huge pressure to do interdisciplinary stuff, but at the same time, there's a remarkable pressure from the same sources to maintain disciplinary boundaries. When you do any sort of research framework, assessment framework, whatever it's going to be called the next one, it's going to go through units of assessment which are effectively disciplinary, despite the fact that it kept going on about the importance of interdisciplinary work and interdisciplinary working and having some poor sap to say how important it is on each board. Now that, all right, it's just a – is it a tension? I don't know, it seems to me that it's inconsistent actually, those two things are inconsistent, or whatever else we're saying, and – of course, there may be a resolution to the contradiction which is to have somebody with many heads, but it's a – it's a tension which I think is really quite an important one, and it's difficult to sustain and it's difficult to imagine how it can be sustained in those terms. So, there's that feeling which … in the social sciences has been borrowed from a scientific study where you have all these huge teams, and on the other hand you have Einstein or whoever it is who's the great thinker, Stephen Hawking, becomes the person who is the figurehead, the icon. That difference, that tension between – within the world of intellectual … what intellectuals are supposed to be, I think is an interesting one and I – having said that, I think it is possible and we've done it, actually, even in discussing this, we've done it; it is possible to imagine a situation in which we do work together, but we can recognise that there are some people who play a significant leadership role, a role which if you like opens up and makes possible some of that collaborative working in productive ways, even if – in some cases it's what they intended but in other cases it's maybe a side-effect. I think that's important too, so we do recognise – it's not that we don't recognise – that Stuart Hall was a significant figure who opened up all these sorts of things, or that Doreen [Massey] was a significant figure because she made us think about geography differently, which opened up ways in which we might work together sometimes. Sometimes with them, sometimes independently of them; I think that's maybe that's how you resolve it.

…

8

Fiona Williams

Fiona Williams is Professor Emerita of Social Policy at the University of Leeds, where she worked after North London Polytechnic, Plymouth Polytechnic, the Open University and the University of Bradford. At Leeds she was also the director of CAVA (the ESRC research group on Care, Values and the Future of Welfare). Her work explores gender, 'race' and ethnicity in social policy, while recent research has addressed the employment of migrant care workers in Europe and the transnational political economy of care.

Her 1989 book, *Social Policy: A Critical Introduction – Issues of Race, Gender, and Class*, has been one of the defining sources for critical work in social policy. Her other publications include *Welfare Research: A Critical Review* (1999, with Jennie Popay and Ann Oakley) and *Rethinking Families* (2004). She is also a published poet.

I first got to know Fiona in the early 1990s, somewhere between the early days of the *Critical Social Policy* journal and Social Policy Association conferences. From the start, she has been one of the people who kept me interested in and attached to Social Policy as a field. We have continued to talk about the problems and possibilities of the field and our troubles in writing in and about it.

More information can be found at: https://essl.leeds.ac.uk/sociology/staff/57/emeritus-professor-fiona-williams-obe.

This conversation was recorded in Sandsend, Yorkshire on 26 June 2017.

Themes and topics

- Coming to terms with social policy
- Resistances and refusals
- On contradictions and complexity
- Back to social policy

Coming to terms with social policy

John: So, Fiona, I wanted to begin with social policy because I think you were probably, certainly the first, and possibly the only, person who made social policy imaginable for me as a place to be and think. So, I'm sort of intrigued about what it was like for you to take over a field like that.

Fiona: Well, originally I'd done a degree, my undergraduate degree was in what they then called sociology and social administration, and that was at LSE [London School of Economics] and Bedford College. I was at Bedford College and it was a joint degree with LSE, and so the people who I was taught by were the people who then became quite famous … Richard Titmuss, David Donnison, Oliver McGregor, [who] was at Bedford College, history of the family and family law. I can remember Basil Bernstein giving us a visiting lecture, so there were quite a lot, which I kind of only half realised at the time, I suppose, that these were the shining lights of the time. And in a way it was good that I only half realised that and that I wasn't as au fait with the whole academic business as other students with me. And that was partly, you know, I was a girl, like a lot of our generation, the first in the family to go to university, my brothers hadn't gone to university and I'd been to a mixed grammar school up North and arrived in London, and it was a very different world, you know, and I felt a very small person in it all. And I thought sociology was very interesting; I liked some of the history that Oliver McGregor taught, but on the whole I just thought it was tedious – I mean, you know, even though people look back at Richard Titmuss's work and, you know, it is very good but he wasn't particularly appealing as a person … And at that point, I mean I went to university in 1965 and of course those years leading up to '68 when I left were very active years, and even though Roy Parker, for example, gave really interesting lectures on council housing and the importance of council housing and the Milner Holland Report … and things like that, it just had no relationship to the sorts of demands that students were beginning to make. And that student movement actually had come out, or where I had come out of it, was in the anti-Vietnam movement, and so I think those demonstrations were around '66/'67 and then it moved into the kind of occupations and so on.

And seeing someone like Daniel Cohn-Bendit, you know, talking at LSE, and thinking that these were two different worlds really. I think the main thing for me was that it was so focused on Britain, you know, and at that point I think a lot of the struggles had a kind of anti-imperialist kind of backlash to them because of Vietnam.

John: *Well, I think they do but I think one of the things that I'll push a bit more about is ... making those crystallise in terms of a sort of intellectual politics of contesting and rethinking a field of ... I mean, a discipline, a field of study, whatever, and you know, mine's an odd one because of cultural studies giving, you know, a backdoor into social policy, but yours is much more about confronting and transforming social policy as the thing, the heartland even.*
...

Fiona: ... [B]ut I think having been involved in revolutionary politics as we called it from the early '70s until ... only until '87-ish I suppose. That gave you the confidence to think in terms of taking your knowledge and having a different way to look at it ... But even that frame I used to question because I never really saw myself as somebody who would just go along, I was kind of suspicious of ... it's that very process on the one hand you have to crystallise and consolidate a view of the world on a particular subject, you know, you have to do that in order to communicate it, in order for it to become generalised, in order for it to become a demand or a claim or whatever. But at the same time you always have to be standing on the edge of it, and not letting that become an idea that dominates other ideas. I think I've always been interested in that process, that process between ... well, I think I've called this in this another situation, the melting and freezing of ideas; you know, you have to freeze the ideas at some point in order to move on. In order to effect change you have to, right, even though you know there are a few queries around this, but also you have to know that the edges can melt and they can absorb other ideas.

John: *I like the metaphor because it is for me, I mean, it's the one that operates with ... crystallise and then fall apart... And it seems to me it speaks to ... to a long-running process where that's always happening, so for whatever you need to do, whether it's a class that you're about to teach, the chapter you're about to write, the conversation you're about ... you need the things solidified enough to get them out there.*

> *And I think it's always haunted by the notion that actually by the next time you say something it probably won't be quite the same.*

Fiona: Yes, that's right.

John: *For me, one of the great liberating things in cultural studies was the notion that the house journal was called* Working Papers *and it left I think all of us, most of us, who were there with a sense that actually that's what you do, I mean that's what you write, you don't write the definitive, eternal, finished version, you write this week's working paper. But it's not ... I mean the reason I like the melting– freezing metaphor is it's not that everything is in flux all the time, it's that there are some things that you are more secure about and there are other things where you're still feeling where things mightn't ... And sometimes you get taken by surprise that even the things that I thought I knew turned out not to be quite as reliable as I hoped for.*

Fiona: Yes, I know, yes, well, that happens all the time doesn't it? Well, I kind of wait for those things to happen, yeah.

John: *But I don't know, one of the things that I'm puzzled about – and it's one of the reasons why these conversations are happening at all – is that I hear, sometimes, and read, more often, people for whom that seems not to be true, that I read a lot of academic work where people tell me that what they always knew turns out to be true all over again with another example ... Right, so I don't know. With Janet I've been doing a lot of work around the Brexit thing and I know of at least seven positions which say what Brexit proves is they were right all along, right, whether it's, you know, class politics, it was the working class what won it or political theories of populism tell me that, well, that's populism and it's sort of secure knowledge.*
...

Resistances and refusals

Fiona: Yes, yes, that's right. I think as well, you know, what's been different over the past five years say, maybe ten years, is that, you know, as the kind of resistance to, for want of a better word, neoliberalism, as the resistance to that has sort of started from Occupy onwards to kind of develop, the most challenging thing I think for people in social policy is just to stop people thinking that we just need to go back to '45, you know? And it's happening all the time, it's happening all the time. So part of me was saying, you know, we were just shouting in the 1980s about what was wrong about the post-war welfare state, you know, look at what they did, look at this, look at how they treated women, look at how they treated gay men and lesbians, you know, look at it in a way that we kind of weren't able to 20 years later. But now we've got to say it again actually, we've got to say it again simply because it is so easy. ... A couple of years ago I went to the university to watch Ken Loach's film on the welfare state, what's it called?

John: *I, Daniel Blake.*

Fiona: No, no, not that one, the one that came out a couple of years ago, it was a series of interviews.

John: *Oh, this is one of those moments.*

Fiona: Yes. Anyway.

John: *We'll insert the title later [The Spirit of '45]*

Fiona: Yes (laughs). Anyway, it received rapturous reviews, and you know, when it was put on in cinemas people got up and clapped at the end and I was horrified, even though I love Ken Loach, right? I was horrified, and what I was most horrified about was the way in which the young lecturers in my department got up and spoke in these, you know, applauding terms about what it was about 1945 that had formed the welfare state ... And you know, in Ken Loach's interviews he interviewed no black people. There was one woman, and they were mainly kind of old trade unionists, old Labour Party people, who were talking in these terms about, you know, how won– ... which, of course, the welfare state was wonderful, of course it changed lives, you know, our parents told us how dreadful it had been before, so we knew, we liked the little orange bottom of the cork of the orange juice that we used to get, you know, how it's got a little cork and it turned orange so you'd lick it because it was so nice, the fresh orange juice. All of those things we knew that, but we also knew that it hadn't been good and that it'd been deeply authoritarian in many ways.

John: *Indeed.*

Fiona: And the idea that we wrote all that stuff and now people are saying, you know, we just have to go back to '45, the spirit of '45 and all the rest of it and a welfare state and, you know.

John: *Like you I'm gobsmacked because I feel as though ... I feel cast out and possibly – and I don't mean this self-pitying – as though I and we might have done a lot of work that nobody's noticed. (Laughs)*

Fiona: Yeah. (Laughs)

John: *Look, you know, this is an academic world, you write things and*
        nobody notices them, so it's not that problem but it is a political
        problem, I think, about forms of nostalgia that ignore – I mean not
        just academic critique but real politics that grow up to contest those
        things as well. I mean, you know, I was at some event where ...
        I think there are two versions of it, one is 1945 and the other is
        anything up to the month of May in 1979 when we had possibly
        constructed the next best thing to a socialist paradise ... And then
        Margaret Thatcher came along and it all went wrong. And I was
        having an argument with a Labour MP at a conference who said there
        was nothing wrong with, you know, the welfare [state] ... Camden
        Housing was the best thing in the world in 1978. And I said there's
        a generational problem here because I was on the other side of all
        those issues. ... You know, I knew people who were involved in
        housing rent strikes, I knew people who were involved in anti-racist
        struggles at that time, there was another politics to that period and,
        like you, even 1945 or 1978 will not do if you forget, if you forget
        the – I'm going to sound like an old Marxist – the contradictions of
        the institutions. I don't mean that the institutions did not do good
        things but that both the contradictions and the costs and the struggles
        over them can't then just be written out. A politics of nostalgia seems
        to me to be, I mean, both dangerous and likely disastrous, because
        even if you could reconstruct the conditions of 1945 the consequences
        will be ... we should know what they'll be, we've seen that happen
        and I mean ... blurgh, this has just got me over-excited ... How do
        you, how do we make those interventions without just saying ...

[0:41:55]

Fiona: We were right.
John: *... right boring old farts.*
Fiona: I know, I know. Well, on this occasion when I watched the
        Ken Loach film I was too speechless to stand ... and also I
        didn't want to say, well, look at ... I've written things that
        didn't say that, you know, you don't want to kind of put
        yourself into the middle as the only one who had ever said
        anything relevant but, well, it's difficult isn't it? I suppose
        because I'm rewriting some of that stuff from the '70s and
        '80s and '90s, I kind of find it a bit boring really. What
        surprises me is, though, how much other people don't
        know and how interested they are, so let me give you an
        example. I sit on a very interesting research project advisory

board and this is a project that's run by Jenny Phillimore at Birmingham University on – it's called 'Superdiversity and Welfare Bricolage', and I was interested because it uses those two terms which themselves, I mean I'm not so happy with superdiversity, I have to say, but actually I know the new configuration of the population that it is trying to describe, right?

John: Yes.

Fiona: It's about the multiplicity of migrants who now live in particular areas in the city, and it's not the postcolonial situation that we were often analysing, so it's a recognition of that change that's taken place, but in and of itself it only describes it, it doesn't analyse it, and it certainly doesn't analyse it in relation to the postcolonial, [which] it has to be seen in relation to and in relation to the kind of wider society. But also I like this idea of taking a notion like welfare bricolage, you know, to have a kind of operational concept that acknowledges that thing that we fought for, you know, at the end of the '90s, the acknowledgement of agency, which in social policy had been so ... kind of the whole tradition of policy being things that were done to people meant that conceptually the idea of agency was lacking, to say the least. And here we have a way of conceptualising the fact that people put together their own well-being, they draw from services and they actually construct in relation to, not necessarily to professionals, sometimes, but in relation to people that they work alongside; the family, people in the neighbourhood, you know, the local acupuncturist or whatever, they construct their own sense of well-being and how to improve it, and in this case it's health, this is what the study is about. So, wonderful, you know, and here in four different countries, right, Sweden, Portugal, UK and Germany, they've got these super-diverse neighbourhoods where they're doing intense anthropological work on how people explain their illnesses, what they do about their illnesses and so on and so forth from these, you know, very multiply origined people, right? ...

John: *Well, it has two important echoes for me. One is I think that it speaks to something which we're not very good at which is ... I mean the shifting, but always recuperating, patterns are power and inequality, which is ... they're not the same.*

Fiona: No.

John: *I don't think what I'm observing now is … I mean in London after the Grenfell Tower event, it's not the same as what we were encountering in Birmingham in the 1970s, but the dynamics and the relations and the forms through which it's organised look sort of familiar. And so I think you're right that as it was the concepts that one might want to deal with some of those things are important. But one of the other things is, and the other echo is an event I was at on a research project, which was about a project that's been dealing with co-production in research and in community life, so it's complicated and they are subtle and sophisticated and yet there were all these things in the writing where I wanted to say you know that every study of participation, involvement, community engagement has ended up with at least four of these troubles, right, one of which is people that want to do it, one of which is people feel engagement-exhausted, one of which is somebody thinks that somebody also ought to surrender power. So, it was just that sort of sense that, yes, they're dealing with a specific new configuration of things that I don't know but there are all these things that I did know and so the academic history gets … I mean it's partly because there's so much stuff to read but it means that there's not … I mean there's not any sense of accumulation of knowledge about these things.*

Fiona: Yes that's right, yes, and in fact that was the thing that we ended up with exactly, was it's actually about power this, you know, you need an analysis that puts power central and you have to understand what sorts of power are at play because it's not just, you know, your race, class, gender, it's all sorts of different sets of social relations of power are involved here. I mean, that was where we ended up. I think what I should have said – scrap what I've said before, I should have said was that some of the dynamics were the same but a lot were different, so for example that whole self-responsibilisation agenda, you know, of doctors or choice, right, choice agenda of doctors saying well you can choose, you can either have a bandage or you can have a plaster, you know, it's your choice.

[0:53:57]

John: *Yeah, do you want this scalpel or this scalpel?*

Fiona: Yes. (Laughs) Which hospital would you like to go to, you know … one that's 100 miles away or one that's 75 miles away? So, you know, things like that had changed but the effects were the same, the unequal effects around access and the disempowerment of people were the same, so that's what I meant to say, that the effects were the same and the effects were to do with power, right, and how you analyse power. So, superdiversity and welfare bricolage were helpful in describing something newish, right, but they weren't helpful in describing power, in analysing power, and in fact that's why they said oh yes that's what we need to provide ...

John: *But I mean, you know, there's a wonderful anthropologist [Čarna Brković] I know who's been working in the former Yugoslavia precisely around questions about how people make up welfare for themselves but the question of power and the unequal distribution of consequences really then always comes back in, and it does seem to me that it's one of the few things that I think I know, right, you know, it doesn't mean I have a theory of power but I know that if you don't notice it there's something gone awry.[1] ... And the complexity of the social configuration of differences and inequality and differential forms of power are all important, but power articulates them in a really crucial way.*

Fiona: Yes, that's right, that's right I mean, and what I was suggesting to them is that, you know, maybe superdiversity is a way of describing it but actually the analysis you need [is] an intersectional analysis of power, you know, and you need to know the layers, the layers of power, not only the intersections at that sort of horizontal level but the way that things are overlaid, you know, and how they're reconstituting everything.

          ...

On contradictions and complexity

[1:05:06]

John: *I think, you know, shouldn't we know that capitalism and its apparatuses are at least contradictory? ... You know, never mind anything else and, I don't know, I just have this sense that ... I mean this is ... I just have this sense that the word 'contradiction' has sort of lapsed somewhat.*

---

[1]   I was introduced to Čarna Brković by Paul Stubbs and found her work on welfare fascinating. She currently works at the University of Göttingen. Her book *Managing ambiguity. How clientelism, citizenship and power shape personhood in Bosnia and Herzegovina* was published by Berghahn Books in 2017.

Fiona: Yes, it has, or else it's become something else, it's become complexity actually, don't you think?

John: *That might … yes, I think you might be right.*

Fiona: Because all the work on institutionalism which I ploughed through …

John: *Oh dear.*

Fiona: Actually, I was quite interested in how some of it is quite good in a way, you know, I mean, you know, it was good to take on what the Marxists never really took on, which is that institutional complexity and how … I don't mean just you have to understand how governance is done or which departments they're operating, but the kind of the pulls and the tugs around reforms and, you know, forms of politics and so on. I think it's actually better than I thought it was going to be when I read it all. But I think the problem with something like that is that it becomes a kind of, it becomes a focus in and of itself, so it then, when it refers to a backcloth, it can only be neoliberalism or something like that or global capitalism or something … And it's then having to … I think that that's what's really hard, having to take that further to have that kind of complexity approach to global capitalism as well, which is hard, and to be able to relate them all, you know?

John: *Yes, but it does seem to me that it's the obligation. I mean one of the things that I … Take the words you use, so institutional complexity is important and we should know it and we should know its dynamics and we should know how power works in it, but we should also know how power works on it and through it, so the 'backcloth' thing is sort of too far away and it's sort of inert because what you know about is the institutional complexity, then it turns out it's in a type of neoliberalism, you know. So, the hard bit is precisely to keep complexity, so not to either detach it from the backdrop or, you know, I might think of a word, conversion of causal Marxism, to say and so everything's neoliberal, right?*

Fiona: Mmm, yes.

John: *But to say, okay, how does that work? And why does it work like that? I mean, God, why does it work through New Labour rather than New Conservativism or, you know, there are things … with … consequences for the particular sorts of institutional complexity that were for a while constructed and then changed all over again. And so … the question is how clever do you want to be? And I say this because I saw a really nice piece by a friendly, lovely anthropologist*

[Stef Jansen] about the book that I did with Paul and Noémi and Dave which said, well, yeah, despite all this, these bad things are what we might call rather structural [and] bad things keep on happening...

Fiona: Are pretty fixed really.

John: *Yes, and they keep coming round again and I think there's a sort of terrible tension between, yes, there are structural things and determinations, but don't you want to know how they happen as well as that they do?*

[1:09:55]

Fiona: Yes, yes, that's right. And also even in structures you want to know where the gaps are, you want to know where the weaknesses are ... where the contradictions weaken those structures. So, even one I noticed in the piece that you gave me that you'd written with Janet on ...

John: *On who knows what? Expertise is what it's officially about.[2]*

Fiona: Yes, we've had enough of experts ...

John: *But you might wonder what it's about reasonably.*

Fiona: But I notice, you know, you had a little thing I thought yes, yes, that's right, you know, but even within the World Bank or the IMF [International Monetary Fund], you know, there are these kind of tides that ... riptides, you know, there are these riptides and it's important to know those even though ... Oh, recently I wrote a paper for a wonderful conference ... about women and work, but I was in the bit on care, right? And so I had written for this a piece that was how care is both global and it's local but how it's also a cycle of resistance as well at all these levels. And one of the comments that I got back on it in order to kind of get it ready for publication was that I had underestimated the effect of international financial institutions and of, you know, global neoliberalism upon the capacity for people's claims to get anywhere, you know. I think I spent two working weeks, I mean not all the time obviously, trying to work out how to change my paper to take account of these comments from somebody I have a lot of respect for. And I read loads, I asked my friend Rianne Mahon, she sent me a book that she's edited ... with Steve McBride on

---

[2]   John Clarke and Janet Newman, '"People in this country have had enough of experts": Brexit and the paradoxes of populism', *Critical Policy Studies*, 2017, 11 (1): 101–116.

austerity.[3] And so I altered it to, you know, acknowledge that structural power, but yet I just thought, but that's not where I'm coming from, you know? I'm interested in where the weaknesses are, I'm interested in what these claims mean, I'm interested in what these claims have in common and where there's some strength in them that can kind of batter at some of the kind of weaknesses of the structures that exist. Is there any hope? Is there any hope, you know, that things might change? Right, and if they are going to change, how they're going to change and how do we help?

John: *Oooh. I think for me it's a really critical issue which is how do you ... For me it takes the form of how do you not get depressed, right, because if what you know is that structural power structures, how do you not get depressed? How do you even get to bother finishing the end of the article, because I think we all know that, and part of what I think I'm always stuck with is something that ... and there's a consequence to this which is I think what I'm always stuck with is wanting to say 'yes, but ...'. On the other hand, if you think about contradictions and antagonisms and fissures and fractures and stuff you might see those other things. And I know that I've often been told off for not paying enough attention to a structural power, but the trouble is that's the easy bit, and yeah, I don't mean it's easy, but in one sense it seems to me it's the easy bit — which is capitalism makes the world look like capitalism, yeah, neoliberalism, if that's the word we're going to use, makes the world more neoliberal and di di di di, all of that's true. And then what? ... If you only write structural power structures, I don't know that there's an ... then what? I don't think there's even a question about possibilities, lines of antagonism, why the wheels might come off sometimes, because if you know structural power structures and that's all you know, I think you have a very funny ... There's a story I tell a lot and I shouldn't, because he's much too nice a young man to do it to but in a class at CEU [Central European University] one of my students said, 'Well, the trouble with this piece of writing (by somebody that I liked) is it doesn't really take enough account of, you know, the smoothly running power of capitalism,' and I said, 'Where? When? Tell me where it runs smoothly.' And there was a long silence in the class and eventually somebody said, 'You mean it doesn't, don't you?' And I said, 'No, that's exactly what I mean.' You can tell me about*

---

[3]   Stephen McBride, Rianne Mahon and Gerard W. Boychuck (eds), *After '08: Social Policy and the Global Financial Crisis*, University of British Columbia Press, 2015.

the amount of effort that goes into trying to make capitalism run smoothly, but it's not its normal condition, you know, there's a lot of economic, social, political work goes on to stop the wheels coming off, to stop contradictions accumulating, to stop crises happening, to stop bad things, from a capitalist point of view, to stop bad things happening. But if you only know that structural power structures, you miss any of those questions, so I do want, I do want to align with you on the difficulties are more interesting than the structures.

[1:17:45]

Fiona: Yes, yes.

John: *It doesn't mean they're not there but the weight that you give to things matters.*

Fiona: Yes, yes, that's right. I think the other thing that struck me as we've been talking as well, sort of reflecting on, you know, how I might pick up a concept and run with it sort of thing, is for me, I do feel as though when I'm writing something that the conceptual methodology that I'm using has to somehow have a relevance to a form of politics. And I don't mean that just in that I've got to respect voices and things like that, I mean, you know, I do mean part of that, but that if I'm going to use concepts that somehow they do have their politicising equivalent. So, the most recent thing that I found myself having a theme on, right, is this idea of conceptual alliances, you know, that I think that we have to begin to look for conceptual alliances between different ways of thinking about things. Because what I do think is important at the moment is political alliances; I don't mean politics from the top, although actually interestingly I think progressive alliance from the top is important, but actually the idea of the different movements, you know, all our kind of different sort of grassroots movements that really look for the commonalities, really look for where they can have alliances, really look for the places where they can have dialogue, because that it seems to me at this moment in time is the most important way forward, you know, to push for something progressive. And somehow I feel that it has to be mirrored in my work as well, you know, that I have to look for those alliances across different … you know, across feminist or postcolonialist or disability ways of thinking, you know? … And I was thinking about this recently in relation to something and I kind of look back at my own work and I thought, oh yes, I mean it was there as well, you know, 30/40 years ago much more crudely, but it was there still and I think that that's something that's been helpful for me, you know, a more intuitive thing to think about what I think about things.

John: *I mean, that has three really peculiar echoes for me. One is yes and I recognise it in the way you write, I mean I think it's visible as a Fiona Williams practice, which is one of the things that makes you productive from my point of view, you know, it's generative rather than … what's the opposite of generative? Rather than purely academic, maybe, one of the things. The second is that I think the echo is that it's true about the moment, and trying to think about connections at all sorts of levels looks to me like, you know, an obligation rather than anything else. And the third echo is how ill it sits with the normal mode of conventional critical intellectual work, which is mainly about chopping, drawing distinctions; this is right, this is wrong and it's a different and, I mean I actually think, feminist-inspired effect.*
…

Back to social policy

John: *And so your thing about, you know, the superdiversity project and the things that you had before will not quite do it, so you need to think again but the thinking again should take account of the things that you already knew.*

Fiona: Yes, that's right.

John: *And if I was doing my old Marxist persona that would be the dialectical approach to thinking, I suspect.*

[1:26:54]

Fiona: Yes, that's right. But just to take these thoughts back to social policy, which is where we came in, I mean I would say one of the good things about social policy as a discipline is that it isn't much of a discipline, you know, it is very blurry around the edges, it's very eclectic so it does … you know, when I said, oh I don't know why I didn't go into cultural studies, well actually social policy allowed me to do my own thing, funnily enough. I mean I assumed that it would just get lost but it didn't, and that was just, you know, the time and everything. But I do think that I do remember having that conversation with you, probably the early '90s about, you know, if you need to align yourself to any discipline you may as well do it with social policy because they're kind of generally quite nice people who don't frown on interlopers, you know, they don't put the doors down? And they will let kind of new ideas come in, and they were, I mean in the '80s, that was the discipline that was most changed by feminism, you know, and that was partly because they were prepared to make feminists into professors, and all of that.

John: *No, indeed.*

Fiona: So, I think that the very eclecticism of it, the very blurriness of its edges compared with economics, say, it's almost the opposite of economics and you see this in all sorts of different ways, you know, you see it in the economists in good and bad ways. Economists who assess research applications always praise them up to the hilt because they're economists, whereas social policy people offer their critical assessment of it ... So, economists get the money. (Laughs)

John: *No, I think that's true.*

Fiona: Porous boundaries, that's the word.

John: *Porous boundaries, and it is one of the reasons why doing social policy at the OU was a lot of fun because we moved in and out of those boundaries, you know, and my relationship to social policy remains profoundly contradictory, which is I'm still haunted, and I think haunted is probably the right word, by a final session at a social policy conference somewhere which had presentations on the future of social policy. And I remember, having heard three of them, standing up and saying in none of these visions for social policy can I see any future for myself, I mean I have friends elsewhere so it's okay, don't feel bad about me, but none of them look like anything that I or my colleagues do. On the other hand, getting a lifetime award from the Social Policy Association is one of the more unnerving moments of a person's life, as you know Fiona, and I think you're right, I think its porous boundaries made it possible for a lot of us, for a lot of us actually to inhabit it in more or less comfortable ways. But I also think that there's large bits of it that remain strangely untouched.*

Fiona: I think you're right, yes, yes, we inhabit it but we don't represent it in a way, yeah.

John: *Yeah, I mean my suspicion is that's true of many academic fields if I talk to other people ...*

Fiona: Yeah, true in sociology.

John: *Yeah, indeed. But I certainly think that it was ... God, I don't normally use the word fecund but it was a strangely fecund field for doing lots of that sort of rather incursionary work and there's something about … I remember having arguments at the OU about we were better doing this than being in sociology because there's something about the issues, the social relations, the state, everyday lives, the nation. I mean all of those things were there, even if not drawn to great attention by previous … they were there and available to us, and so when we were doing social policy courses it meant we could do them about things that we thought were important.*

9

Davina Cooper

Davina Cooper is Research Professor in Law at King's College, London, having previously worked at Keele and Kent universities. Her work engages issues of transformative politics: their possibilities, limits and conflicts as these take shape in relation to law, the state, experiments in living, gender and sexuality and cultural diversity. Her research and writing explore the challenges which governing beyond the conventional 'order' generates; her work also focuses on bringing new conceptual thinking to contemporary innovative spaces and politics, and in turn works from these sites to explore new ways of thinking about core socio-legal and political concepts, including the state, power, care and equality.

Her publications include *Governing out of Order: Space, Law and the Politics of Belonging* (1998); *Challenging Diversity: Rethinking Equality and the Value of Difference* (2010); *Everyday Utopias: The Conceptual Life of Promising Spaces* (2014); and *Feeling Like a State: Political Withdrawal and the Transformative Imagination* (2019). With Nikita Dhawan and Janet Newman she is editing a collection on *Reimagining the State* (2019).

I first met Davina in 1989 to explore our mutual interest in processes and relations of governing (after *Governing out of Order* came out). We have continued to find things to talk about around issues of power, politics, states and the possibilities of thinking and doing 'otherwise'. I like the way she is consistently imaginative and inspiring.

Her university web page provides more details: https://kclpure.kcl. ac.uk/portal/en/persons/davina-cooper(01148c13-6cd0-4a19-92ea-267acefee0f0)/biography.html.

This conversation was recorded in London on 10 July 2017.

Themes and topics

- In a world of disciplines?
- Thinking beyond boundaries
- The consequences of talking to people
- Emerging projects and emerging identities

In a world of disciplines?

[0:00:00]

John: *What I wanted to start with was where you think you fit in a world of disciplines. I know you are in a school of law, and I know you know about law, but you are, I don't know, what is the word, I am going to say, more mobile than that, that is the nice version. So just where do you think from?*

Davina: It is a good question, because when I started off I would have probably said I was a political theorist or an interdisciplinary political theorist, and my PhD focused on a political theory question. But I have always worked in law schools and I have always done socio-legal research in different ways. Probably the questions that I ask are mostly political theory questions, but I draw on different intellectual resources to do so. Socio-legal studies but also cultural geography, organisational, policy studies, and gender and sexuality, so ... the resources really vary. Sometimes I wonder about the term post-disciplinary, because it's a way of recognising one's relationship to a set of disciplinary fields and frameworks, but there are too many 'posts', so I don't really like the phrase. But it is about that relationship – but also distance from – disciplines, so that, at least in some ways, one's intellectual questions or projects aren't discipline driven.

John: *I share that thing about the post-disciplinary, I think (a) I am uncomfortable about 'post' but (b) it is much too optimistic. So much of what still goes on is organised and disciplined by disciplines that I don't think that is true, but there is something noteworthy about your work for its capacity to mobilise lots of very complicatedly distributed resources. It is one of the things that makes it gripping all the time, and so what does being in law mean, if that is the case?*

Davina: I think there is a way in which you get socialised and acculturated by a discipline beyond what you are conscious of. My first degree was a law degree, and I think – some of the work I do which is conceptual work, although on its face it really isn't about law at all, I sometimes wonder how much it was driven by spending three years reading judgments, which are all about conceptual questions. A vehicle mustn't cross the grass. Is this a vehicle? What constitutes a vehicle? What constitutes grass?! So, I think there is a subterranean way in which one's background informs how one approaches subjects, but law comes in and out of my work in different ways. One of the things I have found quite useful more recently has been some of the discussions about legal pluralism, and law in everyday life, and actually using them to think about the state. Because it is a way of thinking about the state which isn't that developed. There is state pluralism, but that means something different to the way in which legal pluralism thinks about pluralism, which is more critical. And law in everyday life is about how everyday life constitutes law and a lot of the work on the state doesn't really see the state as something that is produced and reproduced by everyday social practice. So, there are ways in which law feeds the work I am doing, sometimes by its parallels and its analogies, and more generally as a set of resources to draw on.

John: *I think that's true about the state, and one of the things that it just made me remember is that most ... some, who knows, writing on the state always says, well of course the state is not just the law, or coercion or ... but it certainly says it is not just the law, and one of the things that another friend of mine said to me was, well you say that in this case citizenship isn't just a legal question, but you can't stop there because it is also a legal question, and unless you go back — I mean the bracketing of the law seems to me to be strange, and not least because it leads it to socio-legal scholars who are both exciting and weird! So I have been to a couple of socio-legal studies events, and they are wonderful and they don't know lots of other stuff! Just have these strange conversations, where they think they have discovered hegemony. And I think, well can I just stop you there? So ... and socio-legal studies seems to me to be about the unbounding of law and to get stuck by the slight stickiness of law and legality.*

Davina: Yes, and policy can often get lost there because ... well, people can think of law and soft law, but actually recognising that so much of governance, decision making, implementation and the distribution of public resources is through policy, and that is something not adequately understood as just being soft law. I have been recently re-reading work on regulation, and been struck by how, for lots of academics, their concepts expand to cover terrain that other people would read through other concepts. It is interesting how, if that becomes the concept you stake your career in, it just expands and moves out. A lot of the discussion in regulation studies, I thought, was really interesting. But a lot of it you would see in governance studies using the concept of governance instead.

[0:06:43]

John: *Yes, I have had recent encounters with exactly that concept, and wanted to say well 'But at what point do you stop?' and somebody was saying well, I can't remember what it was, but somebody said, well this is really Foucault, and the conduct of conduct. And I wanted to say well yes it is, but if regulation — it is a bit like Foucault, if regulation becomes everything that is done to conduct conduct, why would you bother having a concept of regulation? I mean, is there not a sort of distinction between regulation and other modes of, and I don't know, I am ... as usual I get lost in these debates because I keep thinking 'yes, but ...' Probably all of us want to make whatever we are interested in —*

Davina: Expand.

John: *— expand, yes. Cultural studies was pretty expansive in my experience, probably the world, probably the galaxy.*

Davina: And I suppose part of me thinks does it matter? Because if concepts provide entry points into a terrain, and what you are doing with that terrain is interesting, then I think it doesn't matter ... Where I get frustrated is when it seems that the discussion becomes so internal, and so much requiring knowledge of a set of literatures and conversations, that it stops being available for contact by somebody else who might be having a conversation that's running closely parallel.

John: *Well, one of the things I am starting to think about the people that I am having these conversations with is that ... and I still don't know what the right metaphor for talking about it is — they are relatively undisciplined. Or at least they operate in ways which place them ... if it is a spatial metaphor, it is on the boundaries, it is about not being tied to the reproduction of a discipline rather than the exploration of things that are interesting. And I do think that is beginning to feel like a recurrent thread, and I am interested in how it is that people I know manage to be both interesting and ... I mean is it marginal? I don't — I mean I honestly don't know whether the right word is marginal, I mean do you experience marginality? Oh God, it sounds like a research question doesn't it!*

Thinking beyond boundaries

Davina: Mmm, do I experience marginality? I talk about this with PhD students who I try and encourage to think in interdisciplinary or post-disciplinary ways. But I do also want them to think about the material and professional costs [this can also bring]; that if you don't have an academic plot which you cultivate, and tend and water and get known for, it can be professionally harder. For me, doing academic work is more like a journey. Looking back, you see the paths, you see what is coherent, but you don't necessarily know in advance where it is going to go. I wouldn't want to have it all plotted out. It is about travelling with a certain set of political commitments, and wanting to think about what can ... I suppose, what can academic methods contribute to transformative, progressive politics. And that takes me to different places.

John: *Say more! Say more, because I think that there is something then about, as it were, being disciplined by different things, not by academic disciplines, but by commitments and attachments and obligations and desires, even ... that make it work differently.*

[0:11:23]

Davina: I think that is right, because if you leave that to one side, it just looks random and arbitrary. At one end of the spectrum, work is directly politically relevant; and my work hasn't ended up being that. I might have wanted it to be. I know when I wrote *Sexing the City*, which came out of thinking about [structuralist Marxist] state theory, and also my own experience of being in local government, I thought the book might be interesting to people who were also part of that practical political project. And they either were irritated by it or it was just irrelevant; they didn't engage with it. So I think I have realised the kind of work I do is politically committed but it is not always directly applicable. Like the work I did at Summerhill School about property ... I went there not thinking I would write about property at a free school, but I also went there with a critique of property. However, doing research made me think, does Summerhill provide a site through which one might rethink what property could mean, [and does one need to rethink what property might mean] in order to understand more about the school? Although it didn't take me to quite wanting to recuperate or retrieve property, there was an openness or contingency that developed which was prepared for property to be useful, or to see that property could do work. In this case I thought property did some work in maintaining the school as a space where people could have intimate relations and lives; as well as more public lives. And that required rethinking property, conceptually, in order to see it do that [and to move beyond an account of property just as ownership]. There had to be that openness to hold on to property as somehow helpful or relevant in that context – analytically if not normatively. And so I suppose you can be doing work that feels politically committed and that creates a certain kind of discipline, but maybe it is not so tight that it doesn't allow you to then reflect on places you get to on that journey, and think, hmm I hadn't thought I would get there, and what do I think about it, and …

John: *One of the things that I … I like, admire, enjoy, all those things, about reading you is that there is always, it seems to me, the mixture of, I don't know, political sensibility – that you have a sense about why things might matter. In more than their academically interesting terms. But it is not a political disciplining of intellectual possibility, so precisely the moment when you think something might be interesting, no matter what its apparent attachments are, is the moment where you are not stuck with official, sanctified critique as the only way of thinking about those relations. And I … the first thing I read from you was* Governing out of Order, *and it seems to me that what it … even the title announces a wonderful problematisation of governing is important and interesting and the out of order bit then is 'hmm should we not be more careful and attentive to' … rather than the presumption of order that disorders. And that is a constant about identifying the political of the social, the legal, the institutional, the personal, without … and there was something you said, and I know can't – I have babbled so much that I have let the words slip away, but it is looking for what might be discovered there, rather than knowing what is to be revealed there.*

Davina: Yes, so it is the creation of something as well; it is both there but it is also about creation rather than just exposing things that already exist. And people can get quite irritated with that.

John: *(Laughs) Oh yes they can!*

Davina: I mean the *Everyday Utopias* book, some people have really liked it, I think, and some people have really not liked it, and been very irritated. And one thing people have been very irritated with is because the book isn't ethnographic in trying to stay with different communities' understandings of what care and property are. It tries to work with the nuance and understanding of how people think about or practise care and property. But it is not trying to just extract or interpret what people think. So some people find it annoying because they think well, who are you to be creating a conceptual line? At the same time I don't want to say this is the *right* conceptual line and the *only* conceptual line. It is about engagement in a democratic process of reflecting on social contexts; and immersion in different contexts.

[0:17:23]

John: *Yes, but that then means a commitment to a democratic understanding of argument that if you say something, it is both as it were what you want to say and you don't necessarily presume that it is the absolute truth, that is … I mean one of the reasons for doing dialogues is that I think things emerge, in argument, in conversation, which … the cultural studies thing that kept me going, still keeps me going, I guess, is the notion that you write things to start conversations, not to announce the definitive end of any discussion. So … I do know some academics who do write definitive conversation-ending statements, but they are not very interesting.*

The consequences of talking to people

Davina: People get dug in and you can end up defending what you have written, even though you didn't necessarily think you would, because you have said it quite certainly. It is also why I feel very committed to doing empirical research where the people I'm interviewing, I mean, having conversations with – they are not vertical discussions, which so much traditional interviewing still is. I try out ideas, and people will often say no, no, you are wrong, and I have never found that people have been deferential to me as an academic, which is also one of those assumptions – that as an academic people won't want to disagree with you, I find they are very ready to, and thank God really!

John: *There is clearly something about how you talk to people! But I think it is true, people say no no no no no that can't be right.*

Davina: Well, they always say to me, it is much more complicated than that!

John: *And I think no, no, I'm the academic, I am supposed to say [that] – but I think that part of the joy about doing empirical work is that for me it is increasingly driven by an understanding that people are engaged in personal, political, organisational sense making of a complicated, multi-vocal kind. And they are neither witnesses to the world, the truth of the world, nor are they any dumber than I am, and I think one of the terrible things about conventional academic research is the assumption that academics know things that people don't, and all the stuff that I have been involved in says, do you know, actually given this is where they work and spend much of their lives, they know much more about it than I do.*

...

Davina: Yes, and have to think about it, because they are engaged with it. I mean, have you found that your conceptual work has shifted through talking to people? That it has made you have to rethink the ... what one takes from the literatures?

John: *Oh how embarrassing, yes! I mean massively. In one research project, where we set off to see whether people thought they were citizens or consumers, it was the big deal for New Labour public service reform, and we rather happily went into it thinking, well nobody will think they are consumers, but people will think they are citizens. Well, indeed, nobody thought they were consumers, but not very many people thought they were citizens either, and they started talking about other relational categories, that they lived their relationship to public services through. And it taught me much about research design, which is you can always have another go, keep some money back because when you discover you have asked people the wrong thing, you should go and ask them [again] – but in the process, I mean one of the things it did for me was to leave me with a view of, precisely about that sense-making work, that people are actively constituting the relations and the processes [interruption] – should I stop, should I pause this?*

[0:23:19]

John: *And one of the things it has made me start doing a lot more is to write about the nature of subjects, and little Bakhtinians, they are heteroglossic, they draw on lots of different repertoires, they do sense making, they are plural and they are not singular, and so it is partly a critique of the stuff in policy studies, where what you do is people do opinion surveys, and people can only have one opinion! It is a sort of doomed and desperate project.*[1]

Davina: But what you are saying about heteroglossia is interesting. The academic training is to remove all that natural sense of being part of lots of worlds, bringing in lots of different sets of meanings, so that people feel they haven't got the confidence, I am only an expert in this, so I really shouldn't talk about any of the things around it.

John: *Indeed, indeed. Yes, and it drives me crazy, and one of the examples of it has been around Brexit, and I was at a workshop where we were talking about Brexit and populism and racism, and somebody said well, but ordinary people aren't racist and misogynist, they are ordinary, decent people, and it is a debate I have heard a lot. And I sat there and said I can't have this conversation, I don't know why you wouldn't think that ordinary, decent people aren't also racist and misogynist. I grew up in an area stuffed full of ordinary, decent people, and they were also patriarchal bastards who were racist, and it is all tucked – and I don't even have to go and do the research – it is all tucked away in my head, because I know that I was formed by those things as well as being better brought up by feminists and anti-racists and so on. But I know that there is a sort of heteroglossia in me, which knows that all those things flow around, and they are evoked and elicited and seduced into being at different moments by different forces. That matters, but I don't see why I should be required to decide whether, on the basis of a single vote, that somebody is a racist, misogynist bastard, or an ordinary, decent person, because that doesn't … none of my world works on those meanings.*

Davina: No, and I mean with the whole debate around anti-Semitism and the Labour Party, it becomes so much about people being anti-Semitic or not being anti-Semitic, and so the question is where you draw the line since people are either one or the other. If you draw the line too high, too many will be defined as anti-Semitic, and if it is too low, then too few … which doesn't really get at how knowledge and ideas travel. Aside from the institutional structural factors that shape and produce racism, we carry – I'm Jewish, but I carry anti-Semitic imagery. I might have other sets of imagery to offset against it, or complicate it, and I don't believe it, but

[1] This Bakhtinian view of subjects was later developed in a piece with Janet Newman about political subjectivity: 'What's the subject? Brexit and politics as articulation', *Journal of Community and Applied Social Psychology*, 2019.

this approach also reduces anti-Semitism to a sense of, 'do you think people are good or bad?' so that anti-Semitism becomes, 'I don't like Jewish people,' or 'I think Jewish people are bad,' or 'I think Jewish people are this.' But actually there are much more subtle sets of knowledges about other people and cultures and notions of Britishness. And there needs to be a better language to talk about a lot of it. This might be where law is helpful, paradoxically, in illuminating critically what is going on, because law is often about line drawing; and sanctions when you fall on the wrong side. This juridical imaginary erases the fact that … we live in a social world which has histories that have produced these ways of thinking. It is much easier to be able to say these are the bad people who carry anti-Semitism and we have to target them.

John: *Yes, I think you are right, and it is both punitive and … it is not self-serving, it is self-saving. That those people, that cluster of people, are like that, and the rest of us are innocent of those things. Well, I have to say I have spent so much of my life being trained to be a real man, that it seems to me that it is unlikely that I will ever lose all its traces, so why would I say oh no, it is okay because I am a feminist? I mean, it is a ritual of purification, is what it is, which cleanses all of us who are good people from all those things that those few bad people have. And if we saw it anywhere else, when the Metropolitan Police says it is – as they used to do in my younger days – it is just a few bad apples, you would say, no it is not, it is institutional, and that means people live in it. It doesn't mean they are it, but they live in it, and I think I live in it as well.*

[0:28:50]

Davina: And we all do. I think part of the problem was that the rejoinder to the 'there are bad apples' was 'we are all bad apples'; and 'we are all anti-Semitic'; 'we are all sexist'; 'we are all racist', which still treats what it is to be racist or anti-Semitic or misogynistic, in a very thin way. And doesn't really deal with how you create other cultural knowledges, as well as the institutional questions and the systemic questions. I wonder also how much the shift to more identity-driven notions of the subject is actually reinforcing the idea that sexism, homophobia, transphobia are attached to particular subjects. I have become quite interested recently in the ways *property* paradigms get used to frame people's relationships to their beliefs, and to their identities; that these things belong to you, these sets of attitudes are yours and you hold them. This is usually a framework which declares, 'You have religious beliefs and those beliefs are worthy of protection because they are part of what belongs to you.' And someone else has a gender that is deemed worthy of affirming and protection because it belongs to them. But there is also a kind of negative property. 'You have these bad beliefs; they are equally your property, a kind of dangerous property that is attached to you and...'

John: *... Now I see why you might hang on to 'property'. I think that is really interesting, and I now want to – when I go on the train ride home, I am going to lie there worrying – I am not going to lie on the train, I am going to sit on the train and worry, because it is interesting that that does speak to something about the way in which we understand persons, as ... the owners of them, not just of themselves and their ... but the owners of their attitudes, orientations, dispositions.*

Davina: Yes, that whole stuff about the possessive self, that you own your capacities and your labour. It was a core liberal tenet. But then human rights and anti-discrimination law extended it to you owning your beliefs and you owning your gender, and these things are your properties, and the question then becomes what can you do with them? And what attempts to use them will be legally and politically supported? The book I am currently writing is about reimagining the state. But it does it through a legal drama over conservative Christians [in common law jurisdictions in the global North] who won't provide goods and services to lesbians and gay men. So, they are withdrawing benefits from lesbians and gay men, and liberal state and public bodies in response are withdrawing contracts and accreditation and promotions from conservative Christians. I am interested in this politics of withdrawal, and how, and indeed whether, conservative action can, paradoxically, provide a resource for reimagining the state in progressive ways. But one part of this project is how the courts treat beliefs in gay sexuality's wrongness as *belonging* to conservative Christians. The courts aren't supposed to interrogate the beliefs and say are these really Christian beliefs [although sometimes they do]. Rather, the question becomes, what are those beliefs allowing conservative Christians to do? How far can they work as property? How expansive are they?

Do they allow you, if you are a marriage registrar, not to marry someone? If you make wedding cakes, can you refuse to make a cake for a gay couple? Or if you are a religious organisation, do they allow you to throw someone out because they are gay? So, the questions are framed in property terms, recognising that these things belong to you as property, that is, as an interest that you possess.

...

Emerging projects and emerging identities

Davina: I have just got funding for a new project which asks the question: should we reform legal gender identity?[2] One possibility would be that people no longer have a legal gender status; that would make gender identity analogous, in Britain, to religious or sexual identity. It would mean your gender identity could change, could be different in different contexts, and you could choose to give it or not give it when asked. It feels quite exciting to do this project and be able to talk with people about the investments, if they have any, in legal gender. To explore the challenges and difficulties of different reform options – recognising that people will have different perspectives on it. But I also want to see whether this law reform method works as a way of exploring fundamental questions. Because you could then imagine trying it with other issues; issues the Law Commission probably wouldn't touch or would do very differently. I am interested in this space, as a kind of small, minor space, but just ...

[1:35:20]

John: *Yes, but they are small, minor spaces where you can condense, as you just did in the discussion, in the presentation just then, you condensed a whole variety of things that might be pursued through that small space. And that, as you were talking about it, I was thinking 'and what a very Davina Cooper-like project that sounds'. Law-ish, yes, well politics of identity, subjectivity, gender, rearticulated, reform, and yet doing it by talking to people about their relationship to both gender and the law. And it ... do it! Do it, just because it is ... it*

---

2   *Reforming Gender Identity: A socio-legal approach* (ESRC project): https://gtr.ukri.org/projects?ref=ES%2FP008968%2F1

is exactly the thing about your capacity to see a conjunction of things, that might be … might at least be interesting, might at most be transformative. And what I think is great about it is precisely there is a whole set of intellectual, political, personal, cultural conditions that lead you to spot it, but you don't know what the answer is.

Davina: No, and I would be interested if I end up thinking there is a place for legal gender status, which there might be. Because an abolitionist stance might mean gender becomes incredibly privatised as simply a matter of personal preference. Deregulation can also generate conflicts between gender-based organisations who say we should be able to set the criteria for what our gender involves and an individual saying no, I have the right to determine whether I come within your gender category. So, even if you talk about self-regulation, once the state no longer defines your gender, it can still get involved in mediating conflicts and determining where the power of decision lies. Part of the rationale for the project was to shift the debate from the narrower question [that currently dominates but which seems to normalise gender difference] about how you accommodate a minority whose genders don't seem to fit the genders they've been assigned. It was to ask a more inclusive and structural question, why do any of us need a legal gender? What is it doing?

John: *That is sort of Cooper-esque in my view, and it is precisely, it seems to me, the important thing about interesting, and good, who knows, radical, critical, intellectual work, is to be able to not be stuck, and that is not to be stuck with the marginality, the inscription of it as a small minority problem, but nor to be stuck with 'and we know what the answer would be', because we know what current politics are. But it is precisely to be able to turn it around and say 'so what questions does this pose?' What possibilities does this open and close?*

Davina: That is exactly right. Because one way of doing this project would be to start with the question: what are the problems with gender today? But actually, I think it may be interesting to start with the question – how does a project of law reform refract both the present and our investments in the present and ideas about change? Because people will talk about what gender means to them differently, if you say, 'Well, how would you feel about this possible scenario involving change and something new?' than if you just say, 'Well what is your experience of living as a man or a woman, or gender minority?' It may seem counter-intuitive to use the possibility of reform as a lens through which to think about the current moment [because reform options are usually where projects end up, not where they start]. In a way, this is really coming full circle, both in terms of our conversation but also for me with academic legal work, which is to think about whether legal form is helpful in – not exactly a pedagogic way but as a way of framing or opening up questions. One of the things that will come out of the project is a draft Bill, which feels quite an ambitious and daunting prospect, but forces us, at least provisionally and temporarily, to resolve some of the difficult questions about what is the best model (although it might be models) for reforming gender, and what would it actually look like as a piece of legislation. An important dimension of law is its reform, but law more generally has a range of forms that can be taken into other disciplinary fields and used for different kinds of interdisciplinary work. There is a move at the moment to go beyond critique. I am not against critique, but I am interested in what else progressive academics can do. And law has some forms that might be productive for this post-critique moment, just as utopian fiction might offer other forms. If you aren't constrained by what is legally possible, law reform projects outside the terrain of formal law offer a structured process for thinking beyond the now. The feminist judgments project [where feminist academics write new judgments for past cases] has been doing something similar. There's a large, long-standing literature from progressive legal scholars that critiques legal form. And its limitations and problems are easy to see. But can legal form, when it's taken up by institutional outsiders or border-crossers, contribute something to interdisciplinary or post-disciplinary projects about change, something maybe quite unexpected?

[1:41:36]

John: You just made me think about … I mean fictions … utopias, legal forms, those genres, rather than as law but as genres, and genres always enable and disqualify. I mean, they make some things possible, and they rule out non-generic – Okay I am going to stop, that was wonderful. Thank you very much!

10

Gail Lewis

Gail Lewis is Reader in Psychosocial Studies at Birkbeck College in London, where she works on the shifting political, cultural and lived intersections of gender and race. Before this she taught at the Open University (OU) and the University of Lancaster. I first met Gail when she came to study for a PhD at the Open University – a process which happily taught me a lot. She has continued to help me to think ever since, even as she explores new ways of thinking that open up new possibilities. Her 2000 book on *'Race', Gender and Social Welfare: Explorations in a Postcolonial Society* remains a vital starting point for rethinking social welfare and social policy, but her published work and other interventions range much wider.

More information can be found at: www.bbk.ac.uk/psychosocial/our-staff/academic/gail-lewis.

This conversation was recorded in London on 3 April 2017.

Themes and topics

- Thinking with others
- Between certainty and uncertainty
- Thinking with and through race
- Dimensions and dynamics of crisis
- Imagining other connections

Thinking with others

John: *So, I'm going to start by going back to the conversation we were just having about thinking in conversation with others, and just tell me what that means for you.*

Gail: (Laughs) Gosh! What it means for me? Well, I suppose it's sort of ... I suppose there's a couple of things that come to mind immediately. One is about how, if I have a, you know, a thought comes in your mind, I don't know, as you're walking along or something, when you kind of literally say, 'Oh, what do you make of what we heard?' Or, 'What's your response to that terrible attack on that Iranian Kurdish guy in Croydon?' You know? I'm terrified that it's going to be black kids who did it. You know?

John: *Yep.*

Gail: There's going to be a similar issue into the national story and all this kind of stuff ... and mindset and, you know, so then I, kind of, it's that. Then I might ... but, so ... It's more that I would pose questions in that sense, and that partly then helps me to articulate what I think the questions are in my head.

John: *Yes.*

Gail: I don't know whether I get answers back so much though, which is the bit where I get stuck. (Laughs) But I think the other thing is it's a way of placing myself not just in a set of voices, but in a sort of time–space formation in a sense, because I might, for some things, I might find I call up my generation as it were. And then that would then make me think, 'Oh okay, so the kinds of ways I'm ... the questions are coming to me are out of our generation. Out of our time–space, our moment of formation.' So, I might, you know, call up people in the Brixton Black Women's Group, for example, for that kind of stuff.

John: *All right.*

Gail: Or even speak back to, I mean thinking with Darcus Howe having just died.[1]

John: *Yes.*

Gail: The way in which we, in the Brixton Group, might have argued with him and the *Race Today* Collective, but argued from a point of view of, you know, a common

---

[1]   Darcus Howe, broadcaster, writer and activist, was one of the founders of the *Race Today* Collective.

vision, a common pursuit, a kind of internal conversation, argument, that was about how do we get to the place we want to get to?

[0:02:52]

Gail: [That] we feel we need to get to. What's the political vision at the end of this? But I suppose I also more and more, kind of, have in my mind the conversations with some of the younger people that I am connected to through, people like Rehana Zaman, for example, who is a kind of artist, art practitioner, who I met at a group relations conference but who has put me in contact with all sorts of other people, so in those younger people, they, you know, are both sort of saying to us, 'Well, tell us about your histories because we need to know for where we want to go now.'

John: *Yeah.*

Gail: But also when they ask you that, they pose the questions in slightly different ways. Like, not so much… It's sort of… well the secondary bit of their vision is how we collectively … what's our collective goal? But the first one is, 'How do I get on in life?' 'How do I get on as a black woman in the academy?' 'How do I get on as a black woman in the world?'

John: *Yep.*

Gail: And where it can seem like … The phrasing of the question is in the sort of liberal, individualised context, but when you probe a bit deeper, it's not that some sense of a collective story is not there, but it's how you articulate the question, so.

John: *Yes. And I mean, my guess is I'm going to say they're right, but there is something about the configuration of this time-space moment and the academy in particular which I think both induces that as a mode of relationship and thinking, and leaves me feeling entirely disempowered.*

Gail: Yeah, I know.

John: *Because I, you know, I mean, if I talk to young people, graduates, students, around the edges, they're asking calculative questions, and I don't mean they're calculating, but their circumstances require them to make calculations that I never made.*

Gail: Exactly. Exactly …

John: *I don't know, 'Which journal do you think would be best to publish in?' So, there's a set of things about the present that make me feel slightly, make me feel slightly old, but also make me disjunctured from it.*

Gail: Yeah, yeah.

John: *And I worry. (Laughs) – I worry that my solutions are not transferable and that I should be careful about it as well.*

Gail: That's right. Yeah, yeah. But I think that … I suppose … Okay, what I think is, so, the kind of conversations that are in my mind now as you ask me about, 'What does it mean to be in conversation?' are things like where younger black women might say, 'How do we empower ourselves in each other?' So that discourse of empowerment. So it's not quite the same as, 'Where do you publish?'

[0:06:37]

John: *Right.*

Gail: So, it's not quite so much, kind of, framed as though this is about career, although of course it is.

John: *Yes.*

Gail: We've all got to survive and live, and all that … And have ambition, but it's more, 'How can I generate in myself the capacity to survive this that I'm in?'

John: *Yes.*

Gail: When it constantly moves anyway. Like, apparently, you know, widening participation, increase in diversity, all that kind of stuff. But actually, it all … I don't know where the avenues are and how I will survive it. So, that's what I mean that it seems like an individual question, but actually it does speak to something more collective if you can kind of decode it, I think.

John: *Yeah.*

Gail: And then that makes me think, I suppose, is that there is a real hunger, there's a hunger for a kind of intergenerational learning and sharing. I really think that. I really think that … I think that the people that I'm in conversation with, at least the young people, there is a real hunger for that and it's true. It's not that you can give them, you know, we didn't know solutions for ourselves. Look, we're here! (Laughs)

John: *Yes. (Laughs)*

Gail: But we can't know the solutions, but something about sharing intergenerational experiences to think together about, 'What's the terrain we're in now and how might we begin to create the resources that might be called empowering?' I suppose I mean. It's not the language that I'd use. And then that makes me think … then of course the other people that are in my head all the time actually, are people like Jacqui Alexander, Gloria Wekker, Angela Davis, but I'd particularly say Gloria and Jacqui and Lata Mani, where things that were squeezed out of an earlier terrain, for me at least, the idea of something called the spiritual, whatever that might be, but also the idea of the body, not as something that gets ill or anything, but the body as another way of, another feltness.

John: Yep.

Gail: You know, all this stuff about the body's marked and inscribed and all that kind of stuff, but beyond that, on another register, a register that isn't … that doesn't come from critique but comes from construct, comes from saying something about … We do have some resources, ancestrally if you like, another version of the intergenerational.

John: Yes.

Gail: If we can only really go to them and try to mobilise them [I mean the ancestral knowledges] as they live in our bodies and spark our imaginations. I mean, that's the only access we have to them, by how we get sparked in our imaginations [and become an embodied feltness].

[0:09:49]

John: *And trying to make them speak into the conversation.*

Gail: Yeah, yeah, yeah. But often times, through the feltness. And if you can articulate the … it's hard to explain. I'm always doing this these days to go to stuff, you know, the feltness of stuff.

John: *(Laughs) No, I think textures, stuff and all those slightly elusive things.*

Gail: So, it is like, you know we were talking about *Moonlight* earlier, it is like the rebirth scene in the water where, you know, you've got that Juan the drug dealer, you know, but somehow this *ability* and *need* to father, in some sense. … And take him into the water, take Little into the water so that you can float in something that is much bigger than yourself. That's how you get them to speak. That's how you get the ancestral voices to speak through the water, and the water is a kind of figure in these other modes of knowing, these kind of … part of a black Atlantic story of the importance of water, not just as a place where you're going to die, but the place where you can be held in the thing in which you cannot be held. It holds you even though it can't –

John: *In suspension.*

Gail: Yeah … But suspension is something that can go on.

John: *Yes.*

Gail: You can survive in a sense. So, when he takes him into the water, I think the allusions in that, sort of, so many registers of black life, but importantly, 'Look, you can do this and I can hold you here. Fall into my arms. I've got you, I've got you.'

John: *I've got you, and you're safe with me.*

Gail: Yeah, yeah. Exactly. And he tells him, you know, the Cuban woman tells him that, 'In the moonlight, the black boys look blue.'

John: *Blue. Indeed.*

Gail: So, that's what I mean. That stuff, and it's those kinds of ways of thinking, of analysing, of visioning of politics, that's summed up in that scene that's in the writing of people like Jacqui Alexander and Gloria Wekker that are there in my head.

Between certainty and uncertainty

John: *But the bit that fascinates me, you know, there are two lines at least, at least, if not three, if not four, out of this and I'll come back to some of them, but one of them is precisely the peculiar oscillation, I think, as I experience it, so this might just be projecting wildly, is the oscillation between thinking that I know where I am and thinking that I don't know where I am, and that the conversational mode of being with others is in part trying out the confident bit and saying, 'If I say I think it's about this, does that make any sense?' And the other bit is about being able to say, 'And there's stuff here, but I can't get my head around but I know you've thought about this before?' So, it seems to me that there's something about that interplay of conversations that are about having something to say and asking questions that have sustained me in … not just sustained, it won't do. Sustained is not a good enough metaphor. Has dragged me along in its train that's been vital.*

[0:13:58]

Gail: No, absolutely. Absolutely. And I think, I suppose, it's precisely in that kind of dialectic or whatever between having something to say or having a sense of some semblance of a sense that you know where you are and another one says, 'Well, I don't at all know where I am. I don't know how I got here. I don't know where I can go from here. I don't know?' You know, I know something. I don't know something is precisely in that dialectic, that third pathway if you like.

John: *Yeah.*

Gail: Or another pathway can emerge to another point where you're caught between those two poles and you go on again … And that's the spiral space, you know?

John: *Oh! Yes.*

Gail: Because it's not that it's just an iteration.

John: *It is not.*

Gail: And it's not just a return to the same, it's a moving on, even as we go around if you (over-speaking).

John: *I should have brought a movie camera for the hands today because I can feel it coming! (Laughs)*

Gail: (Laughs) Yeah, yeah.

John: *But I think the spiral's right and I don't necessarily think it moves in any given axis.*

Gail: No, no.

John: *But I do think that one of the strains, and this is to go back to institutional settings, is about an academic life in which saying, 'I'm not sure,' 'I'm uncertain,' 'I don't really know about this,' or, 'I don't know what's going on?' are at least frowned on, and are I think also a problem about what expectations are held out for young people, and I think the models of certainty, certitude, definitiveness have a sort of even bigger hold than they used to. I'm bored by, and I shouldn't say this, I'm bored by reading people who know things.*

Gail: Yeah, I know what you mean. Yeah, absolutely. Absolutely. Usually nothing to say. (Laughs)

John: *Well, and the ones I read have said it before and it just turns out that today is just another day where the thing that they knew is still true and I mean, I think one of the hard … I mean, I think it's always been true, but one of the hard things about the present moment is I'm even less sure about the things that I thought were true, you know?*

Gail: Yeah, absolutely.

171

John: I mean, you know, I think people have tried to teach me how to think, but I don't think I have a set of ten points that I could write down and say, 'There you go. That's today!'

Gail: Yeah, exactly. Exactly. And, you know, and isn't that just another way of saying that actually we can't do it on our own? Nobody can do that. It's not just who do you have in your mind as being the people you are in conversation with and that that gives the vitality. It's absolutely essential, it's vital to have conversation because we can't do it on our own. But of course, that makes you vulnerable too, you know?

[0:20:19]

Thinking with and through race

John: But I want to go back because the other thing that you said right at the start and is part of our ongoing conversations, even if they've not happened very much lately, is thinking with and through race. And I remember when I first met you that you were one of the few people around the Open University who had it in their head as a category (over-speaking).

Gail: Yeah. (Laughs)

John: Much less as a lived experience.

Gail: Yeah.

John: Much less as a politics, but one of the things that's been clear ever since I did meet you is how do you think the present without that? All right? How is this moment imaginable without racialisations, multiple effects, presences, relations?

Gail: Yeah, yeah. No, I mean, you absolutely can't. You can't even begin to make sense of it, I don't think. You know, the formation that we're in, without thinking about, as you say, racialisations, multiple, and how complex it is because on the one hand, you know, you've … it's sort of everywhere, I think, you know, I really do think there's a return to an earlier structure of feeling, I guess.

John: Yep.

Gail: Where it does feel, to me, much more like the sort of mid-'70s than the late '90s, say, in the sense that it feels frightening, that all, everywhere as you walk around, you hear racist epithets. You know, it could be all kinds, it's not necessarily only anti-black, it's, you know, anti-Semitic, anti-Arab, anti-Eastern Europeans, or European generally, where there's another –

John: *Yes. Indeed.*

Gail: – you know, all sorts of ways in which the world is made ... seemed to be made meaningful in people's mouths through some kind of racialising process of us and them, you know? Insider or outsider and all that, and of course led by politicians, media, just often through a failure to address it properly ... in its ordinariness, so you've got that, but you've got the multiplication, the ways in which, you know, that people seemed to be offended if some European people speak in whatever their European language is to each other. As though this is the most outrageous offence to their very core, the core of the listener, you know? And, like, that's just so frightening and at the same time you think, 'What has happened that people's cores are so unravelled to even hear a European language ...' and we're not talking about someone from Africa or East Asia, you know, or Asia, or East Asia ... that that feels so dismantling of their core, that they, kind of, have a right, but also they have a right too.

John: *Ah. Right.*

Gail: So, they're dismantled or crumbling on one hand and at the same time they have a sovereignty (laughs) through which they can, kind of, express their hatred and all that kind of stuff. So that ... all of that, alongside the mobilisation of the so-called settled minorities, that was the term for a while wasn't it, you know of the people who come from ... people like me who come originally from the Caribbean, or South Asia.

John: *Yep, yep.*

Gail: The settled minorities, and, you know, an incorporation into the national bigotries. 'You too ... We must make sure that when we do our vox pops for the TV and the radio, it's going to be your voices that say there's too many of them here now. Too many immigrants. We've got to stop. And I noticed that you might ... Did your parents come from ...?' 'Ah yeah, but when my parents came, we worked.' (Laughs) I mean, it's like it's through the paradox of the ... it's sick paradox of the same mobilisation.

[0:24:56]

John: *It is. Indeed. Or both paradox and parody! I mean the ...*

Gail: Yeah, yeah, yeah. So, we've got all of that, but the ways in which, you know, you ... Every ill, every kind of hurt, every dispossession is encoded through those languages of immigration, otherness, racialised in some way as not legitimate, and it's really, really frightening. I'm frightened! (Laughs)

John: *I mean, I think that frightening is different, differently embodied, no doubt about it. But I think it's frightening, and it's partly because I think both the proliferation that, I think you're right, there's hardly anything which is not coded into that register and the speed of it as a default reaction, so I do think that, I mean, when you say that there's a sort of doubleness, or fragility, I mean, what is going on that means whatever we're going to call it, the white, English, British-ish identity, and the legitimation of that as the mode of expression is, and … I mean, you know, I've been trying to write something with Janet about what the sense of loss around Brexit and Trump might mean, and what a complicated set of losses that might be that they are both, you know, material losses of jobs and industry and places to live, and there are also psychic losses about a sense of life, you know, the famous 'way of life' that we used to have and, but how wrapped up, I mean, both nationally and internationally in privilege all of that is and that the loop back is, and the privilege is to be able to express it in that register and I've no idea.*

Gail: Yeah.

John: *I have no idea, but every time I read about journalistic and academic versions about the left behind, the sense of loss, the … you know, I think, 'Yeah, but there are many psychic dimensions to the loss that you're talking about.' And, you know, especially having just come back from the States, the Trump question about the loss of supremacy seems to me to be a really contradictory and unnerving, and scary … and I mean, I think you're right about scary, political formation and it's a political formation drenched in, I don't know, you know more about this than I do, psychic, affective stuff that profoundly unsettled, I don't mean it's not been there for a long time, but it's out and about in an entirely new … Well, not in an entirely new way, it's more out and about than it used to be.*

Gail: I mean, certainly the licence to speak in ways that … at least, the very speakers would say that they were not allowed to speak.

John: *Yes.*

Gail: You know, I don't know if that's right, but that's what they often say, or at least I overhear people say it, and it's kind of interesting. Sometimes, I do want to say, 'What happened?

Has it changed? I hope you don't mind, I just overheard you say ...' (Laughs) But I don't in case I get hit or something!

John: Yes.

Gail: But what I can't fathom really ... well, I suppose the question in my mind is, so when Brexit happened, as I was saying to you, I was in hospital and I was reading in the paper, I think it was maybe one of the weekend papers, and there was a lot of kind of interviews with people from different areas that had been heavily leave.

John: Yep.

Gail: And one of them was Wales ... and they had a picture of this town or whatever, and there were all these EU signs, you know, with all this money ... indicating all this money that had come in, and the person they spoke to was a young guy, in his 20s or something, who said, 'Oh yeah, it's great. Brilliant, brilliant. I voted ... I absolutely voted Brexit. Good, we ... bit of ... get our country back.' This is Wales, so they're not getting it back from England, but you know?

[0:30:21]

John: Yep.

Gail: Get our country back and stuff, and you know it went on like this and, 'They've done nothing for us, nothing for us, but we're paying billions and they've done nothing for us.' And then the interviewer said, 'I've noticed all these signs ...' and they were plants for jobs, you know, jobs, the industries had been supported and that kind of stuff, and the guy sort of laughed and he said, 'Yeah, I suppose so actually. Yeah, I suppose they've put quite a lot in here. It's true. But I don't care. The main thing is that those London elite, they got it, didn't they. We showed them in our vote.' So suddenly, the whole shift ... to, 'I know we might have been a bit of a material struggle here, but actually the people who we're voting against is really the London elite,' and that gets on my nerves anyway as though they're ... You know, because they've never even been to London to see all the poverty and material deprivation in London anyway, but nevertheless, I do live on the edge –

John: Yeah, but we know where the elite lives.

Gail: Exactly, and I live on the edge of the City, so I do know about finance capital, and the kind of global side in London and all that. There's all that. But what I … in that register of, sort of, triumph, the triumphalism against the kind of an idea of an elite that's taken from you, taken all of your rights from you, that runs right alongside that is some kind of … could care less about the possible material effects of Brexit on you as well. So it's not like a sustaining of a … It's such a flimsy moment of victory. It seemingly, you know –

John: *Indeed.*

Gail: It seems to be a flimsy moment of victory against some, you know … Again, it's an 'other' over there; not a racialised other now, a classed other in that sense because it's about those people there.

John: *Yeah.*

Gail: And then more and more of those sort of conversations that go on where people say on this sort of terrain of, 'Get our sovereignty back.' 'Get our country back.' 'Get our thing back.' And you know that … of course, at one level, there has been massive material dispossession. People don't have jobs. People don't have … men don't have the possibility of the masculinities that their fathers had in those places, if they wanted them, you know. There are real losses in that sense, but I get stuck. How does it travel out to this? And the Marxist version can't … doesn't, you know, that it's dividing the class and all that, doesn't help me because I don't get it. You know, it's one of those points where I'm lost. I don't get it.

John: *I think, I mean, I think you're right about the Marxist versions of 'get it' because the worst one ends up celebrating Brexit as a working-class victory.*

Gail: Oh, I know.

John: *And I just want to cry.*

Gail: Well, that's just pathetic, infantile.

John: *Indeed. (Laughs) But the other is that, I mean, you captured it in the description of the particular interview with the slide and it seems to me that there are three or four slides, I mean, one of which is, 'You're a sovereignty, we want our country back.' 'Yeah, but, you know, is it going to be a material disaster?' 'Yeah, but we stuck it to the London metropolitan, multicultural elite.'*

[0:34:02]

Gail: I don't even know for this particular person. (Over-speaking) It was, yeah, it seemed more, yeah –

John: *But there's a gloss there about, 'London is different than the rest of us.'*

Gail: Definitely that. And London has imposed all this on us.

John: *Its will on us, yes.*

Gail: Yeah. Yeah, and some of that is to impose multiculturalism on us.

John: *Yes, indeed.*

Gail: There's definitely that.

John: *And then there's … but then the next little beautiful slide is immigration, which is something to do with both of them, but it isn't quite the same thing.*

Gail: Exactly.

John: *And one of the things I think … I mean, you're right about the racialisation of immigration because it now carries the capacity to hit one of about ten registers … we've always hated other people. (Laughs)*

Gail: Yeah.

John: *Sorry, I speak on behalf of the white British here, we have always hated other people anyway, and then, you know, we hated Europeans and then we hated East Europeans. They're not black, so it's not racist.*

Gail: Exactly, exactly.

John: *It was just that we hate them. We don't want them –*

Gail: They come to you with 'just an island' …

John: *They cook pickles! They're … you know, it's just. So, it seems to me that one of the really … actually, I do think one of the unnerving things is the ability of those to fold into the next one.*

Gail: Yeah, sure.

John: *At almost any moment, right? So it's not … there's this thing which has happened, Right?*

Gail: No.

John: *It's this combination, articulation, set of half-connected things that are at stake.*

Gail: And it's that they're relatively empty that allowed the slide because they can be filled in by any one of the bits that can happen, any one of the kind of narratives, or the elements of a narrative can fill into any point of the story. That's the thing. So, there's always that slide, and then in the end, in that case, you know, a young man who's still not going to have a job. (Laughs)

John: *Yeah, yeah.*

[0:36:06]

Gail: Or anything … And about whom nobody cares.

John: *Well, I … that's the awful bit, isn't it?*

Gail: Certainly, the Farages of this world do not care.

John: *No. You know, we have a government that announces that it's going to be for everybody as it dismantles yet more of the welfare system and –*

Gail: Exactly, exactly.

John: *But there was one horrible, I mean, there have been several, but one particular horrible crystallisation of those narratives into one person and one place which was Gina Miller.*

Gail: Yeah.

John: *How awful to be part of the cosmopolitan/metropolitan elite, a liberal constitutionalist … And not British, or not the right sort of British, or not white British. And then suddenly you have the, whatever the opposite of perfect, focus for all of those things to condense into, right? So, not that they're the same, even when they go for Gina Miller, but she becomes a point of condensation for almost all of them; she is in the wrong place, of the wrong sort, doing the wrong thing and I wouldn't have wanted to be Gina Miller at that moment.*

Gail: No. Absolutely. And of course, there's Gina Miller and there's Jo Cox.

John: *And there's Jo Cox.*

Gail: So, there's the two together. There's the one who, you know, the white woman who is clearly a fabulous MP. Really cares, but who must be taken out because she's a betrayer. She's absolutely a betrayer.

John: *Yes. Yes. From the inside.*

Gail: From the inside. And she's a she … And Gina Miller is also a she. Yeah, yeah. I mean, the point is that the kind of gendered terrain, the way in which what is felt to be lost is so much a kind of gendered terrain as well.

John: *Yes. Yes.*

Gail: That gets represented by these two women, I think, in particular ways. The kind of fantasy of whiteness. Of the kind of the voice of the nation. The critical … the voice that can indeed represent the constitution and try to hold the nation to the constitutional process, but in the wrong body, and that wrong body being both a wrong-raced body and a wrong-sexed body … And then Jo Cox, the wrong kind of … doing the wrong kind of work as a woman and not doing it in a way that tends to the white boys.

[0:38:48]

John: *Yes, yes. Indeed.*

Gail: But actually tends to everybody, so not doing the right, kind of, womanly stuff. So, I think that speaks to, you know, the ways in which what feels in crisis and we've known it for so long, is precisely the normativity of gender that have been collapsed by all sorts of cultural pluralities really. You know, in the sense of not just … I don't just mean in that sense of ethnicities, but the ways in which, you know, the diversification of kind of the sexual life and its visibility.

John: *Yep.*

Gail: Diversification of, kind of, ways of doing gender and its visibility. All of those things that lead to a kind of crisis of, 'What does it mean?' 'What does it mean?' There is a, kind of, in that sense, a multicultural crisis [emerging from challenges to ideas of the normal]. (Laughs)

John: *Yes. And it does seem to me that it's right about the different registers of that, and that I'm despairingly struck by one of the key terms in the online discussions after Brexit has been, 'Grow a pair.'*

Gail: Yeah. (Laughs)

John: *Well, (laughs) if you want to find the correct register for the reassertion of a masculinity of a rather, would-be to fantastical, I mean, you know, in the fantasy sense, fantastically tough version, it would be the injunction to everybody to grow a pair … Because this is the only way of being a person.*

Gail: Exactly. Exactly. And it's so captured in that, you know, that's just … It is scary though.

John: *Well, I mean, I'll have the next bit of the conversation which I had in the States which is we had a long argument about whether the moment of Trump was the moment of fascism. Some of us said, no. You know, there are conditions about fascism that this doesn't quite … I mean, it's horrible. It's, you know, executive authoritarianism, but my response was … My worry is in one sense is not Trump. It's when Trump fails on all those promises. So, when … post-Brexit, after we have done all of these horrible things, and then when that*

> *young man in South Wales looks round and there's less, what's the*
> *political repertoire that … I mean, my current version is, I keep myself*
> *awake at night worrying about … and that's when you want a strong*
> *leader because, you know, the political parties are clearly not capable*
> *of delivering on the insane, fantastic promises that were made, you*
> *know? We know that NHS money on the bus from 'Leave' went*
> *the day after. We know that, you know, actually we might not be*
> *able to control immigration because corporate capital needs some.*

Gail: Yeah. Exactly, exactly. (Laughs)

John: *Well, you know, we might not be able to give you any houses because*
            actually, we're going to give the rich a tax cut.

Gail: Exactly. And the jobs? Well, we'll see.

John: *Yeah, well, you know, in another generation. They'll be a couple of*
            apprenticeships down the odd street.

Gail: Yeah, exactly.

[0:42:53]

John: *But they might not actually lead to jobs.*

Dimensions and dynamics of crisis

Gail: Exactly. Exactly. No, it really is … And I suppose that kind of
            crisis of, I mean, profound crisis in a kind of belief of liberal
            democracy, or the delivery of what it can deliver, how it can
            kind of govern in a way that feels sufficiently satisfactory to
            those who are invited to invest in it in particular ways. But,
            there was this programme on the TV, I don't know if you
            saw it, about young people, sort of, post-Brexit? And some
            of them … What were they …? They don't call themselves,
            the alt-right here, but they were kind of alt-right but I
            can't remember what they called themselves, something
            conservative. Some of them were social conservative, kind
            of people, but some were something else and they were
            all certainly authoritarian, kind of right authoritarian,
            economically liberal, and they ranged between, the people
            they interviewed, sort of 18 and 25 or something like that, all
            speaking to this thing … And some had come from the Left
            or something, 'Yeah I used to think and then I realised and
            got mobilised on the net, or from social media …' And then
            connected up into things and all these instances, you could
            see what they could be invited to. Because the thing about

the Trump thing I suppose is that it's not so much him, on his own, you know?

John: Yes.

Gail: It is when he fails. But most importantly, and it's about the kind of international formation as well.

John: Indeed.

Gail: The right-wing formation, led by Bannon and his whole kind of architecture that they fund and then kind of set up institutionally with all the links to ... That's the thing. It's about the kind of Right axis. ... So, they are not fascists and they're not fascists here, but they may be linking with fascists. (Laughs) ... And helping them to mobilise elsewhere, all in this much more Right authoritarians and white supremacist, male supremacist. I don't even want to call it patriarchy in a sense, but kind of supremacist because of a particular kind of masculinity that must be in control in the image of a class, and in the image of whiteness ... Not white-skinness, but whiteness of the horizon and what it means to be a human, you know?

John: Yes.

Gail: And that's why I think it's so frightening because what ... Thank God, Wilders, in the Netherlands, you know, didn't get in. But we don't know what's going to happen with Le Pen. ... We don't know what's going to happen just with the gathering of forces, that's the point.

John: And one of the things is, I mean, you know, they don't have to win everywhere to be connected ... Or to be effective.

[0:45:56]

Gail: Exactly.

John: And I think, I mean, I don't, I probably don't think Bannon and his connections are fascist, but they're certainly not liberal constitutionalists either.

Gail: No, but I was thinking about the connections into Putin and these other and they're setting up.

John: And the old hard Rights around Europe.

Gail: That's right. And they're setting up. They're setting up, you know, they're going to. Oh, I can't remember the name of the site that they've got on the kind of TV or something, but they're going to set up in difference places in France.

John: Yeah, yeah. Breitbart?

Gail:	With the Breitbart people. That's right … So, to give a kind of an infrastructure into which, you know, the fascists can kind of lob their stuff … and gather up more people.
John:	*And where the distinctions don't matter, at least. You know, whether it's Putin. Whether it's Putin. Whether it's the Klan. Whether it's Le Pen, the distinctions matter less than their connections.*
Gail:	And we know here in this country, we know how successful, kind of, Right, small Right, semi-fascist, authoritarian, profoundly racist organisations so easily pull everything rightward … So easily do.
John:	*And, you know, and there's the, I mean it's not an area of knowledge of mine, but there's the thing about Wilders losing in the Netherlands. Well, yes, he lost … But on the other hand, the political culture –*
Gail:	Took up a lot of his stuff –
John:	*Took up half at least of those things … And there have been moments in France where one view of how to outflank Le Pen is to be more anti-Muslim with [than] the Front Nationale.*

[0:47:45]

Gail:	Exactly, exactly … And knowing what it's like for people who are obviously identified as Muslim, whether they are or not, out there, you know, this is in London let alone anywhere else.
John:	*Yep.*
Gail:	It's a complete nightmare … And just the kind of ordinary, everyday insults, micro-aggressions that have just become part of the fabric.
John:	*The texture of the everyday.*
Gail:	Yeah, yeah. Exactly, exactly. And that's what's so awful and that … I suppose, the worry is how much, and this comes back to the collective conversations really, how much we, whoever 'we' is, might be able to mobilise a kind of another vision that can just be a bit like Velcro, you know? And just connect a bit … Stick to people, say, 'Actually, no I want to think through this other frame? I don't know the answers, but I want to think it through this other frame, not what you're offering me. I can imagine myself differently and in relation to others in a different kind of way than what I'm being invited to do.'

Imagining other connections

John: Yeah.

Gail: And that's what I think is so frightening that, how do we make that intervention? Because partly, because we used to be able to do it more through the formations of the welfare state.

John: *Indeed. And through bits of the local state and all those things.*

Gail: All of that, that's what I mean, all that stuff that were ... that gave an institutional infrastructure and a sort of, a distorted, difficult, wrong culture, or cultural form that said, 'We have a relationship to strangers.'

John: *Yeah.*

Gail: I don't mean foreigners, I mean strangers. Those who are living in Birmingham, John ... Or, those who live in Sunderland.

John: *Yes.*

Gail: We are connected.

John: *Yes.*

[0:49:49]

Gail: Not those elite in London – we're going to kick it to death ... But actually ordinary, working-class Londoners ... Connected to ordinary, working-classes people from Llandudno or wherever it was, you know?

John: *Yeah, it's true. It's true.*

Gail: That sense of a connection, you know, it is the bloody thing, isn't it, about the blood transfusion as the metaphor for the welfare state (laughs) I mean, God! (Laughs)

John: *I mean, only last week, in Nashville, somebody said, 'We don't have the, the Left doesn't have an imagery like, you know, ethno-nationalism. It doesn't have that visual thing.' And I said, 'Well, I think we have had. You know, the NHS and the blood transfusion as an example connected, both materially and emotionally, 96% of the people in this country, but why didn't we ever know how that worked!' (Laughs)*

Gail: (Laughs)

John: *And why did we think it could be mobilised just by saying, 'Let's see if the National Health Service', you know ... in that sort of rather flat tone ... because it did connect. And it was, you know, it was the blood transfusion, it was the notion that you'd have shared*

183

experiences, and so I think you're right, there is something odd about the way that London is talked about as if there is not misery, impoverishment, homelessness etc, as well as wherever finance capital lives, you know?

Gail: Yeah.

John: *But the breaking of their imaginary, that sense that other people share good things and bad things, that you know, in different registers of all sorts of things, but that was both a national imaginary and occasionally, on its good days, wandered into being an internationalist imaginary that, you know, there are people like us all over the place to whom we are connected.*

Gail: Yeah, yeah. I know and because we also know that what a long journey that's been because we, you know, obviously all that work that we did in the OU, we are making an intervention into this field called social policy, we are trying to say something really, really serious is happening here ... And the distortion of the movements, the claims of the movements, exposing the problems with the old version that distortion into that ... but we're saying that ... because this is the continuation that the Thatcherite Project began.

John: *Absolutely, absolutely.*

Gail: This is where she wanted to take us. Absolutely. This is it, you know, and it's going on into who knows where, but that breakdown as we're trying to say in all that work –

John: *Yeah.*

Gail: That breakdown of the idea of the social relation, and the imaginaries of that that we're dissing it, you know. Why are we connected to anybody other than our families?

    ...

11

Wendy Larner

Wendy Larner is Provost at Victoria University of Wellington in Aotearoa/New Zealand, having moved from the University of Bristol where she was the Dean of the Faculty of Social Sciences and Law and Professor of Human Geography and Sociology. Her work has explored the shifting dynamics of globalisation, governance and gender and has underpinned a wide range of publications, including *Global Governmentality: Governing International Spaces* (2006, edited with William Walters); *Fashioning Globalisation: New Zealand Design, Working Women and the Cultural Economy* (2013, with Maureen Molloy) and *Assembling Neoliberalism: Expertise, Practices, Subjects* (2017, edited with Vaughan Higgins).

I met Wendy for the first time in 2004 at a conference on Contemporary Governance and the Question of the Social at the University of Alberta (along with the other Wendy, see Chapter Three). We continued our conversations when she moved to the UK at the University of Bristol and I think myself fortunate that, despite her move to New Zealand, we have found ways to carry on talking.

More biographical information is available on the Victoria University of Wellington's Senior Team page: www.victoria.ac.nz/about/governance/senior-leadership.

This conversation was recorded in Edmonton on 6 May 2017, during a Festschrift conference to which we had been invited to celebrate the work of Janine Brodie, Canada Research Chair and Distinguished University Professor in Political Economy and Social Governance at the University of Alberta.

Themes and topics

- Conversations within and beyond disciplines
- Changing institutions
- Unorthodox formations
- On discourse as the practice of articulation

Conversations within and beyond disciplines

Wendy: I presupposed conversations were easier within disciplines, because you had the shared words, the shared go-to references, the shared languages. But I wonder whether for people like you and I, because we are undisciplined, and we sit on the edges, it makes you work harder. So one of the things that I have been thinking about is the reflection that Catherine [Kellogg] made yesterday, which I think characterises both of our works. I think there is something about looking really hard at what is in front of you, and then seeking the language and conceptual registers that help you make sense of that. So what holds us together when we are undisciplined is that we take less for granted, so I think there is a degree of reflexivity around the conversations that isn't there when you are in the disciplines. Now whether that makes the conversations easier or not, I am less sure.

John: *I think that's smarter than me, as usual. I mean, I think undisciplined is just fun, but I think you are right about the taking the pull of the thing you are interested in more seriously, so it doesn't simply become a place where you apply the discipline. So, I mean in the present moment, political scientists are writing books about populism, because that is what they recognise in it. And I think oh yes and all the other stuff, and so I think there is a pull. And it is a pull to have to think and I guess that if there is a thread in most of these conversations, it is about people being willing to think, and I guess one of the joys of hanging out with you over the years has been that willingness, that thinking things are interesting and need attention, rather than hey I am a geographer, I know that that is a place, that is fine, or I am a political scientist and I recognise a populism when I see it. So if that is the case, it puts into problematic question the thing that we were talking about at Janine [Brodie]'s event yesterday and at the dinner with Catherine [Kellogg], which is, is it political science if it doesn't look like political science? I mean, how to move back into disciplines as it were, and remake them. I mean my funny relationship was with social policy, yours has predominantly been with geography, and I am not sure that we quite belong in the same way that Alberta's political scientists do, but there is something about the struggle to also remake disciplinary knowledge, to improve it.*

Wendy: So I, looking from the outside in, suspect that your experience has been a bit like mine. For a long time, for the first two-thirds of my academic career, I felt like I slid down cracks all the time, I never knew where I belonged, and I never felt that I had that premade academic community that disciplinary people have, particularly if you are from dominant intellectual places, where you have large cohorts of people. And as an undisciplined New Zealander, there were two different things at play here.

John: *Doubly out of place!*

Wendy: Doubly! We were laughing about it last night, an undisciplined apparently disrespectful New Zealander! Now what was really interesting for me was when the discipline of geography claimed me, which was what the move to the UK was about. This is going to sound a bit arrogant and I don't mean it to sound arrogant at all, but the opportunities I then had to contribute to the remaking of that discipline, in ways that I never expected or anticipated, because the discipline owned me but still allowed me to be me. They wanted me and they wanted me to do things in disciplinary terms, so the work that was I able to do around early-career academics, the work I was able to do around, for heaven's sake, the Royal Geographical Society, who owned me. One of my fall-over, I can't quite believe this, moments was when I got a phone call asking if I would consider chairing the annual Royal Geographical Society conference the following year. We want you! Me, this undisciplined, disrespectful New Zealander, at the Royal Geographical Society? So disciplines need people like us. I am very clear, just as I am about universities, that disciplines are created by people, which is why I am so invested, as you are, in early-career academics, because they are our futures, and the geography of a decade ago, or a century ago, is not the geography of the next decade and the next century. So how do we create the spaces for the conversations that allow disciplines to be made and remade, because in the end, disciplines, going back to where we started, are no more than a shared conversation where we have some taken-for-granted ways of understanding the world and taken-for-granted methodologies, that have always shifted and changed over time.

...

Changing institutions

Wendy: I am very clear that in a previous generation, at a previous time, someone like me, and this resonates with the bits I know of your story as well, would never have gotten anywhere near a university, let alone anywhere near an elite university. I landed at the University of Bristol, I landed in the bastion of hegemonic geography, in extraordinary ways, and I go back to that panel yesterday that tells me that political science is feminist, queer, indigenised, ethnicised in extraordinarily important and powerful ways these days. So I understand part of my role, as someone who was and had lots of help along the way, and what the tape recorder can't see is me creating elbow room. You create elbow room for other people for whom at a different time and in other places would not have been able to find themselves in the academy because universities remain, and we heard echoes of this yesterday as well, incredibly privileged spaces. Despite all our worries about the contemporary university, we have the amazing privilege of having spaces within which to think, within which to ask hard questions, within which to say the world can be otherwise, and these are the ways in which we might think about this, these are the sorts of things we might do, to nudge that along. So that privilege has to be a privilege that is open to all. I am getting a bit high horse about this, but I feel – I mean this is why I do what I do.

John: *Well I mean, I am going to say dead right, because it is the dull, not-much-discussed politics of the institutional struggle, right, and it was powerfully brought home to me one day, after – and it is not just about getting into the institutions, it is ending up occupying senior positions in them as well. So not long after I was made a professor at the Open University, I was having a conversation with Catherine Hall, and I said I can't take myself seriously as a professor. It is such an unlikely title, and I remember professors, and professors were rather serious, rather tedious, rather dull men, and you have this experience. Catherine is smart, and she said, yes of course I have [that] experience, that is what we all have. But isn't the point to make it look and feel different? Isn't it the point to occupy those spaces not just differently intellectually, but as different embodiments, and ways of conducting.*

[0:13:36]

John: *I mean not just the bodies but the modes of conduct that are associated with them, and I thought this is why I need voices in my head, this is why I need people to tell me that I can think better, because that is right, that is part of other people and yesterday's event was exactly that. It would be easier not to say look, look! There is that table full of complicated women and that is partly because Janine Brodie created the elbow room, didn't just pursue her career, but understood transforming the institutional spaces of possibility. And yes, they are privileged spaces and yes, they are squeezed spaces, and that makes it even harder and more important, simultaneously. I did write notes, I did write notes, because it brings me to – oh it perfectly brings me to the second one, which is one of the things that you have said in at least three different forms, in interventions, over the last few days, and I think it is true about who I think you are, is taking the question of the relational work, of being an intellectual, seriously and I think that is one of the things that … it makes you a pleasure to be around, and in the same way that hanging out with Janine has done, it is the understanding that you don't just think and talk, but you construct relationships through it and to make it possible. So, how did you discover that?*

Wendy: Oh … I have no idea!

John: *Oh good! (Laughs)*

Wendy: So, let me just think a little bit out loud about it. So, like you, I am absolutely convinced that good ideas come from conversations. Some people can just shut themselves in a room, and read their books and have the conversations with themselves, in their heads. I am not one of those people, I don't think I have ever been one of those people. I think better when I think out loud, and when I am able to have conversations, and particularly when I can have exploratory conversations. So I know I was a frustrating graduate student, and I know I was a frustrating early-career academic, because I was always interested in the question of 'how can you think like that?' I remember going to a political theory reading group for a while, and I drove them batty because of course I am not a political theorist and I don't have the kind of normative approach that they have. So, I always wanted to ask the question, so how would that work on the ground? What would that mean for, and for whom? The reading group was around different conceptions of justice. Remember, I am working in bi-cultural New Zealand, where we are trying to work through in almost every register and every site that you can think of, what does it mean to walk the walk around bi-culturalism? And these political theorists were sitting in the room and have an angels-dancing-on-the-head-of-a-pin kind of conversation, which just used to frustrate the hell out of me. I had an early formative experience. I have had the fantastic privilege of meeting and engaging with fantastic people over the years, yourself included. But Richard Le Heron was a senior scholar who cleared space for me in extraordinary kinds of ways. He and I did a really important research project together, and we did that research project by going to a café for a couple of hours a week and talking with each other. And then we would go away and write, and then we would come back together to talk again, and then we would go away to write again. And actually, as I think about it, William Walters, again one of my very early collaborators, we met each other as PhD students, and to this day I think a paper that William and I co-wrote together is one of the best pieces of work I have ever done. We did at a time when we were both in the same city and we did the same thing. We would meet on Thursday afternoon for a couple of hours, we would talk, we would go away, we would do some more reading and then we would come back and talk. The result was we wrote something that both of us are clear that neither of us could have done on our own, and it wasn't just that one and one made two. In that case, it was one and one made three or four or five, actually. But those kinds of conversations have to be with people who are also open to the question of what happens if we think like that. Rather than saying Foucault says or Marx says, going back to the disciplines where you have those taken-for-granted explanations. If you did that you wouldn't have to think in the same way, because you are not trying to ask the hard questions, and then using ideas to explore them. I think you talked about this. Kathy Gibson also talks about being a theory slut, you are promiscuous in terms of the things that you borrow from and then try and work together in order to make sense of what it is that is in front of you, that you are trying to think otherwise about, because the existing explanations of that thing don't give you the purchase that you need or require you to unsee some things about that thing.

...

Unorthodox formations

John: *Well ... you know my long story is cultural studies rescued me,*
Stuart modelled all sorts of good behaviour, I think, but one of
the things that was important for me was that I arrived in cultural
studies also without a discipline, my first degree was a mess, I mean
it was management studies, bits of social sciences, and the only real
bit that got me interested was being taught by a young early-career
researcher about new currents in sociology. As sociology was beginning
to break open in the 1960s, Colin Fletcher gave me a good time,
right, and that rescued me from managerialism and the dullness
of organisational sociology and the rest. But it meant that I didn't
arrive at cultural studies with a disciplinary knowledge to undo, so
it seemed familiar and the great ... I mean lots of people have said
it, but the great thing about early cultural studies in Birmingham
was we were making it up as we went along, and that is wonderful.
People hated us, with good reason for that, but it was a wonderful
experience, because it meant ... I know in the reading groups I was in,
we were reading Marx, Gramsci, Levi-Strauss, Raymond Williams,
Foucault, and in an appallingly unstructured way, and that is what
makes the question that we were talking about earlier, about what is
productive for you becomes a much more central question. Rather than
... even now if I hang out with anthropologists, I am not sure that
I understand. I didn't read Levi-Strauss, in terms of Levi-Strauss'
place in anthropology, I read it because I thought – we all thought –
bricolage was a rather neat idea, that had something to do with cultural
practice. But people occasionally think that I am an anthropologist,
and talk to me about all sorts of things, and I go 'I don't know'. I
have not read that long-contested history of anthropological work, but
... one of the things that I did want to talk to you about is about our
mutual recognition and the conversation and the willingness to push,
because I think having my theory about having friends, and making
friends I think is vitally important. Often – somebody picked on me
about it recently, and said 'but that is just soft, that just means you
are only going out with people who think the same as you, nobody
does critical pushing of you'. And so last night I remember saying to
you, and I remember at the citizen-consumer end-of-project conference,
you talking to me, publicly talking to me, about neoliberalism and
saying no, no, you can't think about neoliberalism without thinking
about its mobility and mutation in place across space. And that is
why you need friends who are geographers! And it seems to me it is
now, in terms of voices in my head, between you and Doreen Massey

and one or two others, it is a … it is a powerful, both disciplining and productive, voice, which is – and I read lots of bits of sociology and political science and economics, every now and then, and I think they oscillate between things being universal, like Putnam talks about modern societies, as if a colonial-settler-slave society like the United States of America is the model of a modern society. And/ or the purely national, right, and what you and Doreen and others have pushed me, and anthropologists sometimes, is thinking about the complexity of place relationally, but powerfully, and avoiding – I don't know, what is it my friend Paul calls it, that you can either have methodological nationalism or you can have methodological globalism, but there is nothing more complicated than that. So, how did you get a geographical imagination?

[0:37:40]

Wendy: … So, this is a story you have heard before. To a certain extent, I have a disciplinary formation, but an unorthodox disciplinary formation. My undergraduate degree in geography was at Waikato University, which geographers may know was an incredibly heterodox department at an incredibly unusual time. In the early 1980s this was a geography department teaching Marxism, Māori geography, feminism and anarchism as core parts of the academic curriculum. And I would name-check people like Ann Magee and Evelyn Stokes in that context. As undergraduate students, we didn't know any better, we thought this was geography. And actually, when I look at where my friends and colleagues from that era went to, we went to all sorts of interesting places, social movements, the unemployed workers union, some of us stayed in academia and did other things. We were politicised, as well as educated, in a rural university in the heartland of conservative New Zealand. Quite extraordinary, it is a bit like the political science department here in the heartland of conservative Alberta … so is that a geographical imagination or is that a political imagination?

John: *Indeed.*

Wendy: … I think the other thing I would talk about is that someone yesterday or in the last couple of days talked about 'following the thing'. I can't remember who they attributed it to, but I didn't know that was where political scientists thought it came from, but there is something about being process orientated and watching something mutate and change. As I began to think about what, at the time, was called economic restructuring, and then morphed into debates about globalisation, and then morphed into discussions about neoliberalism. In the New Zealand context you couldn't think about those processes without thinking about the ways in which ideas and ways of doing things and indeed actors were coming from elsewhere as well as from there. So there might be something about – indeed I know there is something about – small places where you can see things and see connections in ways that are much harder to see in bigger, denser kinds of contexts. When I think back to the 1980s in New Zealand, even though I didn't know them personally I knew that our treasury economists, who at that stage were understood as the culprits in terms of the radical reform programmes going on, I knew they had been US educated, I knew the university departments they had come from, I knew the ideas that they were bringing as new public management was being formed and all sorts of things that are part of that apparatus were being put in place. So, that global sense of place, to use Doreen Massey's term, the idea that things were happening within boundaries, empirically I knew that wasn't the case. So again it is just being true to what you can see happening and really seeing it. There is something about being honest with your seeing, that is not a very good way of putting it. I said this earlier but I do think this is really important, not brushing out of the way the inconvenient things, the things that don't add up, the things that don't make sense, but actually allowing yourself to see those things and then making yourself think hard about them, particularly when they trouble the kinds of explanations you might already have to make sense of what it is you are trying to make sense of. So, being process orientated, and of course this is now in the debates about neoliberalism, as we have moved from discussions of neoliberalism to neoliberalisations, this is the contribution that geography has made to the wider debates. So this is the influence of Doreen Massey, way before I met Doreen herself, with her emphasis on a global sense of place, globalising rather than globalisation, being able to see the ways in which various flows, networks and connections were working in and through the New Zealand context that I was trying to make sense of. Also, and again you have heard me say this many times, the fact that the New Zealand experience didn't make sense in terms of existing explanations about neoliberalism, so that intersection between marketisation and new public management on one hand, and all sorts of progressive things, things like environmentalism, feminism, the Waitangi Tribunal, all sorts of things that were packaged up during the 1980s in New Zealand. All of which required this process, network, flow–based kind of imaginary, to try and make sense of … Sorry, lots of things.

[0:44:07]

John: *No, but wonderfully lots of things. I mean the quick thing is, one of the things that has always struck me as peculiar about social policy was its sense of closure, in geopolitical terms. So the British welfare state was the British welfare state, and there is nothing in the history of social policy analysis in Britain about Britain that thinks Britain was imperial or colonial. How is this possible! And it then triggers all sorts of other things, as a consequence. But the not seeing then is also geographically organised, right, there is something about Britain's both nostalgia for empire and denial of empire, that Paul Gilroy calls 'postcolonial melancholia'. But it's an organising principle, or has been an organising principle, for a lot of British social science I think. The same thing is about the bits that don't fit, and it is I think one of the … oh God, Wendy, joys and frustrations of knowing you, people like you, is the insistence that tidying stuff away, that doesn't fit with the explanation, is the proper work, avoiding saying 'well this neo-liberalism, oh dear', but there is neoliberalism and that seems to me to be the hard bit, the bit that you actually have to think about, because you know it is neoliberalism, so it is not very difficult, you can write another article about it. But actually, that is the only way things occupy the world. They are always in combination, multiplicities, and the difficult question is what difference then do all those bits make? And they make big differences, it seems to me, and we have had these conversations about neoliberalism for as long as I have known you, and mostly it is because from my point of view I am driven crazy by accounts of neoliberalism which don't have any other difficult bits. And then that … and it has occurred again in this conference, because both of us have asked questions about what difference does it make, if you notice the bits that don't add up. And one of the things that really strikes me, and this is going to take us to not quite an argument that I want to have with you, a discussion I want to have with you, but it is about what do you do with mess. So, there is a lot of … science and technology studies, actor network theory, that says attend to the mess. And then they drive me crazy, because they … I mean for all sorts of reasons, but one of them which is, I think, they refuse the challenge of theorising the particular configuration of mess. So, they are incredibly good at drawing maps, grids, pictures of mess, and I am greedy, I want them to do the difficult bit, which is okay how does that hold together? How is that being organised, even as it threatens to come apart? So, given the new book with Vaughan [Higgins,* Assembling Neoliberalism*], why assembling? There is a subtext of … you see I have used it a lot, and I have ended up saying no, I am going to go back to articulation. So why assembling?*

Wendy: So, I am not convinced either. I want to make the mess visible, in part because I want to and in part because I think there is a political purpose to the analytical focus on messiness. This takes us back to where we started our conversation, making visible some of the things that we might be wanting to create new spaces for, open up other ways of thinking about the world. I think in the end for me assembling is descriptive rather than analytical. I think that particularly after having seen the chapters that have come together in that book. Tania [Murray] Li is really important for this conversation, because I think the work she did and that go-to article in *Economy and Society* we all now name-check, that article gave me a methodologically robust way to think not just about the ways in which to use a different kind of language to describe how hegemonic and counter-hegemonic knowledges, actors, understandings, techniques, came together. She also put the academic into the assemblage, to use her language, and I really like that because of that sense that academic work makes a political difference, it allowed me to think harder about that. So for me, that was how assemblage got some analytical purchase. But actually I think I am with you, that question of how things get assembled, how are we going to think about that … rather than just say well look here are all the things that are bouncing around in this context. What are the points of suture? How do things come together? And how does one ask that question rigorously? I think when I think about that book and I think about the work in there, I think assemblage in the end is descriptive rather than analytical.

[0:51:40]

...

On discourse as the practice of articulation

Wendy: One of the reasons why I really like my current university – actually there are lots of reasons why I like my current university – is the emphasis on respect, responsibility, fairness, integrity and empathy. These are the values of my university [Victoria University of Wellington], and I think if we can package academic work in respect, responsibility, fairness, integrity and empathy, and then you need to add intellectual rigour and criticality because the joy of working in New Zealand is that academics are charged by the Education Act to be 'critic and conscience of society'. So I want to think harder about that, but there is something about creating an environment in which we have tough conversations, we have robust conversations, but we have them with respect, responsibility, fairness, integrity and empathy, which means listening hard and asking, to circle around again, how can he think like that, why is he thinking like that? Rather than thinking 'he is wrong'.

John: *Or 'I know where he is coming from'. And I mean, I do think, I think you are right about the practice of that, and I mean I do have a view that even though I am not very good at it, that the listening thing is an absolutely indispensable condition for all of that. But the other is ... is ... is not thinking that because a person uses three words that you know where they are coming from.*

[1:11:51]

Wendy: Absolutely.

John: *That means you borrow some words that you think will be plausible, and you borrow some words that you think are necessary, and you leave out some words that you think might tip it. People ... my early admiration for Margie Wetherell was always about moving the concept of discourse to discursive practice, people make it and that is political, relational work. That is then trying to ... I even went back to my little Bakhtinian phrase, 'people are "heteroglossic"' right, and they work stuff from all sorts of places into what they think will build the connection to you, and that means taking them seriously, not second-guessing them.*

Wendy: Yes and the reason I can do those five values off the top of my head is because I very explicitly name those five values in all sorts of places – discursive practice, this is part of my discursive practice. When I talk to my colleagues, I am trying to constitute something through my discursive practice.

John: *Absolutely. And that … I mean that seems to me to be the exciting bit of thinking about discourses, right, which is they are mobilised, situationally, to produce formations, subjects, possibilities and to close off others, and I mean it is what … I have this memory of an Open University meeting, where it was the first time that I thought about Stuart and articulation as personal practice, right. So we were … and I had known it, but I was … so we were sitting in one of those large faculty groups, arguing about what should go in the next 'Introduction to Social Sciences' interdisciplinary entry point for students. So we talked about all the cutting-edge, exciting, thrilling, funky stuff, at which point the slightly … I don't mean to be nasty about her, the slightly conventional professor of psychology, old-school professor of psychology, said 'but we have to do psychology, because individuals matter'. There was a moment of silence, while I have to say I think 9/10ths of the room were thinking: 'Oh God, not Judith and psychology again! If we sit quietly, will this go away?' And Stuart said 'You are absolutely right, Judith, we can't be doing social science about the contemporary world without having the individual front and centre' – everything that is going on around us works through the question of the individual, whether it is consumption and economic life, whether it is identity, whether it is … and he was … it was the most … I mean non-sexually seductive engagement that I have seen, and then he did the other bit of disarticulation, and said, 'but of course that means we can't fall back on older psychologising models of the individual', and I watched it with absolutely awestruck admiration, because it was, it was how do you … micro, micro, micro, micro level, how do you build an alliance, and that is partly about – what is it Gramsci talks about, making concessions, appropriating the language, but also doing the disconnecting from the other places where you were affiliated, to hold you in place. And that looks like discursive practice to me, and I wish I could … I try. And one of the things that I … love and fear about Stuart, I have this conversation with my friend Larry, who loves Stuart as much as I do, and we say … it is one of those little dances. We say who do you want to be when you grow up? Stuart Hall. Who are you going to fail to be when you grow up? Stuart Hall. And there is … he is both exemplary*

and impossible in almost every way, and I think that is a terrible
thing to have hanging over you! I was going to –

Wendy: But I think this circles us back to the beginning again. It
would be interesting to put him into this conversation as
well, because I think what he would say is you are making
him into the heroic individual.

John: *I know.*

Wendy: I couldn't do what I do and I couldn't say what I say without
those wider conversations that you were part of. Stuart was
having those conversations with you and many others, and
then people like me were sitting reading his work in New
Zealand, and it was allowing us to have conversations as
well. So again this imaginary of academic work, where we
name things and we say that Stuart Hall said that, and the
reverberations of what he said which were so important and
powerful in lots of ways that he might have anticipated, and
lots of ways he could never have anticipated. But I am sure
if he was in this conversation, he too would talk about the
relationality of academic work, that is what his work tells me
that he understood and thought about.

[1:18:42]

John: *You are entirely right, because he did, he would, and both you and*
he would be right, and the fetishisation is a real danger. I know in
other contexts, one of the things that drove me crazy in the immediate
period a few months after his death was people saying 'it's awful,
we miss Stuart's voice in these difficult times, because we all want to
know what Stuart would be saying'. And … I remember somebody,
and I can't quite place who it was, saying, 'No no, no no, none of
us should do that to Stuart. What Stuart did was give us the ways
of thinking about things, and what we should be doing is trying to
think, instead of thinking Stuart should tell us.' And I just thought
that was wonderful, and actually I do think that is true. And that is
without fetishising it, because I think what he tried to practise, and
I have had enough conversations with him where he has said 'and
there are moments where I am not the generous person you think
I am either, where I get bad-tempered and closed, so that is worth
remembering'. But it was always a notion that there are ways in
which we might think together, and we would almost certainly think
better if we thought together.

Wendy: So, I am sitting here wondering about insider outsiders, or outsider insiders. If you are an insider outsider, or an outsider insider, if you are for whatever reason ambivalently positioned vis-à-vis the places of academic power, whatever those might look like, does that then have something to do with this predilection for relational academic work? Now the conversation I have been having with myself, which I am now going to have with you, is that I think it does, but only if there is some sense of being okay with your insider outsider status. Because otherwise you would be busy trying to make yourself an insider. I think you can only be relational, do the kind of relational academic work that we are talking about if – and I know all academics have deep insecurities, and I am sure you and I have them as well – but there is something about being comfortable enough in your own skin to say 'this is what I know and this is how I think and I am going to think out loud with you about this'.

John: *Oh yes.*

Wendy: So I can see the contradictions in what I am saying, and I would be interested to hear what you think – because you have talked about being a working-class lad and what that means, and how that shaped and what cultural studies allowed, in terms of insider outsiders, and the kinds of conversations you then had. I don't know, does that fit into this?

John: *Well I mean, at a … biographical 'personal is politicised' sort of level, it certainly does. And I think it does so in a … I want to end with a contradiction, because I think there is something in there that is … at least paradoxical if not contrary. I think I have lived off … I mean almost entirely lived off insider outsider-ish-ness. One is about class and place, I am not just a working-class lad, I am a Northern working-class lad. I am one of what Richard Hoggart called the 'grammar school boys', that tiny window where clever working-class boys, more working-class boys than working-class girls, got enrolled into the briefly expanding middle classes, through grammar school education. And that was an ambivalent experience too. And then cultural studies, which at least then and still to some extent, was an insider outsider formation, and so was thrilling and explains why I think everybody, not everybody, large numbers of people in the established disciplines were so irritated by us. I cannot tell you the number of times in print, in person, we were shouted at, by people who said 'this is just stupid, this is just stupid, stop it, go away'. But then there is … my teaching life has been first in a polytechnic,*

with sort of working-class teachers teaching working-class young people. So a marginal, not 'properly' academic space. And then the Open University, which was in part a joy because everybody said it is not a real university, to which the answer is 'Yes, we are not a real university, we are better than that!' And so in all sorts of ways, and my relationship to social policy was always ... if I am in social policy, I am from cultural studies. When I am at cultural studies conferences, I insist on ... I once did a keynote which was entirely about the etiquette of talking statistical data at a cultural studies conference. So, and there are ... there are both joys but there are material conditions of possibility about that peculiar relation, peculiar position, in the field of relations. And ... the paradox is of a peculiar ... and I have always thought about cultural studies but I think it is true more generally, which is ... I am saying it about me rather than about anybody else, Wendy, it produces a certain mode of self-confident assertiveness, and in my cultural studies life it was often lived and experienced as arrogance, 'we are smarter than you, we know stuff that you don't know, we have come to tell you ...', but I think for me, around cultural studies and social policy for example, it was always what I can bring disrupts what you think you know.
...

[1:38:29]

John: *If you are going to have a conversation, there is a difference between a conversation and a shouting match. The conversation is about ... invites people who have things in common, but they are not the same. So that there are things to explore. I have been to a couple of grim events at the Open University, where invited speakers have told us things, and one of the things that depresses me most about my life is people telling me what they know, in that definitive ... why would you talk back to them, because they already know all there is to know? So I think ... and I think it means that the conversation is both a metaphor and a practice.*

Wendy: Yes, absolutely.

John: *And I like talking enough that I think the practice is ... and it is one of the reasons why this project exists, which is it has given me a plausible ... it is a bit like your little emails from New Zealand, it has given me a plausible way of writing to people I like, think with, and say would you sit down and talk to me for a while? If we could be in the same place, it is wonderful, and apart from a ... I am not going to cry about this, apart from the ones who have gone missing, it is ... it is wonderful and it is wonderful because it materialises the metaphor. It materialises both metaphors, it materialises conversation, as a proper form of intellectual and personal practice, but it also materialises the voices in my head, and that … in this bizarre moment, one of the other interviews is going to be with Fiona Williams. It is not an interview, the conversation is going to be with Fiona Williams, and I went to Fiona's retirement conference, and you realise what a big deal retirement conferences are. So I stood up and I said well Fiona … love her to bits, great, fabulous intellectual, but most importantly she is one of the voices in my head. And when Fiona got to talk, she said, 'I am very worried about John! He has these voices in his head! And I can't think that is right!' They sit on my shoulder and I just think it is part of the … it is part of the unacknowledged, or not visible, because I mean, students read us singly, sometimes with collaborators and sometimes … but they read us singly and so it looks like a piece of work that has come out of your head and fingertips. And part of a purpose of this is to expose the social relations of thinking.*

Wendy: Which is fantastic, absolutely fantastic.

John: *At this point, is there anything that you thought we should talk about that we haven't?*

Wendy: So what I want to say for the record, and I know that you will do what you want to do with the transcript of this, but one of the things that I and many others actually know about you, John, is your incredible intellectual generosity. So there is something about the space that you created both for those of us who … you always understood about the imperial past of the UK, you always understood about being on a small island and it was actually only a small island, rather than a great island! But also the incredible generosity that you show with those early-career folks and those PhD students, so that practice that we have been exploring over the last while, the way in which you have modelled that for others and the incredible sense of openness with which you inhabit the academy is extraordinary, and I would want to see this find its way into … because the conversations you have in your head aren't just with the big boys and girls. You have conversations, both in your head and in person, with all sorts of people, because there are all sorts of people who have interesting things to say! And you know that!

John: *Oh God yes, and I mean it is … one of the … one of the missing bits of the story is Central European University, so I go for a few weeks each year, I get a few students who are students in my class, but I also take part in the PhD student colloquia, so there are people that I have seen developing their work over two or three years. And one of the deals I have with folk is that if they want to talk about what they are working ... people in my class or the others, we could go to – central Budapest has beautiful coffee shops – so we could go to a coffee shop and sit and talk. And if they come and talk, I will buy the coffee. And there is this really odd exchange that goes on, it is a bit like what you and I have said to Catherine and the conference organisers, which is students say it is really wonderful of you to give up your time to have this conversation. And I look at them in disbelief and say no, the consequences of this conversation is that you have (a) told me stuff that I have no idea about, and (b) you have made me think about it. And it does seem to me that ... I mean it might be an act of generosity, but it is one that is profoundly based in complicated asymmetric reciprocities ... Dear God, I know people who have told me about the modes of management knowledge in state industries, in pre-Soviet-break-up Romania. And I think this is astonishing, right, my friend Alina [Alina-Sandra Cucu] has a beautiful paper about managers as ethnographers, because it is the only way they could know about what was going on ...*[1]

---

[1]   Alina-Sandra Cucu, 'Producing knowledge in productive spaces: ethnography and planning in early socialist Romania', *Economy and Society*, 2014, 43 (2): 211–232.

12

Janet Newman

Janet Newman is a Professor Emerita in Social Policy at the Open University. After a career working in local government, she reinvented herself as an academic, working at the universities of Aston, Coventry and Birmingham before moving to the Open University. Her work has explored different configurations of gender, governing, politics and power. Her publications include *The Managerial State: Power, Politics and Ideology in the Remaking of Social Welfare* (1997, with John Clarke); *Modernising Governance* (2001); *Publics, Politics and Power: Remaking the Public in Public Services* (2009, with John Clarke) and *Working the Spaces of Power: Activism, Neoliberalism and Gendered Labour* (2012).

I first met Janet when we were both tutoring an Open University (OU) summer school at the University of East Anglia and we continued to meet occasionally through the OU. We began a more personal relationship in 1986 and moved towards doing work together, publishing our first co-authored piece (on the new managerialism) in 1993. We have continued to find things to work on, during our time at the Open University and even into our shared retirement.

More details can be found at: www.open.ac.uk/people/jen79.

This final conversation was recorded in Shropshire on 27 January 2018.

Themes and topics

- On collaboration
- The pessimism of critique
- The Marxism and feminism thing
- Looking for the current moment
- Between collaborative and dialogic processes

On collaboration

John: *Okay, so let me start with the writing together issue. So, for more than 20 years now we have been writing together, and I just wanted to ask you about what difference it makes, writing with somebody, rather than writing alone?*

Janet: It makes an immense difference, but we have written together in many different ways, so I think that is one of the things I find most interesting, the different phases we have been through, and the different kinds of engagement we have had in the writing process. Because originally you were the academic and I was the PhD student, having come out of practice, so I wasn't a writer, and you were, already. So, in the early [days] you wrote most and I wrote a bit, but I contributed a lot. (Laughs) So, the thing about *The Managerial State*, which was the first substantial thing we wrote together, I always remember that bottle of wine and the sitting down talking about the principles that were going to inform the book, which came from me mostly, the idea that we should do that. So, my contributions have been different over time, and it has been great having you, because you are so good. (Laughs) But then, sometimes I have [led the writing], sometimes you, sometimes we talk and then write separately and try to join it up. Sometimes I do drafts when you are away, and that is harder, because you come back and think, 'Why has she written that, it is rubbish?' So, if you are distant, it makes it harder to write together, [because] I just write with the imaginary you, rather than the real you.

John: *Right. Is the imaginary me much nicer?*

Janet: Yes. (Laughs) Well, it's different, because I find it difficult to write together with you unless we have talked it through first, unless I am leading on something. And, what interests me is the way in which it has not been very structured. Like, with everybody else I have written with we do, 'I do the first draft, you do the second draft,' or 'Let's work it up in thought, and then go away and write it,' so it has been much more structured. Whereas with you it flows much more.

John: *Right. Well, I mean I think that is partly because it is sort of, in the everyday life, so I think it becomes easier to make it flow. I mean, I don't think it just flows organically, I think it is easier to make it flow. But, it is also I think something to do with, what seem to me*

*to be good habits that we have developed, of being willing to let it
flow, and thinking that things will come out all right.*

Janet: And, they do.

John: *Whereas I think often that the structured planning is the sort of,
slightly careful device for saying, 'We have not done this together
before, how might we go about doing it?' Whereas, I think from* The
Managerial State *onwards, there has been a sense that it might go
round and round and round a bit, and it might not be the thing that
we first thought of … But that it will come out.*

Janet: Yes.

John: *And, that is rather nice.*

Janet: It is.

John: *I mean, one of the things that you have just reminded me of is that,
as a form of thinking together, it is a process in which we typically
bring different things to the starting point.*

Janet: Absolutely. That is one of the big things I have been thinking
about, because it is about difference and intimacy, conjoined
somehow. And that is really weird. (Laughs) So, I am very
aware of the differences that we have come from. So,
difference in [you being an] established academic, me a PhD
student, me coming out of practice, so me coming out of (a)
being politically active and (b) working in local government
for 20 years, and then carrying on engaging with practice …
[You] were more theoretically sophisticated than me, and you
still are because you do conjunctural analysis at the drop of
a hat, and I have to think about it a lot. But the differences
have been productive, I think.

[0:05:09]

John: *I do, too … It does seem to me that part of that dynamic, and I don't
think I read it in quite the same terms as you do, but part of that
dynamic has been about you opening things up for me, and making
me think, not just that they were important, because you know, they
would be, but that they were worth my and our collective attention.
So, I don't think* The Managerial State *would have existed were
it not for your trajectory. So, it is not just about you coming from
practice, and having a practitioner focus. It was partly a way of saying,
'There are things that are going on here that matter, and that are
graspable, in the sorts of terms in which we loosely think.'*

Janet: Yeah.

John: *And, it's not that I didn't think managerialism was significant and important, because there was enough of it in my working life for it to be visible, but I think you dragged me into thinking more carefully both about ... the reform, restructuring of public services on a grander scale. So, I mean there's other things to come back to, but it does seem to me that the differences have been generative, and they are not just differences of who thinks what.*

Janet: Yeah, I think that is right. And, I think, I don't want to set up a practice/theory thing, because one of the big moments of my trajectory was the Women and Work Programme, where I had to teach a subject that I had never [studied] – organisational theory. And they just kept saying, 'That is wrong, that is wrong.' And so, building theories out of the experience in the classroom, or the workshop, or the seminar, or whatever, was wonderful. So, it's something I carried on through my work at Birmingham on the Public Service MBA and MSc, of just having people bring their experience, and their pain, and their anxieties, and their perceptions, and their insights, and trying to help them make sense of it through frameworks I could offer, or frameworks we built together, and then me going away and writing about it. And that has been brilliant, and I miss it, because I don't have that anymore. I got it a bit from the *Spaces of Power* book, because that was talking to practitioners and activists, so that was more political actually, more theoretical, more theoretically driven. But that was the last time I have done it really, and it is sad, I miss it.

John: *Well, it does seem to me it is the equivalent, and it is a complicated equivalent I am sure, but it is the equivalent of what other people in these conversations have talked about as 'the ethnographic moment'.*

Janet: Yes.

John: *You need the sense of how people inhabit the present to work with, rather than ... and there is that thing about, you know, the difficulties of turning up and telling people what their lives are like, and them saying, 'Mmm no'. And that does seem to me to be a healthy moment for doing analysis really.*

Janet: Yeah. But, I have also enjoyed thinking with you, so one of the other key things has been the walking notebook as a token of our relationship, because when we are writing together, we may not actually write together, but we think together.

[0:09:35]

Janet: And, I think when I am walking. We have done a lot of walking in our lives, and I have carried notebooks and had to stop on a rock to write things down, and then go home and write it, and that has been wonderful.

John: *I agree, and I think that the walking, talking, thinking thing has been a sort of constant thread. I mean, what we talk about and think about may change, but that sense of ambling around both physically and mentally has been really productive. And I think there is something about that as a way of, I don't know, taking the thinking bit out of the everyday, slightly out of sitting in a room with notebooks open saying … and the walking … enabled a more expansive version of that, and I still remember walking over the moor in Teesdale, having a long argument about the relationship between state theory and governmentality theory.*

(Janet laughs)

John: *And I just think it was productive for what we were actually doing, but as an experience it condensed a lot of things about our differences, and about being able to work through them. Because, it seems to me even now, 20-odd years on, we are not quite at the point where we don't have differences, and that still feels productive rather than difficult.*

Janet: … I just wanted to say what I get from you, because I just wanted to do a big appreciation. I don't think I am going to talk about it much, but an appreciation of the collaborative relationship with you, because it has been brilliant you know, it really has, because you help me think, in fact you taught me how to think in the Open University units you have written, and you helped knit it together. I have got all these fragments of things that I am worried about, or thinking about, or have read about, or picked up in a newspaper, and we talk about it, and it helps it make sense.

John: *I am both delighted and appalled to turn out to be a knitter. (Laughs) The 'terrible knitters of Dent' are in my head …[1] But, that sense of that dynamic, I think, is interesting. Because I experience it slightly*

---

[1]   We have often visited the village of Dent in the Yorkshire Dales and I have a strong memory of a bit of its history. Women in the village were known for knitting in a fast and furious style that earned them the epithet, 'The Terrible Knitters of Dent' (see, for example, https://rovingcrafters.com/2015/11/05/the-terrible-knitters-of-dent/).

differently, which is I think you enable, encourage, and sometimes even force me to think about things that I won't have thought about. And so I don't know what the opposite of knitting is, unravelling, I think. And one of the things you do is keep my tendency to rush to close things off, you keep it open. So, I think there is a real dynamic there that matters, and it matters because it does stop those easy shortcuts of thinking that you know what the thing is, and you know how to deal with it. And one of the things that runs through the different things we have done is I think, that sense of both opening it up for one another, but opening it up in the practice of writing about it, of saying, 'Well, actually it can't be as simple as that. It isn't as simple as that, and the ways in which it's not simple matter.' And I do think there is something important about that, because it is not just about saying, 'It is more complicated than that,' in that well-known fashion, but it is saying that actually the complications matter ...

The pessimism of critique

Janet: ... I think one of the things that ... I think there is a dynamic about optimism, pessimism, and critique versus hope, that you ... not you, but there is a temptation for theorists to close things down and say, 'There we are, that's it then, closed.' It is all awful, whether it is governmentality, or managerialism, or consumerism, or anything really. And I have really struggled with that, and been quite vocal about it in more recent talks and writing, because I think that as soon as I talk to activists or practitioners, I don't know what to call them. ... It feels different, because people struggle with stuff, and make sense of it, and come out through it. And they get depressed, and anxious, and sick, but they also come back and do things, and that practical politics, the ability of people to shape things out of the everyday life to the sense of 'There is a future,' really matters to me. And it is, in your terms it is the emergent, but the emergent always feels a bit residual in the writing. (Laughs)

[0:15:28]

John: *Well, I think most academic work, including mine, needs to think that it is saying something that people don't already know. And so there is, I think, a tension between wanting, even in the spirit of sort of, goodwill, to be attentive to how people think about things, and act on things, and succumb to things, and fight back against things, and wanting to say, 'Yeah, and there is more than that.'*

Janet: Yes.

John: *And it does seem to me that that is a site of strain, and I think, I mean, we should talk about the critique point in a moment. But I do think that it is one of the things that you have held onto, and it is one of the things that I at least believe rhetorically, I think you are better at holding onto it in practice than I am. But I think, at least as a position, I think beginning and ending with the system works and the system wins is not even critical work, it is just depressing projection.*

Janet: But, nor do I like the six pages of awful analysis, and then resistance in the last paragraph. I think there is a binary at the moment between those who write about how awful everything is, and those who talk about the flowering of new movements. And that dynamic is hardest in the work on the state that we currently do, because I can't see anything optimistic about writing about the state, but there you go, figure that out.

John: *I think, I mean for me it seems that there is a tension between, because I think the divide between writing depressive criticism and writing about the flowering of new things is a distinction that can't and probably shouldn't be sustained, right? ... Because, I think wandering around saying, 'No, things aren't so bad, people are always struggling,' requires the response, 'Well, yeah but actually, things keep on being bad.'*

Janet: Yeah.

John: *And sometimes they get worse.*

Janet: Yeah.

John: *So, you know, there is a need for critical analytics which says, 'Well, why are things bad? And, how have they got like this?' despite, or alongside, but the difficulty seems to me, to be threading those things together.*

Janet: Absolutely, I agree (laughs) ... When I talked about the politics of hope, I do so because I think if we just write depressive stuff, there is no space for thinking.

John: *But I think the difficulty is to find the register in which to, not just gesturally, and not just sort of, the last paragraph taking account of ... but, how do we understand the dynamic relationship between, you know, the capacity of systems, and structures, and systems of power and the rest, to keep on making themselves, and reproducing themselves, and exercising control? Because, I am fairly depressed at the moment. And, yet knowing that not everybody believes, not everybody succumbs, not everything is closed down. And that is, I don't know, that seems to me to be the defining problem of how to write critically now.*

[0:20:00]

Janet: It is. And, one of the things that I have appreciated is you always write about what is currently going on, whether managerialism, or consumerism, or I did more on the Blair moment than you did, but you just shouted at me for what I had written. (Laughs)

John: *Yes, I think that is better coded as disagreement, myself.*

Janet: And austerity, and populism, and expertise. So, we have always tracked … conjuncture spotting is probably what you would call it, but …

John: *Well, only in a self-aggrandising way. I do think there is something about trying to get to grips with the forms in which power and inequality and knowledge, ways of thinking, are working out in the present moment. But I am going to push that a bit, because at a workshop I was at late last year, one of the members of the audience for a series of papers said, 'Aren't you just dealing with ephemera, rather than the stuff that really matters?' and I am both appalled by the question, and take it seriously. How do you know why the thing that you want to look at matters?*

Janet: Yeah, presumably he was a Structuralist Marxist?

John: *He was indeed. And, so there is a problem. All those questions about the 'fundamental' … but there is still a question about, 'Well, am I looking at this because I think it is interesting, or because I think it matters?'*

Janet: Only you know that, but I think it is because it matters. So, this takes me back to the Marxism and feminism thing really, I think.

The Marxism and feminism thing

John: *Go on then.*

Janet: Because the things that feminists have been interested in, Marxists have always said would be ephemera. And, I mean I don't want to paint this too starkly, because you are a funny sort of Marxist, and I was a funny sort of feminist. I am not just interested in women, but the stuff that has come out of the

Women's Movement about personal–political, the intimate and institutional, you know those dynamic relationships, and the relationality of life, and thinking of power as not one dimensional. So, all of those things are things that I have brought, if you like, to the table that we are sitting at. But it was quite hard early on to make space for those, I think, in our conversation and writing. I mean, not very hard, because back in *The Managerial State* you were always interested in the social settlement and its fracturing, and images of the family and so on, so you got it. But I still felt I was coming from somewhere different in the fundamental questions I was asking. But I have got more Marxist as time has gone on. Did you experience it as coming from different places, because I did?

John: *I am not sure about different places. I think I experienced it as coming with different questions, and different problems. But it seems to me that has been part of the productive dynamic tension which is, if I thought the same as you, if you thought the same as me, the conversations would be relatively brief.*

Janet: But haven't we collapsed the differences over time?

John: *No, I think we have collapsed some of the differences, but I think other ones have emerged.*

Janet: Oh, tell me.

John: *Well, I think we have an unresolved tension around some of the work on critique. So even now I am not entirely convinced by the wish to substitute something called criticality, in place of critique.*

Janet: Why?

John: *Because, I think it has a one-dimensional view of critique. But I am also, and let me connect it up, because associated with that, I think, is a rather strange version of a power–knowledge [linkage] which says, 'All ways of thinking and knowing make the world,' and this is a disagreement that we have had on and off. And I think that it may be true that all ways of knowing try to make the world, but some of them are more successful than others. And I think that bit is missing from some of the resources on which you draw, because I think it is too flat. So, I think there are still sites of you know, not, I mean disagreement is too strong, argument, conversation, discussion, because we carry on talking about it.*

[0:25:32]

Janet: Interesting.

John: *Not very, apparently.*

Janet: (Laughs) Well, it goes back to, one of the questions is, 'Who are we writing for? Who are we talking to? Who is the audience for what we do?' And I have always got people who are trying to make the world on my shoulder, and I have always got the women in the Women and Work Programme, or the practitioners on the other programmes I have taught saying, 'What is this for?' and, 'Can I understand this? Can I engage with this?' So, giving people space to think that the way they think can help make the world, has been important to me. But I agree that it is not a theory, it is not a perspective that I want to hold on to … Or, perhaps I do.

          …

Looking for the current moment

Janet: And, the sense of loss that you are writing about now, is the loss of different things. And, I mean, I am currently thinking about other things, I am currently thinking about … so, going back to your ephemera point, I am thinking about the awful stuff around women and power, Me Too [and Black Lives Matter]. And now the fight against the President's Club, and the exploitation of women there, and everything shutting down, and people being horrified, and wondering whether that is an ephemeral moment, or if it is significant. So, it needs a conjunctural analysis of what are the forces that are coming together. So, the capacity of subordinated groups to speak back to power, and to stop things, seems to me to be very, very interesting, but I don't believe that it is going to necessarily alter the deep structures of gender inequality, and I really don't know how to analyse that.

John: *Well, I think you are right. That is a question that requires something like conjunctural analysis, because it is, I mean it is classically a moment in which a whole number of things have come together and they are not a single movement you know, but in which people who have lived subordinate positions are saying, 'Well, no,' and so it is a moment in which, I mean I think you are right to say it, that there is something about both race and gender, that are being visibly contested as well as restorationist retrenchment on the part of those who hold the power, that are in play in the present moment. And, the stuff about, you know, sexual harassment and violence, all going on alongside, and this is what I think conjunctural analysis demands that you struggle with, is, in Britain, in England, is the collapse of a series of rape trials because the Crown Prosecution Service can't manage evidence properly. So, we are against sexual harassment, but we can't organise a criminal justice system that can deliver proper outcomes. So, I think all of those, and I think one of the things that conjunctural analysis should tell us is, 'And, we won't know, and we won't know because it is about what action does to structures and systems.'*

Janet: Yeah. And, there is other things that I thought have been pivotal moments, and I can't tell whether they are going to make a big difference or not. Like, Grenfell Tower is a big one, because it sort of challenges the whole privatisation and contracting, sub-contracting power thing. It challenges the silencing of people who live in shit houses. And they have spoken back. And it seemed to be big, and it seemed to rock a lot of things, including Kensington and Chelsea [Borough Council], and the prime minister, and feeling-less government, but it has made no difference in the end.[2] Or, has it?

John: *Well, I don't know. I think the question is, when the end is? So, like you I thought it was a big moment, so I think there is a question about where the end might be. I thought the Grenfell Tower fire was a sort of crystallising moment, coming as it did so soon after the 2017 election, and the mobilisation of, you know, different constituencies, including the subordinated, the excluded, and the young in new ways. And the Grenfell Tower fire looked like, I mean both the symbolic moment of the culmination of all those bad trends and tendencies about growing inequality, about the degradation of public services, about the degradation of social housing and the demonisation of those who lived in it, and you know, politicians who had no interest in the people that they nominally represented. So, it looked like the culmination, and I think you are right, that it's not for want of trying, but it has gone quieter. It has been moved away from the centre of attention. And one of the things about the question about ephemera is the capacity of those currently in power to declare closure, to move things off the agenda, and I have to say, to be overtaken by new crisis. So, the Grenfell Tower fire is 2017, the Carillion collapse*

---

[2]   At the time of writing, the Inquiry into the fire at Grenfell Tower in the London Borough of Kensington and Chelsea that killed 72 people was continuing. The fire occurred on 14 June 2017; the Inquiry began its work, not without controversy, on 14 September 2017.

of the PFI model of public service provision is the 2018 [crisis].[3] It might be the beginning of the end, sort of thing, and they're perverse moments of horror and hope bundled together ... but, I think you know, those in power have the capacity to try and move things on, but I think they are also increasingly overtaken by the next crisis that they apparently can't see coming. And my prediction about the next one is, well the President's Club is one thing, but the next will be, I think, deaths within the National Health Service, because the sense of strain there is so evident. And the problem is the accumulation of 'And thens', and do they actually accumulate, or are they just a series of one-offs? And I don't know at the moment.

[0:42:15]

Janet: One of the things that I really liked about *The Managerial State*, I keep going back to that, I don't know why ... was the idea of social settlements, and economic settlements, and political settlements. And it seems to me that nothing was settled, but it must be because we still keep on going. The government does function, and people go to work, or not. And the economy isn't working, and yet it does. Society isn't working, and yet it does. And I think the fractures around Brexit have been very, very damaging to any idea of settlement, the eruptions of race and now gender have been really damaging, and what I don't know is whether there is the capacity to shape a new social settlement out of all that, and presumably you can't know that until you know what is happening in the political, and the economic, and the cultural.

John: *I think that is true, because they intersect in peculiar ways. But one of the things you said, which I think is really interesting, is the economy doesn't work, but it does. And society doesn't work, but it does. And I think part of it would be, I mean if we were going to sit down and write about it, would be to take the two centres of both of those words. So, there is an economy, really? And it works or doesn't work. Well, that is interesting, because it clearly doesn't*

---

[3]   Carillion plc was a UK-based construction and facilities management corporation that went into liquidation in January 2018 while extensively involved in Private Finance Initiative (PFI) and other outsourcing work for the UK government. The scale of the liquidation and its consequences for workers, suppliers, ongoing projects and pensioners was enormous. Carillion's collapse raised questions not just about the company's management but also about the PFI process and the efficiency of financial auditing as a regulatory mechanism.

work for most of the people, and I mean, the long stall of wages, the increasing precarity of forms of employment, the degradation of work itself, it doesn't work. On the other hand, it is distributing profits on a regular basis, and there is the question about: [works] for whom? And then the same is true about society. One model of social organisation doesn't look as though it is working, but it is delivering enough for enough people to say, 'Oh well, we can get on with things.' And that seems to me to be what makes the present interesting and dangerous, because the different sorts of investment in keeping things going might be worth thinking about. But the other is that Brexit demonstrates, I mean not just the obvious stuff, but all the different, I mean, all we know is what we have read about it, and it is all the different sorts of disaffection that are around, and I think it would be wrong to assume that the remain voters were happy, content idiots, because I don't think that was true either.

...

Janet: Well, I don't have empirical work anymore, and that is a loss. My best work was when I was interviewing 60 women for the *Spaces of Power* book, because that wasn't a research project, but it offered an empirical richness which enabled me to build theories about different things, whether it was community, or policy, or the state, or the academy. And that was wonderful, and I miss being able to do it.

John: *Well, I think that is true for me too, which is, you know, I mean I have been kept alive by friends who have involved me in their research projects, from Jenny Ozga to Morag McDermont. But the interesting thing, of course, is that our work on Brexit came not through any of those, but through an 'Oh dear God' moment, which is, you know, the collective therapy of trying to think about it, talk about it, and write about it. And from time to time I think, 'I might know enough, I might not know enough to write about it.' And then I write something, and I read other people's and I think, 'I am not sure that you know enough, either.'*

Janet: Is that a kind of collaboration, when you come across people that make you think in a different way?

[01:09:05]

John: *It is, and I think, I mean there is a double dynamic I think, which is about reading people and thinking, 'Ooh, I hadn't thought about that,' or, 'I had thought about that, but actually you have made it come alive,' so it moves from being a footnote to a sort of, central thing to worry about. But it is also about saying, 'No, I don't recognise that, I don't think that is sustainable, I don't think that will do.' And that seems to me to be the double movement of thinking, which is sometimes you think with people, and sometimes you think against them, and the problem is that it is very easy for me, and let me be clear about this, it is very easy for me to turn the 'against' into hardened-up, grimly defended, definitive positions, and I think the good sense of a lot of my friends is to say, 'You might need to think again about that.'*

Janet: I don't think that is something I have learned from you. I have resisted it.

John: *Well, I think you have. I think you are less prone to erecting definitive statements, though I would say that I have seen you do it.*

Between collaborative and dialogic processes

Janet: The other thing that that has just provoked in me, and thinking back to the *Spaces of Power* book, is the relationship between dialogic and collaborative. Because where I have worked with groups of students to develop something, or when I have interviewed women for the book, it has been a very dialogic process, because the meaning is made in the interactive process, even though I am coming with the questions and I have the power to structure the answers, there is something dialogic about the process. But it is not collaborative, because it has never been the co-production of a piece of work, and I have never managed to write it in a way that people will, the people that I have talked to, will value, because it is always too abstract and theorised by then. And that has been a tension for me, trying to think about speaking back to the people that I have worked with who have given me things, but not being able to do it. And I don't think one can co-produce, and I have never been a fan of co-production in the sense that that is now a public service thing, but there is something about not being able to collaborate with the people who give me so much when I talk to them, not be able to give back.

John: *I recognise that as a problem, and as a source of discomfort, but I have to say I think, I mean I think you are right about the problems of thinking this in terms of co-production, because it thinks that co-production is a matter of simultaneity, that you do this together, now. Whereas, it seems to me one of the things, especially about your work, it has a much more long, drawn-out and looped quality, so if*

I think about things that you in particular have done around public services, and practitioners, and activists, it is that you have taken dialogically lots of things from the field, the site.

Janet: We are going to get back to stitching, aren't we? (Laughs)

John: *No, not even stitching, nor knitting. And you have worked on it, and developed it into something else, into an account, an analysis, and then you have taken it back in the form of writing and talking, and one of the things that I know people think, because they have told me it, is that is really important, 'what you have given me is a way of thinking, a way of feeling, and a way of trying to be in this site, in this field'. So, when I was invited, as I was last year, to go to Canada to do some talks, one of the things that happened was, the person who invited me said, 'Would Janet be willing to come as well, because our students read a lot of her, and find her incredibly important and useful?' And it does seem to me that that is a different, I mean that is a stretched version of what collaboration might be, which is learning, and polishing, and developing things from somewhere and taking them to somewhere else, and people saying, 'That helps.'*

Janet: I remember that, yeah. It was wonderful. I remember the decade of summer schools I did, which took things I had been writing or thinking about, from encounters with people like them, and from reading, and from writing. And I was always the first lecturer, and I was always the lecturer that set the scene for the whole thing, much like you do now. And it was wonderful, because people just love it.

John: *Well, I am glad that you get stroked in that form, but I think the question about what they love is then really important, because I think that you know, over the years I have heard lots of people say, 'That spoke directly to how I feel, it allowed me to make sense of the position, state, I was in, we were in,' because it is both individual and collective. And I think it is one of the things that has been a consistent thing in terms of people's responses to your stuff about managerialism, about public services, about publicness, and finally about activism. Because, I mean you know, the response to* Spaces of Power *is people saying, 'You could have interviewed me, that could have been my story.'*

[01:16:11]

Janet: Well, loads of people, yeah.

John: *And so, one of the things that good writing does is to forge those connections.*

Afterword

This short chapter is deliberately called an afterword rather than a conclusion as it's difficult to see how the diverse and shifting discussions captured in the preceding chapters could lead to anything as definitive sounding as a conclusion. Indeed, that would, I feel, miss the whole point of the enterprise. So instead, this is an opportunity to reflect on the processes and relationships that underpin the book and which were the conditions for starting the project in the first place. So, not a conclusion but instead some thoughts about the pleasures and possibilities – and even problems – of thinking together.

I want to celebrate what a joyous project this has been. I have been fortunate in finding people willing to sit down with me and think conversationally, in open-ended ways. In the process, we have explored arguments, exchanged experiences and reactions to them. The 12 interlocutors have explored changing contexts and the angles from which they might be viewed and analysed. They have, even more than I had hoped, been generous with both their time and thoughts. Sometimes these connections were familiar (working at the Open University in course teams), sometimes they were familiar but forgotten (did we really have that argument then?). More often, they involved working across different experiences and locations (spatial and disciplinary) through which we had arrived at the possibility of thinking together. Sometimes the conversations were comfortably familiar – where this dialogue emerges from and circles around established conversations (albeit with the slight strangeness of a recorder on the table). At other points, however, people told me about experiences and encounters that I had not heard before but that clearly shaped their engagement with critical thinking. And, at many moments, these conversations forced me to stop and think again – which is, I hope, one of the recurring themes of the book. The 'turbulent times' of the sub-title (which have got considerably more turbulent since I started these conversations in March 2013) demand that we keep thinking.

What struck me forcefully as I listened to the recordings of these conversation was not so much the intellectual richness of their content (though I am quite impressed by that too) but the amount of laughter that can be heard, such that laughing feels like an integral part of the pleasures of talking together. Larry Grossberg helpfully reminded me that there are many kinds of laughter – and I think these conversations reveal many of them. There is laughter of recognition, of revelation, and of reinforcement. There is laughter that expresses delight, that emerges from being disconcerted and, most strikingly, that results from a moment of discovery. This is not the place to develop a classification system for types of laughter, but I am delighted that there is so much of it woven through these encounters, not least because it captures my sense of pleasure in having these people to talk with.

As I argued in the Introduction, this project was intended as an antidote to two frustrating tendencies in academic life. The first is that thinking 'critically' is generally understood as thinking *against*. It emphasises, perhaps even celebrates, the capacity to deconstruct an argument, to lay bare its logical, conceptual and empirical failings and, in the process, to imply the superiority of one's own way of thinking and analysing. I am not thinking of giving up this mode of being critical, certainly not in a world, and in an academic world, where things that are worthy of criticism continue to proliferate. Yet, by itself, this critical disposition misses something else – the sense of thinking with, as well as against. This process of thinking with applies to both texts and talk, albeit in slightly different ways. This is, as I suggested in the Introduction, one of Stuart Hall's great gifts and it is the quality that David Scott's book about *Stuart Hall's Voice* rightly celebrates, suggesting that this dialogic style involves and evokes an 'ethics of receptive generosity' (Scott, 2017). It is, I hope, a quality that is visible/audible in the dialogues that make up this book – expressed in a willingness to listen, question, explore and think again through thinking with. It certainly marks their contributions: they are people who have created, defended and held open spaces for others to think (institutionally, academically, politically) in very different ways.

This leads to the second tendency that the project is intended to counter: the individualised version of thinking that the academy still promotes. The fetishism of the great thinker – the one whose monograph transforms an entire field or who blazes a trail for others to follow or is simply celebrated as a 'original thinker' – is problematic in many ways. For me, its distorting effect was visible in Tariq Ali's strange observation in his comments after Stuart Hall's death that:

> Unlike almost everyone else of his 1956 and later cohort, he did not write a book. Why, many asked, did he concentrate on the essay? Perhaps he liked the provisionality that lent itself to the shorter form. Or perhaps the masochistic practice of collective composition surrounded by sectarian twentysomethings at the Birmingham centre left him exhausted. I don't have the answer, but it doesn't really matter. (Ali, 2014)

I remember stumbling over this comment when I first read it. I was later asked a question about it at a conference where I was talking about collective work at the Birmingham Centre, and it has continued to puzzle me. The fetishisation of the book – the sole-authored monograph – still seems to me a peculiar measure of anyone's contribution, but especially Stuart's. I also find the dismissal of collaborative work as 'masochistic practice' interestingly revealing, but since I was one of the (not very) sectarian 20-somethings, I might be expected to. But it fits with a wider culture in which collective work, collaboration and collective thinking is disparaged, disregarded or treated as some sort of failure, even on the Left. It speaks to the intensifying fetishisation of individualised production in the increasingly competitive academy – the book, the sole-authored article and so on – as criteria for both recruitment and promotion. I still cherish the bizarre day when I was told that my case for promotion at the Open University had been turned down, in part because I had too many co-authored publications. Later that same morning, I was in a Senate debate about why it was so difficult to promote a collaborative culture of research in the university. My contribution was to suggest that resolving the contradictions between different policies might be a starting point (though I am sure the actual comment was probably more sarcastic). That was a long time ago, but the same obsessions and tensions are still visible – and still tend to be resolved in favour of the 'heroic individual' scholar.

Nonetheless, I am struck by just how fortunate I have been to find institutional settings that actively promoted forms of collaborative working. I arrived at the Birmingham Centre for Contemporary Cultural Studies through an entirely fortuitous encounter with someone already studying there (thank you, Judith Scott) and found people with whom to work and think. It was a revelation to me – nothing like the lonely 'masochistic practices' of trying to be an 'original thinker'. The Open University offered me a second institutional space in which some forms of collaborative working (mainly in the realm of teaching) were central to its way of life. And I have benefited from finding – and exploiting – lots of possibilities to work, talk and think with a range of people through different research and writing projects. These experiences, and the conversations collected here, underscore my sense that I have never had an original thought in my life – and feel the better for it.

In turbulent times

All of these conversations have been with people whose work I admire and enjoy, and whose thinking helps me to engage with contemporary issues and formations. It is a particular sort of privilege to know such people and have them be willing to take the time to think out loud in these conversations. They are, though, as I said in the Introduction, conversations, not formal interviews, so they move in unexpected directions, take short cuts, circle back round things and stop to puzzle over discovered points. I suspect that makes them both rewarding and frustrating to read: we are used to reading texts that move in more structured and linear ways. The dynamic qualities of dialogic thinking are more evident in the audio files, where we can be heard making connections, over-speaking in our excitement and responding to what has just been said in unpredictable ways.

Perhaps most importantly, these are people that I want to be thinking with in these turbulent times. The times, and their turbulence, are not the main or stable focus of these discussions – but they certainly haunt them, either as specific things that focus our attention or as the question that demands forms of critical thinking. One thread that connects all the dialogues is the importance of thinking – thinking hard, thinking again – about the changing circumstances that confront us. When I was conducting the first conversations in 2013, this was a pressing matter: socially and politically things were dismal, whether viewed from a UK stuck in the austerity politics and policies through which national governments were trying to manage the restoration of business – and profitability – as usual, or in wider framings such as those posed by Tania Murray Li's work about the challenges of subsistence and livelihood at 'Land's End'. Not surprisingly, questions of politics, political analysis and intellectual work weave their way through the first six conversations but are tugged this way and that by different locations: the first six dialogists are engaged by places that stretch me beyond my parochial concerns (South East Asia, India, South Eastern Europe …). However, by the second set of dialogues the times had become considerably more turbulent. Brexit and Trump dominated national (British) and international politics but were more troublingly aligned with other incarnations of the toxic mixture of nationalism, racism, populism and violent reaction – from Orbán's Hungary to Modi's India. These configurations haunt these conversations: sometimes as explicit focal points, other times as animating contexts.

The conversations collected here do not address these issues systematically or in a sustained way: there are lots of places where such examinations are going on, including in publications from the people involved here. Indeed, the project was never conceived in such terms and would, no doubt, have taken a very different trajectory if it had been. However, that may be the next project ... What is at stake in these conversations is a concern with the practices and relationships through which such critical intellectual work can take place. The conversations have ranged across the shifting institutional conditions (particularly, the changing university), the organising structures of knowledge (the question of disciplines and interdisciplinarity, especially) and the social relations of intellectual production (the forms of collaboration, collectivity and conversation). What I draw from these conversations is not a conclusion about the one best way, but the importance of the commitment to keep thinking and to keep thinking together about the challenges that confront us. I hope it persuades you to do the same ...

Keywords

Readers have pointed out that a number of distinctive concepts pop up and swirl around during these conversations. These terms animate some of the conversations, they provide temporary points of reference or departure and they shift around as they are put to use in different ways. They emerge from a range of analytical vocabularies – from Marx to Foucault, from feminism to poststructuralism, from anthropology to cultural studies and more. We had a discussion about creating a glossary of terms to accompany the chapters, but I have a difficult relationship with glossaries, since I fear that they tend to tidy up complicated and shifting meanings into one apparently unified and clear definition. Instead, I offer a few notes on the some of the concepts that appear here and indicate something of their range and scope, in the spirit of Raymond Williams's approach to *Keywords* (1976). For those unfamiliar with Williams's wonderful book, he argued that the quest for correct definitions or the 'proper meaning' of words misses the point:

> when we go beyond these to the historical dictionaries, and to essays in historical semantics, we are quite beyond the range of 'proper meaning'. We find a history and complexity of meanings; conscious changes, or consciously different uses; innovations, obsolescence, specialization, extension, overlap, transfer; or changes which are masked by a nominal continuity so that words which seem to have been there for centuries, with continuous general meanings, have come in fact to express radically different or radically variable, yet sometimes hardly noticed, meanings and implications of meanings. (Williams, 1976: 17)

The notes that follow here do not come close to the range and depth of Williams's work, but they are my attempt to indicate why these particular words matter – for me and for others – and why they might be the focus of shifting meanings and uses. The words here reflect something of my trajectory into and through cultural studies, and the continuing encounters with other ways of thinking. I suspect these words are here, in these conversations and in my head, because they are 'baggy' concepts – capacious enough to allow for different uses and shifting inflections.

Ambivalence recurs as a term in these conversations. At its simplest, it refers to a state of having mixed or contradictory feelings, reactions or ideas about something. It is used in these conversations to talk about the condition of not being certain in theoretical or political terms and thereby being open to the play of different orientations or possibilities. More abstractly, it carries theoretical implications from psycho-social studies and some versions of social psychology that think that individual subjects may think or feel more than one thing at a time: they are plural, if not contradictory subjects. For me, this is a critical point of intersection of such approaches with a Bakhtinian view of 'heteroglossia' – the interplay of multiple voices (as explored in the Introduction). It also echoes Gramsci's understanding that 'common sense is a plural noun': that it is composed of many elements rather than being a singular and coherent body of (bad) thinking. Some of these issues are explored (in the context of Brexit and British politics) in an article written with Janet Newman (Clarke and Newman, 2019).

Articulation is a Stuart Hall keyword. Stuart used it to think about the temporary and contingent organisation of different things into a sort of unity: the structure of social formation or a political bloc, for example. But he also used it as a way of talking about the process of coming to voice – articulating positions, points of view, feelings and so on. He saw this as central to the practice of politics in the contemporary world, making cultural studies attentive to the ways in which particular groups or identities were organised through the process of articulation – being spoken to or spoken for. For a longer discussion, of the centrality of the idea to Stuart's work see Clarke (2015).

Assemblage is a concept derived from the French philosophers Deleuze and Guattari, as an English translation of their concept of 'agencement'. It has been taken up in very diverse ways – ranging from the work of Actor Network Theory scholars (see, for example, Bruno Latour's *Reassembling the Social* (2005), through anthropologists such as Aihwa Ong and Stephen Collier's work on 'global assemblages' (2004), to Tania Murray Li's exploration of it as a strategy of governing (2007a). It has proved a fecund idea, primarily because it points to the temporary connections that organise diverse elements (human and non-human) into a formation. In a collaboration with Dave Bainton, Noémi Lendvai and Paul Stubbs, we explored its value for thinking about how policy moves and is translated between locations, suggesting that it was important for us because it draws attention to the heterogeneity of elements that go into making policy, for example, people (more accurately particular types or categories of agent), objects (forms, guidance documents, computers and programs), places (officially defined territories, buildings, offices, meeting places, etc.), as well as different sorts of texts (manifestos, official statements, media commentaries, guidelines for implementation, action notes, training leaflets and more). (Clarke et al, 2014: 31)

Conjuncture has been another key word in cultural studies, or at least, that branch of it that came out of the Birmingham Centre for Cultural Studies' period of working with Gramsci's ideas (for example, Hall, 1986). It was developed as a way of thinking about the composition of the current moment – the 'here and now' as containing multiple crises, multiple social forces and becoming the site of political contestation (in a struggle to direct the way forward). It was most famously developed in *Policing the Crisis* (Hall et al, 1978) and in Stuart Hall's subsequent work on Thatcherism. It remains elusive both as a concept and as an approach. For me, the emphasis on thinking about multiple strands that come together to make up the conjuncture has been a critical element in trying to find a way to think about Brexit and related political and cultural developments (for example, Clarke and Newman, 2017; Clarke, forthcoming a).

Crisis: Societies appear constantly prone to crises – in many different forms and settings (economic, environmental, institutional, political and so on). Not surprisingly there are many different usages of crisis – from conservative accounts of crises of moral order to Marxist examinations of capitalist crises. For cultural studies, however, the idea of crisis has always occupied a double or ambiguous role, both pointing to the ongoing emergence of forms of crisis and the contested cultural work of making a crisis mean something. Crises are variously anticipated, calibrated, denied, exploited, managed, manipulated and more (see, inter alia, Hall et al, 1978; Clarke, forthcoming b).

Discourse has proved to be another popular and productive concept in the social sciences and beyond. Its use ranges from the micro-level studies of conversational analysis, through what has been called Critical Discourse Analysis (for example, Chouliaraki and Fairclough, 1999) as a mode of analysing text and talk, to work based on Foucault's understanding of discourse as an organisation of social practices, forms of subjectification, power and knowledge (see below). Discourse can refer to both the practices of meaning making (discursive practices) and their products (text, talk and so on). The distinction is significant, since a lot of work on discourse concentrates on the products rather than the practices (for an important alternative, see the work of Margaret Wetherell and her several collaborators that attends to the ways in which people are discursive practitioners rather than mere reproducers, for example, Wetherell and Edley, 1999).

Moral economy is a term that has a long and complex history. It first came to my attention in the work of E.P. Thompson on the 'moral economy of the English crowd' (Thompson, 1971) in which he explored how ideas of rights, expectations and obligations bound some sectors of society together. Thompson himself suggested that he had borrowed the concept from the Chartist movement's critique of early capitalism. Subsequently I came across the term being used in anthropological work on peasant societies (Scott, 1976), and it has played a much wider role in anthropology (for a review, see the thoughtful essay by Didier Fassin, 2009, who has himself been making use of the concept involving distinctions between moral economies from above and from below). A rather different take is offered by Andrea Muehlebach's examination of the intertwining of economic and moral imperatives in her work on volunteering in Italy as an instance of the 'Moral Neoliberal' (Muehlebach, 2012).

Popular: The popular is always enmeshed in shifting meanings, evoking both positive and negative connotations. Its basic sense of something that belongs to, is enjoyed by or is of the people indicates why this might be so, since 'the people' have long been an object of fascination, fear and fantasy. The popular is often explicitly or implicitly contrasted with other types of culture. So, popular cultures are set against elite or high cultures, marked by distinctions of 'taste' (Bourdieu, 1984). Elite forms of culture are seen as set apart by the cultural skills and knowledge needed to engage in them or appreciate them. By comparison, popular products and practices are presumed to be accessible or available to large numbers of people. Some, but not all, cultural studies work has tended to view the forms and practices of popular culture as sites of contestation, located in, but not necessarily determined by, the social relations of capitalism (and other systems of subordination). This does not necessarily mean that all popular forms are resistant, transgressive or counter-hegemonic, but it does assume that the meanings within popular culture have to be struggled over –

whether to maintain forms of subordination or to refuse them (see Hall, 1981). And, of course, it shares the same root – and the same current mix of fascination, fear and fantasy about 'the people' – as populism. But that needs a different story.

Power-knowledge is a phrase derived from the work of Michel Foucault (*pouvoir-savoir*). In *Discipline and Punish* he argued that: 'There is no power relation without the correlative constitution of a field of knowledge, nor any knowledge that does not presuppose and constitute at the same time power relations' (Foucault, 1991: 27). Alongside the entanglement of forms of knowledge and modes of power, this way of looking also brings into view the specific types of subject (or agent) who are empowered by this particular formation, and the sorts of practices that are enabled and legitimised by it. The idea has been a fecund one, underpinning the exploration of very diverse forms of knowledge. For those of us working on questions of policy, it has been particularly significant as a means of refusing claims about abstracted universal reason and apolitical empiricism through which policy is often constructed. It is an orientation to thinking about knowledge claims rather than a clear analytic framework or method – which is part of its attraction.

References

Ali, T. (2014) 'Stuart Hall's message to those who want change: think, debate – and get off your backside', https://www.theguardian.com/commentisfree/2014/feb/10/stuart-hall-radical-thinker-thatcherism.

Billig, M. (1987) *Arguing and thinking: a rhetorical approach to social psychology*. Cambridge: Cambridge University Press.

Bjork-James, S. and Maskovsky, J. (eds) (forthcoming) *Beyond populism: Angry politics and the twilight of neoliberalism*. Morgantown, VA: West Virginia University Press.

Bourdieu, P. (1984) *Distinction: A social critique of the judgement of taste*, trans. Richard Nice. London: Routledge, Kegan and Paul.

Brennan, J., Cochrane, A., Lebeau, Y. and Williams, R. (2018) *The university in its place: Social and cultural perspectives on the regional role of universities*. Heidelberg: Springer.

Brković, Č. (2017) *Managing ambiguity. How clientelism, citizenship and power shape personhood in Bosnia and Herzegovina*. Oxford: Berghahn Books.

Brown, W. (1995) *States of injury: Power and freedom in late modernity*. Princeton, NJ: Princeton University Press.

Brown, W. (2015) *Undoing the demos: Neoliberalism's stealth revolution*. Cambridge, MA; Zone Books.

Butler, J. (1998) 'Merely cultural', *New Left Review*, 227: 33–45.

Chakrabarty, D. (2000) *Provincializing Europe: Postcolonial thought and historical difference*. Princeton, NJ: Princeton University Press.

Chouliaraki, L. and Fairclough, N. (1999) *Discourse in late modernity: Rethinking critical discourse analysis*. Edinburgh: Edinburgh University Press.

Clarke, J. (2009) 'Programmatic statements and dull empiricism: Foucault's neoliberalism and social policy', contribution to a symposium on Michel Foucault, *The Birth of Biopolitics. Lectures at the College de France 1978–1979*, *Journal of Cultural Economy*, 2 (1–2): 227–231.

Clarke, J. (2015) 'Stuart Hall and the theory and practice of articulation', *Discourse: Studies in the Cultural Politics of Education*, 36 (2): 275–286.

Clarke, J. (2016a) 'Hierarchies and beyond? Staff, students and the making of cultural studies in Birmingham', in K. Connell and M. Hilton (eds) *Cultural studies 50 years on: History, practice and politics*. London: Rowman and Littlefield International, pp. 101–110.

Clarke, J. (2016b) 'Doreen Massey (1944–2016): making geography matter', *Cultural Studies*, 30 (3): 357–361, http://dx.doi.org/10.108 0/09502386.2016.1172751.

Clarke, J. (forthcoming a) 'A sense of loss? Unsettled attachments in the current conjuncture', *New Formations*.

Clarke, J. (forthcoming b) 'Crisis', in R. Ballard and C. Barnett (eds) *The Routledge Handbook of Social Change*. London: Routledge.

Clarke, J. and Newman, J. (1997) *The managerial state: Power, politics and ideology in the remaking of social welfare*. London: Sage Publications.

Clarke, J. and Newman, J. (2017) '"People in this country have had enough of experts": Brexit and the paradoxes of populism', *Critical Policy Studies*, 11 (1): 101–116.

Clarke, J. and Newman, J. (2019) 'What's the subject? Brexit and politics as articulation' *Journal of Community and Applied Social Psychology*, 29 (1): 67–77.

Clarke, J., Coll, K., Dagnino, E. and Neveu, C. (2014) *Disputing citizenship*. Bristol: Policy Press.

Clarke, J., Lendvai, N., Bainton, D. and Stubbs, P. (2015) *Making policy move: Towards a politics of translation and assemblage*. Bristol: Policy Press.

Clarke, J., Newman, J., Smith, N., Vidler, E. and Westmarland, L. (2007) *Creating citizen-consumers: Changing publics and changing public services*. London: Sage.

Cochrane, A. (2007) *Understanding urban policy: A critical approach*. Oxford: Blackwell.

Cohen, M. (2015) *Critical thinking skills for dummies*. London: John Wiley and Sons.

Connell, K. (2015) https://www.birmingham.ac.uk/Documents/college-artslaw/history/cccs/Interview-Transcripts/John-Clarke.pdf.

Cooper, D. (1998) *Governing out of order: Space, law and the politics of belonging*. London: Rivers Oram Press.

Cooper, D. (2010) *Challenging diversity: Rethinking equality and the value of difference*. Cambridge: Cambridge University Press.

Cooper, D. (2013) *Everyday Utopias: The conceptual life of promising spaces*. Durham, NC: Duke University Press.

Cooper, D. (2019) *Feeling like a state: Political withdrawal and the transformative imagination*. Durham, NC: Duke University Press.

Cooper, D., Dhawan, N. and Newman, J. (eds) (forthcoming) *Reimagining the state: The challenge for progressive transformative politics*. London: Routledge.

Cucu, A. (2014) 'Producing knowledge in productive spaces: ethnography and planning in early socialist Romania', *Economy and Society*, 43 (2): 211–232.

Fassin, D. (2009) 'Les économies morales revisitées', *Annales. Histoire, Sciences Sociales*, 64 (6): 1237–1266.

Ferguson, J. and Li, T. (2018) *Beyond the "proper job": Political-economic analysis after the century of the labouring man.* Institute for Poverty, Land and Agrarian Studies, University of the Western Cape, PLAAS Working Paper 51, www.plaas.org.za/sites/default/files/publications-landpdf/WP%2051_Beyond%20the%20proper%20job_12%20Apr%20%282%29tl2%20FINAL.pdf.

Foucault, M. (1991) *Discipline and punish: The birth of the prison,*trans Alan Sheridan. London: Penguin Books.

Freire, P. (1970) *Pedagogy of the oppressed.* New York: Continuum.

Gibson-Graham, J.K. (2006) *The end of capitalism (as we knew it).* Minneapolis: University of Minnesota Press.

Goode, J. and Maskovsky, J. (eds) (2001) *New poverty studies: The ethnography of power, politics and impoverished people in the united states.* New York: NYU Press.

Grossberg, L. (2017) *Under the cover of chaos: Trump and the battle for the American Right.* London: Pluto Press.

Hall, D., Hirsch, P. and Li, T. (2011) *Powers of exclusion: Land dilemmas in Southeast Asia.* Honolulu and Singapore: University of Hawaii Press/National University of Singapore Press.

Hall, S. (1981) 'Notes on deconstructing the "popular"', in R. Samuel (ed) *People's history and socialist theory.* London: Routledge and Kegan Paul, 227–239.

Hall, S. (1986) 'Gramsci's relevance for the study of ethnicity', *Journal of Communication Inquiry*, 10 (5): 5–27.

Hall, S. and Jefferson, T. (eds) (1976) *Resistance through rituals: Youth subcultures in postwar Britain.* London: Routledge. (Originally published as *Working Papers in Cultural Studies*, 6/7.)

Hall, S., Massey, D. and Rustin, M. (eds) (2015) *After neoliberalism? The Kilburn Manifesto.* London: Lawrence and Wishart, https://www.lwbooks.co.uk/soundings/kilburn-manifesto.

Hall, S., Critcher, C., Jefferson, T., Clarke, J. and Roberts, B. (1978) *Policing the crisis: Mugging, the state and law'n'order* (2nd edn, 2013). Basingstoke: Macmillan.

Henriques, J., Morley, D. and Goblot, V. (2017) (eds) *Stuart Hall: Conversations, projects and legacies.* London: Goldsmiths Press.

Higgins, V. and Larner, W. (eds) (2017) *Assembling neoliberalism: Expertise, practices, subjects.* Basingstoke: Palgrave Macmillan.

Holland, D. and Lave, J. (2001) 'History in person: an introduction', in D. Holland and J. Lave (eds) *History in person: Enduring struggles, contentious practices, intimate identities*. Santa Fe: School of American Research; Oxford: James Currey Ltd.

Holquist, M. (ed) (1981) *The dialogic imagination: Four essays by M.M. Bakhtin*, trans C. Emerson and M. Holquist. Austin, TX and London: University of Texas Press.

Jackson, J.L. (2001) *Harlemworld: Doing race and class in contemporary America*. Chicago: University of Chicago Press.

Jackson, J.L. (2005) *Real black: Adventures in racial sincerity*. Chicago: University of Chicago Press.

Kirwan, S., McDermont, M. and Clarke, J. (2016) 'Imagining and practicing citizenship in austere times', *Citizenship Studies*, 20 (6–7): 764–778.

Larner, W. and Walters, W. (eds) (2006) *Global governmentality: Governing international spaces*. London: Routledge.

Larner, W. and Molloy, M. (2013) *Fashioning globalisation: New Zealand design, working women and the cultural economy*. Hoboken, NJ: Wiley.

Latour, B. (2005) *Reassembling the social*. Oxford: Oxford University Press.

Lewis, G. (2000) *'Race', gender and social welfare: Explorations in a postcolonial society*. Cambridge: Polity Press

Li, T.M. (2007a) 'Practices of assemblage and community forest management', *Economy and Society*, 36 (2): 263–293.

Li, T.M. (2007b) *The will to improve: Governmentality, development, and the practice of politics*. Durham, NC: Duke University Press.

Li, T.M. (2014) *Land's end: Capitalist relations on an indigenous frontier*. Durham, NC: Duke University Press.

Longden, E. (2013) *Learning from the voices in my head*. TED Conferences.

McBride, S., Mahon, R. and Boychuck, G. (eds) (2015) *After '08: Social policy and the global financial crisis*. Vancouver: University of British Columbia Press.

McCarthy-Jones, S. (2012) *Hearing voices: The histories, causes and meanings of auditory verbal hallucinations*. Cambridge: Cambridge University Press.

McCarthy-Jones, S. (2017) *Can't you hear them? The science and significance of hearing voices*. London: Jessica Kingsley Publishers.

Massey, D. (2005) *For space*. London: Sage.

Muehlebach, A. (2012) *The moral neoliberal: Welfare and citizenship in Italy*. Chicago: University of Chicago Press.

Neal, S., Bennett, K., Cochrane, A. and Mohan, G. (2017) *Lived experiences of multiculture: The new social and spatial relations of diversity.* London: Routledge.

Neveu, C., Clarke, J., Coll, K. and Dagnino, E. (2011) 'Introduction: questioning citizenships/questions de citoyennetés', *Citizenship Studies*, 15 (8): 945–964, DOI: 10.1080/13621025.2011.627759.

Newman, J. (2001) *Modernising governance.* London: Sage Publications.

Newman, J. (2012) *Working the spaces of power: Activism, neoliberalism and gendered labour.* London: Bloomsbury.

Newman, J. and Clarke, J. (2009) *Publics, politics and power: Remaking the public in public services.* London: Sage Publications.

Ong, A. and Collier, S. (2004) *Global assemblages: Technology, politics, and ethics as anthropological problems.* New York: Wiley.

Pennycook, A. (2007) *Global Englishes and transcultural flows.* London/New York: Routledge.

Reinarz, J. and Wynter, R. (eds) (2014) *Complaints, controversies and grievances in medicine: Historical and social science perspectives.* London: Routledge.

Scott, D. (2017) *Stuart Hall's voice.* Durham, NC: Duke University Press.

Scott, J.C. (1976) *The moral economy of the peasant: Rebellion and subsistence in Southeast Asia.* New Haven, CT: Yale University Press.

Scriven, M. and Paul, R. (1987) 'Defining critical thinking', The Foundation for Critical Thinking, http://www.criticalthinking.org/pages/our-conception-of-critical-thinking/766.

Sharma, A. (2008) *Logics of empowerment: Development, gender and governance in neoliberal India.* Minneapolis, MN: University of Minnesota Press.

Sharma, A. and Gupta, A. (eds) (2006) *The anthropology of the state.* Malden, MA and Oxford: Wiley-Blackwell.

Thompson, E.P. (1971) 'The moral economy of the English crowd in the eighteenth century', *Past and Present*, 50: 76–136.

Vincent, H. (2013) 'Hudson Vincent interview with John Clarke – 31 May 2011', *Cultural Studies*, 27: 729–743.

Werner, M., Peck, J., Lave, R. and Christophers, B. (eds) (2018) *Doreen Massey – critical dialogues.* London: Agenda Publishing.

Wetherell, M. and Edley, N. (1999) 'Negotiating hegemonic masculinities: imaginary positions and psycho-discursive practices', *Feminism and Psychology*, 9 (3): 335–356.

Williams, F. (1989) *Social policy: A critical introduction – issues of race, gender, and class.* Cambridge: Polity Press.

Williams, F. (2004) *Rethinking families.* London: Calouste Gulbenkian Foundation.

Williams, F., Popay, J. and Oakley, A. (1999) *Welfare research: A critical review.* London: UCL Press.

Williams, R. (1976) *Keywords: A vocabulary of culture and society.* New York: Oxford University Press.

Index

A

Aam Aadmi Party (AAP) 79
abstraction 54, 55, 63
  and Marx 64
academic research 158
academic work 1–2, 8–9, 155
  cataloguing 32
  certainty and uncertainty 171
academics 12, 99, 117–18
  deference to 157
  and lack of activism 99
  and trade unionism 96–7
ACT UP 95
activism 99
agency 113–17, 141
agrarian capitalism 28
Agrawal, Arun 27
AIDS 95–6
  activism 96
  targets for anger 96
Alexander, Jacqui 169, 170
Ali, Tariq 220–1
Allen, John 119, 125
Althusser, Louis 14, 15, 50, 57–8, 107
Althusserian Marxism 107
ambivalence 58, 118, 226
  moment of 66–8
  movements of 97
  politics and certainty 94–102
  zone of comfort 98
American Anthropological Association
    (AAA) 87
Anglophone Foucauldians 55, 56
anthropology 23, 61, 70–1
  micro-studies 81
  particular to the general 81–3
  provincialising effect 80–1
anti-imperialism 137
anti-Semitism 159–60
anti-Vietnam movement 136
Applied Social Sciences 127
archives 23
articulation 16, 51, 52, 195, 226
  and discourse 196–202
assemblage 90, 111, 195, 226–7
Association of University Teachers 97

B

Bainton, Dave 116
Bakhtin, Mikhail 7, 10, 11, 12, 108
  dialogism 10–11, 12
Bannon, Steve 181
beliefs 160, 161–2
Bernstein, Basil 136
bi-culturalism 190
Big Boys 58
Billig, Michael 6, 10
Birmingham Centre *see* Centre for
    Contemporary Cultural Studies
    (CCCS)
Bjork-James, Sophie 87
Black Lives Matter 212
Blair, Tony 94
boundaries, thinking beyond 154–7
Brazil 35
Breitbart people 181–2
Brexit 11–12, 138, 159, 175–6, 214,
    215
bricolage 141, 142, 143, 191
British Labourism 94
  labour exchanges 99–100
  right to work 99, 100
Brixton Black Women's Group 166
Brkovic, Carna 143
Brodie, Janine 185, 186, 189
Brown, Jackie 88
Brown, Wendy 53–68, 71, 83

C

capital 67, 68
  subsidised 34, 35
Capital (Marx) 64
  reading group 57, 60
capitalism 28
  contradictions of 143–4
  running smoothly 146–7
  thingness of 30
capitalist relations 28, 30–2
care 145, 156–7
Carillion 213–14
cataloguing 32
Central European University 129,
    200–1

Centre for Contemporary Cultural
    Studies (CCCS) 2, 4, 9, 14, 90, 221
certainty
  politics and ambivalence 94–102
  and uncertainty 95, 97, 98, 99,
    170–2
citizenship 8, 11, 74–7, 85, 94, 158
Citizenship Studies 74
civil rights movement 100
clarification 8
closure 8, 9
co-authoring 24
co-production 216
Cochrane, Allan 119–34
Cohn-Bendit, Daniel 137
Coll, Kathy 8–9, 69
collaboration 2, 204–8
  and dialogic processes 216–17
  Glasgow Media Group 114
  London Edinburgh Weekend Return
    Group 114
  multiple authors 115–16, 132–3
  at the Open University 121–2
  pains and pleasures of 44–9
  promotion of 221
collaborative-working puzzle 22–30
collective course production 45–6
collective sensibility 46
collective writing 45–6
Collier, Stephen 226
coming together process 132
common sense 12, 49, 226
Communist Manifesto, The (Marx) 67,
  68
complexity 143–8
concepts 30–3, 147, 153–4
conceptual alliances 147
Conference of Socialist Economists
  119
confidence 124
congenital borrowing 15, 16
conjunctural politics 130
conjuncture 17, 33, 52, 129, 131, 227
  conjunctural analysis 114, 131, 132,
    205, 212–13
consciousness 74
conservative rule 33–4
constructive criticism 24–6
consumers 158
contradictions 129, 140, 143–8
conversation(s) 1, 9–10, 18
  among unknowns 47
  within and beyond disciplines 186–7
  continuing 48
  initial thoughts 45, 48, 157
  known positions 47
  modes 47–8
  surprises 47

through questions 43
conviction politicians 97
Cooper, Davina 151–65
cosmopolitanism 88
Cox, Jo 178, 179
crisis 28, 42, 179, 227
  Carillion collapse 213–14
  dimensions and dynamics of 180–2
  of work 35
Critical Discourse Analysis 227–8
Critical Policy Studies 3
critical thinking 3–4, 220
  definition 5
  information about 5
  at the Open University 120–4
  performing and judging 6
  re-articulation 5
  thinking critically about 6–7
  see also thinking critically
criticality 211
criticism see constructive criticism
critique 164, 211
  pessimism of 208–10
cultural studies 5, 37, 48, 52, 90, 131,
  191
  British 104
Cure for Marriage project 45
current moment 212–16

D

Dagnino, Evelina 8–9
Dahlie, Chris 19
Davis, Angela 169
Davis, Ann 10
Deacon, Bob 105
Deleuze, Gilles 226
demobilisation 34
demoralised discourse 75
dialectical approach to thinking 148,
  170–1
dialogic selves 10–12
dialogic thinking 19
  dialogic processes and collaboration
    216–17
dialogism 10–11, 12
dialogue 9
differences 205
  talking through 38–42
dilettantism 108, 117
disaffected consent 34, 35
disciplinary formation 60
Discipline and Punish (Foucault) 55–6
disciplines 126–34, 152–4
  conversations within and beyond
    186–7
discourse 49, 109–10, 227–8
  of belonging 76

as the practice of articulation 196–202
on rights 76
displacements 40
dissertation workshops 26–7
Donnison, David 136
Dunleavy, Patrick 123

E

economic 149
economic restructuring 193
economic settlements 214–15
economies 41
Economy and Society 195
elite 175–6
empathy 196
empirical research 157–8
employment 34–6
empowerment 70, 72, 76, 112
ephemera 210, 212, 213
essentialist categories 110
ethics 15–16
ethnographic moment 206
ethnographic work 31, 32, 33
ethnography 74
Everyday Utopias (Cooper) 156

F

fairness 196
faith 100
false consciousness 74
fascism 179, 181–2
Fassin, Didier 228
feedback 24–6
feltness of things 169
feminism 70, 74, 93
feminist judgements project 164
and Marxism 210–12
and social policy 149
Ferguson, Jim 24, 34, 75–6
fetishisation
of books 221
of individualised production 221
of thinkers 220
field notes 23
Fletcher, Colin 191
formations, unorthodox 191–5
Foucault, Michel 7, 41, 55–7, 90, 154, 229
Freire, Paulo 112
fusion 52

G

gay sexuality 161–2
gender 90, 100

as property 161
and race 179
gender identity 162–4
genealogies 56
genealogy 61
geography 131, 187
Gibson-Graham, J.K. 84, 107
Gibson, Katherine (Kathy) 84, 190
Gilbert, Jeremy 34
Gilroy, Paul 194
Glasgow Media Group 114
global capitalism 144
global neoliberalism 145
global sense of place 193
global social policy 104, 105
Global Social Policy 104
Goode, Judith 87
governmentality 27, 31–2, 71–3, 85, 107
Graham, Julie 84
Gramsci, Antonio 12, 17, 57–8, 60–1, 197, 226, 227
grassroots movements 147
Grenfell Tower 142, 213
Grossberg, Larry 37–52, 219
Guattari, Felix 226
Gupta, Akhil 81, 82

H

Hall, Catherine 188
Hall, Derek 28, 29
Hall, Stuart 3, 8, 9, 14–16, 45, 90, 120, 125, 126, 197–8, 220–1, 226, 227
conjuncture 17
on popular culture 49
on theory and politics 64
Hamnett, Chris 123
head notes 23
hearing voices 3
heteroglossia 10, 11, 158–9, 226
Himmelweit, Sue 119
historians 62
Hobbes, Thomas 59
Hoggart, Richard 199
holistic outlook 130
Holland, Dorothy and Lave, Jean 10–11
homework 27
Howe, Darcus 166

I

ideas 189
identity 162–4
immigration 177
India

corruption 77, 78
  decentralisation 78
  independence 77
  Right to Information (RTI) Act 2005
    76–7, 78
  and the state 73, 83
  welfare measures 83
India Against Corruption (IAC) 78–80
  Last Fast 79
Indian Spring see India Against
  Corruption [IAC]
individual ideas 2, 3, 12, 22, 44, 45,
  46, 114, 126, 133, 168, 198, 217,
  221
individual, formation of the 10, 197,
  226
individualised conceptions of thinking
  and working 2, 6, 167, 220, 221
industrial working class 91, 92
institutional complexity 144
institutions 188–90
integrity 196
intellectual formation
  feedback 23
  group work 22
  PhD process 23
  undergraduate process 23
interdisciplinarity 30, 120, 121
Interdisciplinary Social Sciences 127
interdisciplinary thinking 126–34
intergenerational experiences 168–9
international financial institutions 145

J

Jackson, John 71
Jansen, Stef 145

K

Kellogg, Catherine 186
Kerjiwal, Arvind 78
Kilburn Manifesto, The (Hall et al) 16,
  17
Kingfisher, Catherine 87

L

labour exchanges 99–100
Labour movement see British
  Labourism
land issues 28, 29–30
  dispossession 30
Larner, Wendy 185–202
Latour, Bruno 226
laughter 219–20
law 152–3, 160
  gender reform 162–4

Le Heron, Richard 190
leadership 134
left-wing politics 66–7
legal gender identity 162–4
legal pluralism 153
Lendvai, Noemi 105, 116
lesbians 161–2
Levi-Strauss, Claude 60, 191
Lewis, Gail 165–84
Li, Tania Murray 21–36, 226
Li, Victor 24
liberal democracy 180
lists 28–9
Loach, Ken 139, 140
London 175–6, 177, 184
London Edinburgh Weekend Return
  Group 114
lone scholars 132–3

M

Madonna 95–6
MaGee, Ann 192
Mahon, Rianne 145–6
mai baap 75
Managerial State, The (Clarke &
  Newman) 204, 205, 211, 214
managerialism 112, 116, 117, 125, 206
Mani, Lata 169
maps of the world 59–60
marginality 154–5
Marx, Karl 7, 30
  and abstraction 64
  and ambivalence 67
  Communist Manifesto, The 67, 68
Marxism 73, 90, 115, 129, 176
  categories 31
  and feminism 210–12
Marxism Today 16
masculinism 65–6
masculinity 176, 179, 181
Maskovsky, Jeff 87–102
Massey, Doreen 16–18, 125, 126, 192
  conjuncture 17
  and the Open University 127
McBride, Steve 145–6
McDowell, Linda 123
McGregor, Oliver 136
Me Too movement 212
meaning making 228
means of production 31
middle classes 91–2
Miller, Gina 178
misogyny 159
Mitchell, Tim 91
MKSS (Mazdoor Kisan Shakti
  Sangathan) 77
Moore, Donald 27, 30

moral consensus 84
moral economy 38, 41, 42, 76, 228
morality 76
Morgen, Sandi 87
Muehlebach, Andrea 228
multi-authored works 115–16, 132–3
multicultural crisis 179
multiculturalism 177
multiple resources 70–2

N

Narotzky, Susana 67
National Council for Excellence in
    Critical Thinking 5
national popular 50–1
negative property 161
neoliberal discourse 75
neoliberal governmentality 71–2
neoliberalism 54–5, 71, 82, 144, 193
    global 145
networks 126
Neveu, Catherine 8–9
New York City 88
New Zealand 189–90, 193–4, 196
    Education Act 196
    treasury economists 193
Newman, Janet 11–12, 106, 138,
    203–17
NGOs (non-government organisations)
    76–80, 80, 85, 109
    discursive production of 85
    moral consensus 84
NHS 183–4, 214
nostalgia, politics of 140
notions 33

O

Official Secrets Act 76–7
Ong, Aihwa 226
Open University 25, 44
    Applied Social Sciences 127
    collaborative working 121–2
    collective course production 45–6
    disciplines and interdisciplinary
        thinking 126–34
    diversity of backgrounds 125
    Faculty of Social Sciences 120
    Interdisciplinary Social Sciences 127
    networks 126
    opening up possibilities 125–6
    Patterns of Inequality course 120
    Social Policy 127
    Social Policy and Criminology 128
    as a space for critical thinking 120–4

P

paid labour 35
paradoxes in popular politics 88–91
Parivarthan 77
Parker, Rory 136
Phillimore, Jenny 141
place(s)
    being dragged out of 104–7
    making up 111–13
pluralism 153
Policing the Crisis (Hall et al) 4, 48, 93,
    114, 115, 132
policy 107–11, 153, 226–7
    see also social policy
political alliances 147
political economy 61, 70
political ideas, compatibility 25
political positions 62–3, 64
political science 186, 188
political settlements 214
political theory 152, 189–90
political trajectories 91–4
politics
    certainty and ambivalence 94–102
    popular politics 88–91
    and theory 62–6
    of withdrawal 161
politics of nostalgia 140
politics of resignation 34
popular culture 49, 50, 228
popular politics 88–91
popular, the 49–52, 228–9
populism 132, 186
positions, taking provisionally 42–4
possessive self 161
postcolonial melancholia 194
post-disciplinary 152
post-war culture 50
postcolonial state 73
postcolonial studies 70, 73
postcolonialism 76–7, 81, 141
    in India 77
power 142, 146
    and institutional complexity 144
    intersectional analysis of 143
    social relations of 142, 143
power-knowledge 210, 229
President's Club 212
production 31
property 155–6, 156–7
    and beliefs 161–2
    negative 161
    paradigms 160–1
provisional positions 42–4
provisional resting points 9

Q

queering 93
questions 43

R

race 90, 93, 100, 172–80
  and Brexit 175–6
  English/British identity 174
  epithets 172–3
  and the London elite 175–6, 177
  and Marxism 176
  and masculinity 176, 179
  and right-wing politics 180–3
  sense of loss 174
  settled minorities 173
  and sovereignty 176–7
  speaking foreign languages 173
Race Today Collective 166
racism 88, 132, 159
  and anti-Semitism 159–60
radical sociology 90
re-equipping 27–8
reading 27–8
  theoretical 32–3
refusals 138–43
regulation studies 153–4
reification 84
relations of production 31
religion 51–2
research
  academic 158
  design 158
  empirical 157–8
resistances 138–43
respect 196
responsibility 196
revelation 64
revolutionary discipline 94
revolutionary politics 137
Right to Information (RTI) Act 2005
  76–7, 78
right to work 99, 100
right-wing politics 180–3
Royal Geographical Society 187
Ruccio, David 41

S

Sabsay, Leticia 117
SANA (Society for the Anthropology
  of North America) 87
scholars 117–18
Scott, David 3, 8, 9, 15–16, 220
Scott, Jim 74
Scott, Judith 221
Scriven, Michael and Paul, Richard 5,
  6

seductions of theory 57–62
settled minorities 173
Sexing the City (Cooper) 155
sexual politics 93
sexuality 100
Sharma, Anu (Aradhana) 69–86
Simmelian position 130
Smith, Dorothy 106, 108
Smith, Neil 94–5
social democracy 94
social displacement 40
social movements 79–80
social policy 90, 99–100, 105, 107,
  131, 135, 148–50, 194
  coming to terms with 136–8
  eclecticism of 148–9
  English 104
  and feminism 149
  and the Open University 127
  porous boundaries 149
  resistances and refusals 138–43
Social Policy Association 149
social settlements 214, 215
socio-legal studies 153
sociology 136, 191
soft law 153
sole-authored works 132–3
Soros, George 112
Soundings (journal) 16
South East Asia, land issues in 29–30
sovereignty 176–7
space 16–17, 104, 112
  and time 17, 113, 114
spiral space 171
Spivak, Gayatri 74
state pluralism 153
state, the
  in Europe 73
  in India 73, 83
  production and reproduction of 153
  provision of welfare 83
  regulation of women 73
  reimagining of 161
  in the US 73
state transparency 71
Stokes, Evelyn 192
structural power structures 146, 147
structure of feeling 50
Stuart Hall Project, The (film) 90
Stubbs, Paul 103–18
student movement 136
student politics 92–3
subaltern studies 70, 72–3, 74
subjectivity 71
subjects
  behaving badly 72–6
  dialogic 10–12
Summerhill School 155

superdiversity 141, 142, 143
Superdiversity and Welfare Bricolage
    project 141
supremacy, white 181
Susser, Ida 87
systematic thinking 28–9
Szanton, David 27

T

talking theory 54–7
talking to people 157–62
technical discourse 75, 76
technology 51
tension 133–4
Thatcher, Margaret 94, 140, 184
theoretical reading 32–3
theory
  importance of 90
  and politics 62–6
  seductions of 57–62
  talking 54–7
theory heads 65
things, making up 111–13
think-tanks 39
thinking 7
  dialectical approach 148
  as a dialogic process 8, 9
  double movement of 216
  with multiple resources 70–2
  new ways of 125
  with others 166–70
  systematic 28–9
  with and through race 172–80
  troubling thoughts 80–6
  see also critical thinking
thinking critically 6–7
  with and against 3, 8, 16, 216, 220
thinking with 3
Thompson, E.P. 42, 228
Thompson, Grahame 122
time, and space 17, 113, 114
Titmuss, Richard 136
totalising ideas 84, 102
trade unionism 96–7, 99
Trotskyism 90
troubling thoughts 80–6
Trump, President Donald 179, 181
trust 39
  mutual 25
  personal 25

U

uncertainty 95, 97, 98, 99, 170–2
unemployment insurance 100
universities 188
University of Bristol 188

unorthodox formations 191–5
urban areas 88
urban studies 89

V

Victoria University of Wellington 196
voices 1–4, 12–14, 169
  missing 14–18
voices in my head 2–4, 33, 46, 169,
    189, 191–2, 201

W

Waikato University 192
Walters, William 190
Wekker, Gloria 169, 170
welfare bricolage 141, 142, 143, 191
welfare state 83, 105, 139, 183
  British 194
Weltanschauung 61
Wetherell, Margaret (Margie) 13, 14,
    196, 228
white supremacy 181
Wilders, Geert 181, 182
Williams, Fiona 4, 135–50, 200
Williams, Raymond 75, 225
withdrawal, politics of 161
women see feminism
Women and Work Programme 206,
    212
work
  false promises of 35–6
  problem of 34–6
workfare 36
working classes 91–2, 98
Working Papers in Cultural Studies
    (journal) 9, 138
wriggle room 71, 72, 73
writing, collaboratively 204–8
writing theory 54

Y

Yeates, Nicola 104

Z

Zaman, Rehana 167